Clash of Generations

ALSO BY LAVENDER CASSELS

The Struggle for the Ottoman Empire
1717–1740

75p.

3.73

Clash of Generations

A HABSBURG FAMILY DRAMA IN
THE NINETEENTH CENTURY

Lavender Cassels

JOHN MURRAY

© Lavender Cassels 1973

Printed in Great Britain by
The Camelot Press Ltd, London and Southampton

0 7195 2731 7

For
W. and L.T.

Contents

vii

CONTENTS

THE HABSBURG MONARCHY
FROM 1848 TO 1890

Miles
100   200
0   80   160   240   320
Kms

R.Danube

Königgrätz

BOHEMIA

MORAV

LOWER

•*Prague*

•*Linz*

Gmunden

Vienna

Salzburg•

UPPER
AUSTRIA

AUSTRIA

VORARL-
BERG

STYRIA

T Y R O L

CARINTHIA

•*Graz*

H

1859

LOMBARDY

Arco•

V
E
N
E
T
I
A

1866

KÜSTEN

KRAIN

•*Agram*

Milan

Solferino•

•*Custozza*

Trieste•

ISTRIA

•*Fiume*

C
R
O
A
T
I
A

MODENA
1860

Venice

BOSNIA

187

TUSCANY

1860

A
D
R
I
A
T
I
C

D
A
L
M
A
T
I
A

S
E
A

GALICIA

•Cracow

•Lemberg

BUKO-
VINA

Danube
Komorn •Budapest

NGARY

TRANSYLVANIA

•Temesvar

SLAVONIA

R. Danube

ERZEGOVINA
•Sarajevo

SANJAK of
NOVI BAZAR

•Dubrovnik
acroma

FRONTIERS OF THE MONARCHY 1848

CADET BRANCH GRAND
DUCHIES LOST IN 1860

ITALIAN PROVINCES LOST IN
1859 AND 1866

MANDATED TERRITORY GAINED IN 1878

Illustrations

All the illustrations are reproduced by kind permission of the Bildarchiv der Österreichischen Nationalbibliothek

Foreword and Acknowledgements

In 1880 the House of Habsburg, encrusted by tradition, was within a few years of celebrating the six hundredth anniversary of its foundation. As every Habsburg was proudly aware this was an achievement which no other reigning house in Europe could match, and they were united in a determination that it should be perpetuated. Most of them believed that to do so innovation must be resisted. Two of the younger members of this remarkable family disagreed. They were convinced that many of the convictions rooted in tradition held by their elders were outmoded; they were certain that progress and change were essential to secure the future of their dynasty. Such differences of attitude between the old and the young are endemic to the human race. Rarely, however, have they been accompanied by such drama as was the clash of generations within the House of Habsburg which is the theme of this book.

*   *   *   *   *

I am greatly indebted to the Directors and officials of the Haus-Hof- und Staats Archiv, the Kriegsarchiv and the National-bibliothek in Vienna for the help which I received during my research for this study of the Habsburgs. In particular I wish to thank Dr. Richard Blaas the Director of the Haus- Hof- und Staatsarchiv for directing my attention to documents relating to Archduke Johann Salvator, and two members of his staff—Dr. Anna Coreth who generously gave me the benefit of her advice and scholarship, and Dr. Rudolf Neck. I received similar invaluable assistance from Dr. Rainer Egger and Dr. Edith Wohlgemuth of the Kriegsarchiv. In London Fräulein Erika Strobl of the Austrian Institute eased my task by answering innumerable queries; I am most grateful to her, as I am to the staffs of the British Museum and the Foreign Office Library and the Institute of Historical Research. In common with many other authors I owe a very great deal to that unique institution the London Library.

Extracts from published transcripts of papers in the Royal Archives are quoted by gracious permission of Her Majesty The Queen. Quotations of Crown-copyright records in the Public Record Office appear by permission of the Controller of Her Majesty's Stationery Office. I thank Lord Salisbury for allowing me to quote from the papers of the Third Marquess of Salisbury in Christ Church Oxford.

My husband was unfailingly patient with the demands which the Habsburgs made on my time, and I owe much to him for his sustained encouragement. Finally I wish to record my debt to Mrs. William Younger with whom every stage of the book was discussed, and without whose help it would never have been completed.

Prologue

The year, 1880: the scene, the Hofburg in Vienna. In the snow-covered courtyard of the Imperial Palace hussars wearing scarlet shakos and green cloaks mounted guard, the lamplight gleaming on their drawn swords. On the first floor in the Rittersaal, an immense room decorated in white and gold, banked with palms and exotic flowers, lit by hundreds of candles in crystal chandeliers, the Emperor's guests were assembled for the Hofball. The ladies, covered though they were with diamonds and priceless jewellery (for which as an Ambassadress later recalled 'the well developed expanse of their person afforded ample room')[1] were quite outshone by the men. The uniforms of the officers of the best dressed army in Europe were a galaxy of colour, the Life Guards in scarlet, the Halbardiers in black jackets frogged with gold, white breeches and high black boots, artillery and infantry officers in black trousers with scarlet stripes and brown or pale blue tunics. 'They do not seem to have any connection with fighting.' wrote one bedazzled observer, 'but . . . they were a joy to behold.'[2] The nobility of the Monarchy were an even greater joy to behold with their cloaks of deep violet, cardinal red, royal blue, trimmed with sable and fastened with silver clasps, the Poles wearing birettas edged with fur and ornamented with diamond aigrettes, the Croats in their semi-Oriental robes covered with precious stones, and the Hungarians in skin tight blue breeches embroidered with gold, high yellow boots, scarlet tunics adorned with large turquoise buttons, attilas of pale green velvet bordered with beaver flung over one shoulder. Glittering with orders and decorations, bedizened with jewellery, the assembled company presented a magnificent spectacle as they lined up to await the state entry of the Emperor.

At 8.30 p.m. precisely the Grand Master of Ceremonies advanced to the end of the room and struck three times on the floor with his double eagle headed staff of office. The doors were flung open and, as the men stood to attention and the women curtsied, Franz Joseph I, the Empress Elisabeth at his side, followed by a procession of Archdukes and Archduchesses, entered the ball-room.

The Emperor, then aged fifty, was tall with the slim figure of a fine horseman, good looking rather than handsome. Out of uniform, bewhiskered after the fashion of the day, he would not have been outstanding in a gathering of civil servants, and his uniform —the white tunic and scarlet trousers of a Field-Marshal—was sober by comparison with the splendour of some of his subjects. But as he advanced slowly down the room with the impersonal aloofness of a general inspecting his troops on parade, he carried himself with an air of extreme distinction which placed him above and apart from everyone else. The Empress beside him, looking neither to right nor left, moved so lightly that she seemed to float rather than walk across the floor. She too was tall and slight, her dress of mauve shot with silver designed to show off her superb figure. Her chestnut hair was looped under a coronet of diamonds and emeralds with matching gems at her throat, on her bodice, round her waist. Already a grandmother, she looked no more than thirty-five, and was acknowledged to be one of the most beautiful women in Europe—'supernaturally lovely', 'dazzingly beautiful' according to contemporary observers. It was generally agreed that no portrait or description did justice to her.

After escorting the Empress to a dais at the far end of the room, Franz Joseph walked round talking to his guests. Meanwhile senior ladies from the diplomatic corps and the aristocracy were presented to Elisabeth. Then the band struck up. The dance programme was timed with military precision—seven minutes for a waltz, five minutes for a polka and twenty minutes for a quadrille. The ball invariably ended at midnight.

The German Emperor Wilhelm II later described the Court of Vienna as 'the most elegant court in Europe'.[3] The ceremonial of the Hofball was faultless and the music at it unsurpassed, for in Johann Strauss the Emperor possessed a conductor of the Court orchestra envied by every other ruler. There were, however, a number of discomforts to be endured. Apart from the chairs on the dais for the Imperial family, there were only two small marble seats; most people were therefore compelled to stand throughout the evening. A privileged few obtained some respite in that they were able to sit down for supper, which was served in a separate room at small tables each presided over by an Archduke, but rigid protocol decreed that at this, as at the smaller and more exclusive Ball bei Hof, the same people invariably sat next to one another. It was difficult to get near the buffet where refreshments were provided for lesser mortals, and success in doing so was unrewarding. A leading member of the aristocracy voiced the feelings of many when she grumbled about '10,000 dried up patties which for years they have had the effrontery to serve at the Hofball'. [4] It was rumoured that the soup, which was disgusting, was brewed up from a three-hundred-year-old recipe. There was also a strong and most disagreeable smell. Franz Joseph insisted on all officers being dressed in accordance with army regulations. Army regulations included no provision for patent leather. Officers therefore wore their field or riding boots, and the smell of boot polish was overwhelming. Finally, everyone, from the Emperor downwards, complained of the excessive heat.

As his letters show, Franz Joseph did not enjoy the Hofball, but it was an opportunity for the House of Habsburg to parade its unity before the world, and therefore an ordeal which he never contemplated evading and in which he required all Archdukes and Archduchesses to participate. His conviction of the necessity of demonstrating this unity was vehemently supported by his older and ultra-conservative cousin Archduke Albrecht, and to it most of the Imperial Family were content to conform. By 1880, however, some of the younger generation were not. Crown Prince Rudolf, the twenty-one-year-old heir to the throne, appeared reluctantly at the Hofball to endure a tedious evening making conversation to people with most of whom he had nothing in common. Rudolf's cousin Archduke Johann Salvator absented himself from what he considered to be a farce. Two Habsburgs, although the Emperor did not realise it, no longer subscribed to his belief that *en masse* ceremonial appearances of the family contributed to the prestige of the dynasty.

Prologue

Although he preferred to go to bed by 8.30 or, at the latest 9 p.m., Franz Joseph did not allow the ending of the Hofball at midnight to affect his rigid timetable and at 5 a.m. on the following morning started work as usual, reading through files in his study, a plain but comfortably furnished room devoid of ornament except for a portrait of Elisabeth by Winterhalter. His breakfast consisted of a cup of coffee and two rolls which he ate at his desk, receiving ministers and giving audiences from 8 a.m. onwards. After a short break for lunch, which again he often ate at his desk, he returned to work. The volume of papers which he had to consider was formidable. Memoranda addressed to him by his ministers averaged about four thousand annually, and in addition to these there were despatches from ambassadors abroad, press summaries and police reports to be studied. He insisted that all recommendations for the promotion of middle and high-ranking army officers and civil servants should be referred for his personal decision, and dealt with all correspondence with foreign royalties. Some forty thousand petitions were addressed to him every year, and he received up to one hundred and sixty people a week in audience.

For over thirty-one years the Emperor had worked harder than any of his officials, and in spite of this had experienced very little triumph and suffered a great deal of disaster. But by 1880 it seemed that he had reached a watershed, and that after much adversity the position both at home and abroad was more secure than it had been for a considerable time. As he continued to labour without remission Franz Joseph at last looked forward with some confidence to the future.

PART ONE

Age and Experience

CHAPTER 1

The Emperor—Ruler and Statesman

(i) HIGH CONFIDENCE AND BITTER DISILLUSION

Franz Joseph was eighteen when on December 2nd, 1848, his uncle Ferdinand I abdicated, and he was proclaimed 'by God's grace' Emperor of Austria, King of Jerusalem, Apostolic King of Hungary, King of Bohemia, Galicia, Lodomeria, Lombardy, Venetia, Illyria and Croatia, Archduke of Austria, and Grand Duke, Duke, Markgraf, Prince or Count of some thirty other places in a vast realm inhabited by over thirty-five million people. It had been put together in the course of five and a half centuries by the House of Habsburg, a dynasty which, imbued with the conviction that more acres meant more power, acquired them whenever the opportunity offered without regard to the problems involved in retaining them. The result was a domain which sprawled across Central Europe and northern Italy. It was not a geographical unity, and it had no ethnic coherence. It contained eleven nationalities speaking as many different languages, each in varying stages of social, cultural and economic development, so scattered within its boundaries that in virtually every province there was a minority group. It was a Monarchy rather than an Empire, for the Habsburgs regarded it as their dynastic property.

When Franz Joseph succeeded to this conglomerate of a heritage it was in a state of grave disarray. Throughout 1848 as in most European countries, there had been popular uprisings demanding political liberty and self-determination. Imperial authority had to be reasserted. This took the Prime Minister Prince Schwarzenberg and the army the greater part of a year to achieve, and the rebels in Hungary who had followed up their proclamation of independence by a declaration deposing the 'perjured House of Habsburg-

7

Lorraine . . . for ever', were only subdued with the assistance of two hundred thousand Russians sent by Czar Nicholas I in response to Schwarzenberg's appeal for help.

During this difficult time the young Emperor was evidently making an excellent impression, both on the public who liked his good looks and natural dignity, and on the army who applauded his disregard for danger under fire when he visited the troops in Hungary. When he had been on the throne for eighteen months Schwarzenberg, who was in a better position than anyone to judge, praised his sovereign's intelligence and 'diligence in affairs'; dignity and courtesy, 'his behaviour to all is exceedingly polite though a little dry'; integrity, 'he has a rooted objection to any kind of lie', and above all his courage, 'physically and morally he is fearless, and I believe the main reason why he can face the truth, however bitter, is that it does not frighten him'.[1] The Prince did not, however, refer to the fundamental conviction which would always sustain and determine the actions of the Emperor—his sense of dynastic mission. Franz Joseph was certain he was called by God to fulfil a sacred trust, and that this imposed on him two obligations. The first of these was to maintain the power and honour of the House of Habsburg, guarding and if possible enhancing the inheritance which had devolved on him: the second to rule justly and impartially over all his subjects. To him these two obligations were conjoined, for the power of his House was dependent upon the preservation of its multinational domain, and he was convinced that if the Habsburg dynasty prospered all its subjects would also prosper. His duty therefore was to promote the interests of the dynasty, and in carrying this out he was answerable only to his conscience before God. It was a duty from which there could be no abdication, and to which all personal feelings must be subordinated. He and he alone could know what was best for his House and therefore for his subjects. He and he alone had been entrusted with the sword of authority and must carry the whole burden of decision. On December 31st, 1851, it therefore appeared to him logical to take what he described as 'a long step forward'[2] and to proclaim himself absolute ruler of the Monarchy. 'The man who holds the reins of government in his hands must be able to take responsibility,' he declared. 'Irresponsible sovereignty is for me a phrase without meaning.'³

For the next eight years Franz Joseph ruled as an autocrat, sharing his power with nobody, treating his ministers as his servants, there to carry out his orders. All his subjects, regardless of nationality, were administered by a centralised bureaucracy: this seemed to him expedient and right, as did a Press law so rigorous that the Archbishop of Vienna was threatened with police action because he had forgotten to submit a copy of a pastoral letter for censorship. The Emperor was unconcerned by mounting popular resentment, both of the system itself and of the means by which it was enforced—'a standing army of soldiers, a seated army of officials, a kneeling army of priests, and a creeping army of informants'⁴—to quote one radical critic. Provided law and order were enforced and enough recruits and money were forthcoming for the army, the internal situation was he assumed perfectly satisfactory.

Franz Joseph regarded foreign policy as his special prerogative. International stability was essential to him, for the Monarchy resembled a jelly, the only cohesive element in which was the Crown, set in the mould of the *status quo* in Europe, and it was vital that this should remain unaltered. He enjoyed a special relationship with the Czar, who assured him with something amounting to paternal affection, 'I rejoice to see you daily more admired and honoured as you deserve',⁵ and he was convinced that the rulers of Europe shared his views on the necessity of maintaining peace. Unfortunately some of them had other ideas.

There were three wars within the next fifteen years. In 1853 Russia attacked Turkey and the Crimean war began. Franz Joseph ignored accusations of base ingratitude from St. Petersburg and refused to take the field in support of Nicholas I. He then concluded an alliance with Britain and France but did not enter the war on their side, leaving it to them to tie down and defeat Russia in the Crimea, and so safeguard the *status quo* in the Balkans by frustrating the Czar's plans for annexing part of the European provinces of Turkey. This policy of sitting on the fence achieved all he hoped for, but at a price. It wrecked his relationship with the Czar who was enraged by the attitude of his former protégé, 'the Emperor Apostolical has become the servant of the Crescent—a fine thing'.[6] When the war was over the Russian Ambassador in Vienna made a sombre prophecy: 'I am only sorry for the young Emperor, for his bearing has so offended the Russians that he can be certain of never having a quiet hour for the rest of his reign.'[7] In London the Foreign Secretary summed up the feelings of the rest of Europe in a scathing comment to the Austrian Ambassador. 'The Austrians,' he observed, 'lacked finesse and, it would appear, loyalty.'[8] When two years later Franz Joseph was forced to fight to defend his inheritance he had no ally.

The next war broke out in Italy where the suppression of the revolt in Lombardy and Venetia in 1848–49 had not eliminated nationalist feeling. To the inhabitants of those two provinces the continuation of Austrian rule merely, as one of them said, 'gave them the choice of being fried or boiled',[9] and they had the full support of Cavour, the Prime Minister of Piedmont, who found a powerful ally in the French Emperor Napoleon III.

Napoleon III, a nephew of Napoleon Bonaparte, had seized power in France by a *coup d' état* in 1851, and was proclaimed Emperor in the following year. To Franz Joseph, the head of the oldest dynasty in Europe, this short vulgar little man with dull eyes and a large moustache was a parvenu, only reluctantly to be addressed on correspondence by the conventional greeting between monarchs '*M. mon Frère*', to be mistrusted because of his revolutionary and conspiratorial past, and altogether unworthy of much attention. The Emperor's mistrust was justified; his disdain was not. Napoleon was devious, unpredictable and very ambitious. Nobody could forecast what he would do next: Lord Palmerston the British Foreign Secretary said that his mind 'seemed to be as full of schemes as a warren is of rabbits'.[10] In 1858 the French Emperor's pet scheme was the re-establishment of a Bonapartist hegemony in Italy, to realise which the first step must be to drive the Austrians out of the Italian peninsula. His interests and those of Cavour coincided. They concluded an agreement whereby Napoleon pledged French support for Piedmont in a war to liberate Lombardy and Venetia, provided that Austria could be provoked into starting hostilities.

The Emperor—Ruler and Statesman

Franz Joseph considered that there could be no argument about his right to Lombardy and Venetia, for both provinces had been awarded to the Monarchy by the European Powers at the Congress of Vienna in 1815. In the spring of 1859 when France and Piedmont began to arm he sent an ultimatum to Cavour. It was rejected. By the end of May the French had crossed the Alps and joined up with the Piedmontese; on June 4th their combined forces defeated the Austrians at Magenta, and three days later Napoleon III entered Milan. It was not a good start to the war. The Emperor who meanwhile had left Vienna to join his troops in Italy with high hopes of victory, and visions of the day when the Imperial Double Eagle would fly in triumph over the Piedmontese capital, Turin, was horrified by the disaster at Magenta. He dismissed his Commander-in-Chief for 'monumental incompetence' and assumed personal command of the army with a Chief of Staff aged seventy-one to advise him. A week later he was defeated by Napoleon at Solferino, a battle in which over two hundred and fifty thousand men were engaged, and in which both sides suffered casualties amounting to fifteen per cent of their total strength.

Franz Joseph was then twenty-nine. He tried to console himself with the thought that he was not entirely to blame for the defeat, but it undermined his confidence in the army, in himself, in his luck, and the slaughter appalled him. His troops were demoralised and exhausted. He swallowed his pride, met the victor who he referred to as 'that arch blackguard Napoleon'[11] at Villafranca and concluded peace. The terms imposed on him by the French could have been worse. He lost Lombardy but retained Venetia and the famous Quadrilateral of fortresses—Mantua, Peschiera, Verona and Legnano—which formed his main base in Italy, a springboard from which Lombardy might in due course be recaptured. Throughout their history the Habsburgs had been noted for their ability to regain strength after a loss and, having done so, to recoup it. The Emperor returned to Vienna determined to emulate his ancestors, but when seven years later he once again went to war, it was not to recover his lost province but to defend something which he valued above everything, the leadership of the

Age and Experience

assortment of principalities, ecclesiastical states and free cities
which made up the German Confederation.

The German Confederation had been set up in 1815 after the
Napoleonic Wars. Shortly after Franz Joseph ascended the throne
Prince Schwarzenberg defined his sovereign's position within it
in the following terms:

> His Majesty the Emperor of Austria is the first German Prince.
> This is a right, sanctified by treaties and the course of centuries,
> by Austrian political power, and by the wording of treaties on
> which federal relations, still in force, are founded. His Majesty
> is not willing to renounce this right.[12]

It never occurred to Franz Joseph that there could be any question
of doing so. Twenty of his ancestors had been crowned Holy
Roman Emperor of the German 'nation', and when that title was
abolished the presidency of the Federal Diet (the Central Assembly
of the Confederation), had been awarded by the Powers to
Austria. But four years after Solferino the Emperor discovered
that one state was not prepared to accept his primacy in Germany.
When he convened a meeting of the German Princes in Frankfurt
with the object of drawing up plans for a revised Confederation
under Habsburg leadership, the King of Prussia boycotted it.

Wilhelm I of Prussia had been bullied into staying away from
Frankfurt by his Minister President Otto von Bismarck. A tall,
powerfully built man with piercing blue eyes, there was nothing
ordinary about Bismarck, much that was contradictory and little
that was moderate. He chain smoked cigars, had an enormous
appetite, consumed large quantities of alcohol and fussed continually about his health. He was an immense bundle of nerves, but as
a statesman he combined a grasp of detail with a breadth of vision
unique amongst his contemporaries. Unfortunately for Franz
Joseph he was determined that Prussia must become the leader
of the German Confederation.

Bismarck made no attempt to conceal his intentions. In 1865
the Imperial Ambassador in Berlin reported: 'Bismarck placed
before us, in so many words, the alternative of withdrawing from
Germany and transferring our centre of gravity to Ofen,[13] or of

seeing Prussia in the ranks of our enemies on the occasion of the first European war.'[14] In Berlin preparations were already far advanced for that war which, according to Helmuth von Moltke the general responsible for them, would be fought, not because the existence of Prussia was threatened or public opinion demanded it, but because it was:

> . . . a struggle . . . recognised as a necessity by the Cabinet, not for territorial aggrandisement but for an ideal end—the establishment of power.[15]

Von Moltke had spent practically the whole of his military career on the Staff, specialising in problems of logistics, rapid mobilisation and modern weapons. He was a quiet man, clean shaven, thin lipped, exacting in the standards which he set himself, and endowed with a first class brain. Bismarck described him as 'unconditionally reliable and cold to the very heart'.[16] Together they were a formidable combination.

It soon became painfully clear that the Emperor possessed no minister who could in any way match up to Bismarck. In April 1866 the Prussian Minister President concluded an agreement with Victor Emmanuel, the recently proclaimed King of Italy, whereby the latter undertook to attack Austria if hostilities opened within three months. In May he contrived to escalate a long standing dispute between Prussia and the Monarchy over the future of Schleswig-Holstein to the point where only two choices were open to Franz Joseph. He must voluntarily surrender the leadership of the German Confederation to Prussia, or he must fight to keep it. The former alternative he could not as head of the House of Habsburg entertain. Whatever the risk he must fight, and once again without allies. Appeals to the lesser German states to declare themselves on his side met with a tepid response. The best that Imperial diplomacy could achieve was a strange last minute agreement with France which ensured Napoleon III's neutrality (on which he had already decided) on condition that at the end of the war and whatever its outcome, Venetia would be handed over to the French Emperor to pass on to Victor Emmanuel. Also the Prussians were armed with the latest rifle, the breech-loader, which fired at five times the rate of the old fashioned muzzle-loader with which the Emperor's army was equipped. They would be outnumbered on the field of battle for Prussia had a total population of only fourteen million against the Monarchy's thirty-five million but, as Franz Joseph knew, when that ultimate test came, everything would depend on the courage of his troops and on the ability of Feldzeugmeister Benedek who as Commander-in-Chief of the army in Bohemia would face the main Prussian attack.

Benedek had distinguished himself at Solferino and after that battle was promoted over the heads of thirty-seven senior generals. His military luck was proverbial, the troops idolised him, and his panache in the field was in the great tradition of the Imperial army. By contrast with the cold intellectual von Moltke, Benedek was a volatile man, liable to alternating fits of exaltation and depression, who admitted that he knew little about strategy and tactics. But his courage and absolute loyalty to the Emperor were unquestionable. The latter made him accept a command which he did not want, for he did not know the terrain in Bohemia, was doubtful whether he was up to the job and said so. Franz Joseph overruled him, and for Benedek the Emperor's wish was law. The judgement of both of them was put to the test when on June 22nd the Prussians crossed the frontier and the war began.

During the next week the Prussians advanced deep into Bohemia. News from the front was sparse and confused, and Franz Joseph had no clear idea of what was happening until on June 30th he received a telegram from Benedek, drafted in one of the General's blackest moods, imploring that peace be concluded at any price as a military catastrophe was unavoidable. The Emperor was horrified. Apparently no major battle had been fought. Honour apart, to lay down arms in such circumstances would mean the end of the Monarchy as a European power. He replied, 'It is impossible to conclude peace. I command that—if it is unavoidable—you should retreat in good order.'[17] Benedek, that blindly loyal servant of the Habsburgs, obeyed. On July 2nd he reformed the army, its back to the river Elbe, near the village of

Königgrätz to stand and fight the Prussians. Early on the following morning he rode out to review the dispositions of his troops. The day was cold and wet: the uniforms of the Emperor's soldiers were a spectrum of colour—white, green, brown, blue, crimson—splashed across the drab landscape. As Benedek, surrounded by his staff in their gold laced cocked hats with light green plumes passed by, regimental bands struck up and the men cheered. The sight of their Commander-in-Chief was evocative of the great days of the past when the Imperial army had marched to victory on the Rhine, or down the long dusty road through Hungary to defend the outer bastion of Christendom against the Turks. Nearby the Prussians in sober field grey looked forward into the future.

The battle began at 7.30 a.m. Two Prussian armies were on the field. A third was advancing through the wooded defiles of the Bohemian mountains to join them but nobody knew exactly where it was, and von Moltke was by no means certain of victory. In Vienna Franz Joseph waited anxiously for news. The day wore on and none came. At last, late in the evening a telegram arrived from Benedek. It read: 'The disaster to the army which I feared . . . has today occurred.'[18] The King of Saxony was due to arrive: the Emperor went to the station to meet him, his face as white as his uniform.

On hearing of the Emperor's defeat the Cardinal Secretary of State exclaimed 'the world is collapsing'.[19] For Franz Joseph it had broken asunder. As night fell on the battlefield of Königgrätz the final curtain came down on the great role which the House of Habsburg had played through many centuries in Germany. The Emperor was not an arrogant man, but he had his full share of Habsburg pride. This was the harshest blow he had yet suffered, and it scarred him for the rest of his life. The failure against Prussia turned to dust and ashes the successes in Italy, where at Custozza Archduke Albrecht with an army of seventy-five thousand men routed over a hundred thousand Italians, and at Lissa where Admiral Tegethof won a brilliant naval victory. Venetia passed to Victor Emmanuel, and the Monarchy was finally ousted from the Italian peninsula.

In this bitter hour even the consolation of the support and affection of the inhabitants of his capital was denied to Franz Joseph. Morale in Vienna was abysmal, 'people say openly that they no longer wished to be ruled by this dynasty'.[20] The Mayor presented a petition sharply criticising the Imperial Ministers and demanding that they be replaced by more competent men. As the Emperor drove through the streets onlookers shouted for his abdication. He held on and whatever his feelings, his self-control was such that he betrayed little of them in public. No further resistance was possible, and once again he swallowed his pride and negotiated for peace. It was concluded at the end of July. The Monarchy lost no land and the idemnity which had to be paid was not excessive, but the Emperor was finally excluded from Germany and had to recognise the federation of the north German states under Prussia. The war had been fought as von Moltke said not for territory, but for power.

Each defeat abroad compelled a concession at home. Solferino forced Franz Joseph faced with bitter criticism of his policies, an empty exchequer and no possibility of raising foreign loans unless public control of the budget was instituted, to abandon autocracy and promulgate a constitution establishing a central Parliament. He did so with the utmost reluctance, stressing that the new system was a creation of the Crown in whose interests it must be operated. Königgrätz forced him to come to terms with the Hungarians.

'Rather the devil than the Hungarians.' This remark, attributed to the Empress Maria Theresa, epitomised the feelings of her successors towards the most intractable of their subjects, that section of the inhabitants of Hungary who spoke the Magyar language and who, although numerically in the minority, regarded all other races living within its frontiers as their vassals. The Hungarians were a proud people to whom the virtue of moderation was unknown and who looked back to A.D. 1,000 when their kingdom was founded by St. Stephen. Imbued with a strange blend of mystical historical emotion, they acknowledged no King as legitimate unless he had been crowned in Budapest with St. Stephen's holy crown, swearing 'by the living God, by the Virgin

Mary and all God's saints' to defend all the lands of that crown, and these they maintained included not only inner Hungary but also Croatia-Slavonia and Transylvania. Hungary had been liberated by the Habsburgs from the Turks at the end of the seventeenth century. Shortly after that the Hungarians recognised the Habsburg Emperor as their King, and he in return pledged himself to respect their rights, privileges and institutions. Thereafter they enjoyed and jealously guarded a special status in the Monarchy, bitterly resented the loss of it after their revolt in 1848–49, and never ceased to demand it back. The constitution promulgated by the Emperor in his February Patent of 1861 placed them on the same level as the other nationalities and in no way satisfied them. They boycotted the very large numbers of Imperial troops stationed in their country, and refused to send delegates to the central Parliament or to pay taxes to Vienna.

This deadlock continued until 1866, but in the meantime a moderate party was gaining influence in Hungary. Its leaders were a strangely assorted pair. Ferenc Deak was a lawyer and country squire, unimpressive in manner and appearance, and capable of appearing on formal occasions wearing a black cloak and galoshes. Count Julius Andrassy, tall and handsome, was an aristocrat who looked magnificent in his Hungarian magnate's robes. Deak had never travelled outside the Monarchy; Andrassy knew Europe. As a young man he had been involved in the 1848 revolution, when it failed went into exile, and in 1851 was hanged *in absentia* in Budapest. By 1857 when he was amnestied and returned to Hungary, he had acquired the capacity of thinking in terms of European politics which Deak lacked. Courageous, self-confident and sophisticated, quick to sense the mood of the man to whom he was talking, he excelled in handling people and persuading them to do what he wanted. His diplomatic skill tempered Deak's legal pedantry. The two men complemented each other and both were ardent Hungarian patriots, but their patriotism was blended with common sense. Hungary, they reasoned, was too small to be able by herself to play any great role in Europe, but she could become great in association with the Habsburg Monarchy if she could assume her proper place there. 'We are comrades of the Austrians',

Deak said, 'we stand with and beside them, but we will never be under them.'[21]

Defeat by Prussia made a settlement with Hungary imperative. The Emperor saw Deak and Andrassy who told him that they demanded no more than they had done before the disaster of Königgrätz, but also made it clear that they would accept no less. Franz Joseph found Deak wise but timid, and Andrassy honourable, but imprecise in his ideas for Hungary and without the necessary thought for the interests of the rest of the Monarchy. He procrastinated, but eventually allowed himself to be persuaded that a settlement with Hungary would not weaken the dynasty. Early in 1867 the Ausgleich—the Compromise—was agreed, a bilateral contract concluded directly between the Emperor and the Hungarians which established 'the lands of St. Stephen'—Hungary, Transylvania and Croatia-Slavonia—as a kingdom with internal autonomy (thereby placing a large number of Slavs under direct Magyar rule), and left the remainder of the Habsburg lands as a loose federation nominally governed by a Parliament in Vienna. Outwardly, so far as foreign affairs, defence and finance were concerned the Emperor's domain, now renamed the Austro-Hungarian Monarchy (although still referred to for purposes of abbreviation as Austria), remained a unity; internally it was split in two.

The overall political system set up by the Compromise resembled in many ways a secular version of the Trinity. There were three Parliaments, one in Vienna, one in Budapest, and the Delegations which consisted of twenty members of the Upper House and forty members from the Lower House of each Parliament, and sat separately in the Austrian and Hungarian capitals. There were three joint Ministers—for Foreign Affairs, Defence and Finance—who did not sit in either Parliament but reported to both Delegations. There were three armies, a combined army, and an Austrian and a Hungarian militia. The apex and keystone of this triune system was the Emperor in whose person were combined the three roles of Emperor of Austria, King of Hungary and joint Monarch, and who was Commander-in-Chief of the joint army. If the Delegations could not agree, the point at issue was referred to him and his decision was final.

The Emperor—Ruler and Statesman

On March 13th, 1867, a Hungarian Government was set up with Andrassy as Minister President. Three months later, with a pageantry reminiscent of the Middle Ages, Franz Joseph was crowned King of Hungary in Budapest. In Vienna, Parliament was convened, presented with a new constitution embodying the Compromise and grudgingly ratified it.

In Queen Victoria's opinion it was 'a miserable thing to be a constitutional Queen and to be unable to do what is right': [22] all nineteenth century monarchs found constitutions and the Parliaments which stemmed from them irksome. Franz Joseph thoroughly disliked and mistrusted the constitutions to which he had been forced to agree in the Compromise, but he was still left with a great deal more power than most constitutional sovereigns, who according to Bagehot's classic definition have three rights only— to be consulted, to encourage, to warn. The 1867 constitution in the Austrian half of the Monarchy laid down that the Emperor held his position by divine right, not by the will of the people, and stated categorically 'the Emperor appoints and dismisses the Ministers'. [23] In Hungary Franz Joseph had slightly less power— but only slightly less. He remained his own Prime Minister, no minister could survive in office without his support, and in neither half of the Monarchy could any major decision be taken without his approval. Parliament in the opinion of one deputy existed merely to provide the oil for the machinery of government, the machinery was operated by the Emperor. Since he was free to appoint whom he chose as Minister of Foreign Affairs he was able to control foreign policy, and so far as defence was concerned, while the approval of both Parliaments was required for the budget and the number of recruits, his reserved rights were tacitly acknowledged and eventually he got his own way. The Compromise did not to any significant extent diminish the power of the Crown.

(ii) MODUS VIVENDI

In 1871 one of the Emperor's senior officials wrote:

If a Monarch ruled in Austria who had twice as much genius and drive as Frederick the Great, and if this Monarch only wanted to do what was right and wise and logical he would fail. The execution of a consistent policy is not possible in this State for as much as three months.[24]

It was a fair description of the difficulties with which Franz Joseph had struggled since the Compromise which, although it strengthened the Monarchy by ensuring the loyalty of Hungary to the Crown, did not diminish the burden of ruling it. The problem always before the Emperor was how to prevent the Magyars from grabbing still more and—far worse—how to conciliate and gain the co-operation of the other nationalities who considered that they had been unfairly treated by the Compromise and were at loggerheads with each other, without making concessions to them. The Vienna Parliament, dominated by that large proportion of his subjects who were of German ethnic origin, resembled a tribal assembly to which the representatives of each nationality came for the purpose of furthering their own cause and, if they failed to do so, walked out in dudgeon. By 1871 the Czechs, Tyrolese, Poles, Slovenes and Roumanians were all boycotting it, and the Compromise had undergone a considerable strain but, thanks to the Emperor's untiring efforts, it had not collapsed.

Meanwhile, Franz Joseph had suffered another disappointment. He had not been reconciled to his defeat by Prussia and clung to the hope that the day of revenge would come. But the experience of two disasters made him cautious, and when the Franco-Prussian war broke out in 1870 he was adamant that the Monarchy would only come out on the side of the French if it was clear that they were winning. The defeat of Napoleon III at Sedan was a great blow to him, and when congratulating the Prussian envoy in Vienna on his sovereign's victory he made no attempt to conceal his feelings, 'I cannot, however, rejoice at the event, neither would you expect me to do so.'[25] On January 18th, 1871, when the King of Prussia was proclaimed German Emperor, he was finally compelled to accept the fact that the European *status quo* which had existed when he came to the throne in 1848 was irrevocably altered.

What foreign policy would best serve the interests of the

Monarchy in this new and dangerous world? The humiliation of Königgrätz was still bitterly resented by many influential people in the Monarchy who, mistrustful of Berlin, maintained that the only hope for the future lay in drawing closer to Russia. Franz Joseph found what he described as the 'arrogance, vanity, and sanctimoniousness'[26] of 'Old Wilhelm' as he called the new German Emperor almost unendurable. But he also neither liked nor trusted the Czar. Alexander II, an exceptionally handsome man, had an air of freezing hauteur—a junior member of the Diplomatic Corps recalled that when the Czar addressed them 'there was something in his voice and a look in his eye reminiscent of the Great Mogul addressing an earthworm'[27]—was moody and unpredictable, and had never forgiven Franz Joseph for his failure to support his father in the Crimean War. Moreover, it seemed that Alexander was either unwilling or unable to control his Pan-Slavist subjects who were eager to help their fellow Slavs in the Balkans to free themselves from the Turks, and the openly proclaimed aims of this movement had never been reassuring. The assertion by one of its founders that 'Our most helpful and powerful allies in Europe are the Slavs, our kinsmen by blood, tongue, heart, history and faith, and there are ten million in Turkey and twenty million in Austria,'[28] was not agreeable reading in Vienna, and still less in Budapest where the ruling Magyars denied any form of corporate expression to the Slav inhabitants of Hungary.

Altogether there was a great deal about Russia which was alarming. It was remote (St. Petersburg was four days train journey from Vienna) and it was alien, the beginning of Asia rather than the eastern edge of Europe. Also it was a country of over a hundred million people the ruler of which was unfettered by a constitution or the necessity of giving his subjects any account of his policy, and where everything was on a vast scale. The Winter Palace in St. Petersburg was half a mile long, and foreigners returned with stories of Russian Court Balls at which the guests numbered not hundreds but thousands and 'one could literally trample on diamonds . . . one walked on pearls and rubies'.[29] The revolutionary plots, the draconian measures of the

Czar's secret police of which hair-raising rumours reached the outside world, sounded far more savage than anything comparable in Western Europe. And Russia, except in the Crimea, had never been defeated in any war. It was all very well for Disraeli to advise Queen Victoria 'to take no notice of the Czar's caprices'.[30] England was a remote island. Part of the frontiers of the Monarchy marched with Russia and Franz Joseph's sensations with regard to that country resembled those of a timid early Christian contemplating the lions in the Circus, with a fixed resolution to do nothing to cause an encounter with them, for it would quite certainly be final.

But at the same time it was impossible to permit Russian influence in the Balkans to increase unchecked. The Sultan's hold on his European provinces was tenuous. Montenegro, Roumania and Serbia already enjoyed de facto independence of the Porte, and all three principalities were extremely susceptible to Pan-Slav propaganda. There was a great deal of unrest in Bulgaria and Bosnia Herzegovina which were still under the direct rule of Constantinople. If Turkey collapsed, the indications were that the Russians would try and enlarge Serbia into a satellite state wholly under their influence and stretching across the Balkan peninsula. This would create a great deal of unrest amongst the Emperor's Slav subjects, effectively prevent the Monarchy from expanding south-east towards the Aegean (the only direction in which expansion was now possible), and jeopardise the Imperial provinces of Istria and Dalmatia running along the east coast of the Adriatic, to which Bosnia Herzegovina formed the hinterland. Russia must be contained in the Balkans by all means short of war, and to do this the Monarchy must have an ally strong enough to exercise a restraining influence on the Czar. There was only one choice. In 1871 Franz Joseph decided that, much as he disliked it, the interests of the Monarchy demanded that he should seek a rapprochement with Germany. To be successful in this he must have a Foreign Minister who shared his convictions and was acceptable to Bismarck. At the end of the year the Emperor appointed the man whom he had hanged *in absentia* twenty years earlier, the Hungarian Julius Andrassy, Foreign Minister of the Monarchy and Minister of the Imperial and Royal House.

Franz Joseph made this appointment without consulting any-one, and it was not popular. Most foreign diplomats dismissed Andrassy as a political lightweight. The staff of the Ministry of Foreign Affairs regarded him as an amateur and were unenthusias-tic about their new chief. The Count however was agreeable to everyone, entertained on a lavish scale and gave the impression of being entirely at home in his new position. He brought with him an atmosphere of optimism and confidence and when he took up office a new wind blew through the dusty corridors of the Ballhausplatz.[31] The Emperor found his breadth of vision, incisiveness and imperturbability in a crisis a refreshing contrast to the average run of ministers with whom he had to deal. Andrassy on his side openly proclaimed his respect for his sovereign's judgement, describing him as his own Minister of Foreign Affairs, and not a bad one at that. An exceptional working relationship developed between them.

Old enmities had to be abandoned and fences mended where-ever possible. Andrassy steadily built up an understanding with Bismarck, who later recalled that their joint attitude was that of two neighbouring country squires, rather than that of two states-men. The German Emperor, the Czar and Franz Joseph banded themselves together in the Dreikaiserbund or Three Emperor's League, announcing that they were united in their desire for peace. This was not, however, in practice 'a union for mutual advantage' the dictionary definition of the term 'league', for all three were concerned to extract as much benefit as possible from it for themselves. Their association resembled a *ménage à trois* with all the jealousy, mistrust and manœuvring for position inherent in such an arrangement. It offered no firm guarantee for peace, and did not stand up to the strain of the next international crisis when the *status quo* in the Balkans collapsed.

In 1875 Bosnia and Herzegovina rose against the Turks, and in the following year the Bulgarians followed their example in an insurrection which was brutally crushed by the Porte. Serbia and Montenegro then declared war on the Sultan. In April 1877, the Czar announced that he must come to the aid of the oppressed

Christians in the Balkans, and for the ninth time the Russian army took the field against Turkey. When Alexander was asked about the ultimate objective of the campaign he replied laconically 'Constantinople'. Ten months later the Russians were within sight of the walls of the Ottoman capital.

In the spring of 1875 the Emperor had for the first time visited Dalmatia, a tour which filled him with enthusiasm for 'this primitive but loyal province'.[32] When trouble flared up in the Balkans he was thoroughly alarmed and told one of his senior diplomats:

> If for example Bosnia becomes independent we shall lose Croatia and Dalmatia. We can never agree to this, we have already lost enough territory . . . the western provinces of Turkey are my direct concern.[33]

Andrassy agreed with him:

> At this depressing spectacle of oriental confusion we are sitting in the stage box, and . . . in Bosnia and Herzegovina at least we have vital interests.[34]

How to secure these vital interests was another matter. No support would be forthcoming from Bismarck who, anxious about a French war of revenge, publicly declared that Germany had no interest in what happened in the Balkans, and Franz Joseph was advised by his generals that he could not declare war on Russia with any hope of victory.

Happily for the Emperor, Britain too was actively concerned to contain Russia, and reactions in London to the prospect of a Turkish defeat were robust. The Tory Prime Minister Disraeli[35] was pursuing with the enthusiastic approval of his sovereign a policy of Imperial grandeur and, having secured control of the Suez Canal, had proclaimed the Queen Empress of India. The arrival of the Czar's army on the Bosphorus posed a threat to the route to India which Queen Victoria was not prepared to tolerate. Disraeli and Lord Salisbury the Secretary of State for Foreign Affairs were bombarded by letters and telegrams from Osborne,

Windsor and Balmoral in which their sovereign inveighed against the Russians, demanded that the strongest measures be taken, and threatened to 'lay down the thorny crown' and abdicate rather than see Britain 'kiss the feet of the great barbarian'.[36] Fortified by her approval, and secure in the knowledge that a large section of the British public heartily agreed with her, the government on February 9th, 1878, ordered the Mediterranean Fleet to proceed to the sea of Marmora where it anchored forty miles from Constantinople.

The British were now in a position to cut the Russian lines of communication by sea. The Emperor could threaten their lines of communication on land. The Russian supply system was chaotic, and their troops exhausted. The Czar hurriedly concluded the Peace of San Stefano with the Porte. This set up a new nominally independent south Slav State, Bulgaria, enlarged to stretch across the greater part of the Balkan peninsula and bordering in the south on the Aegean Sea. The implications were plain. This greater Bulgaria which would undoubtedly be under Russian influence, would serve the dual purpose of blocking Austrian expansion towards the Aegean and acting as a shield to the Russian lines of communication when they next attacked Turkey. The Peace of San Stefano was therefore unacceptable to the other European Powers. Diplomatic pressure was brought to bear on Russia from all sides, and finally St. Petersburg reluctantly agreed that those clauses of it which were of general European interest—which in effect meant most of them—should be discussed at a Congress in Berlin presided over by Bismarck.

Andrassy now saw an opportunity which might never recur to 'bring the western half of the Balkan peninsula permanently under our influence—I do not want to conquer it'.[37] By this he meant to gain not only control of Bosnia Herzegovina, but an assured outlet for the Monarchy from these provinces through the Sanjak of Novi Bazar southwards to Salonica, to safeguard which, the frontiers of the new State of Bulgaria as defined at San Stefano must be pushed back. In this latter point the interest of the Monarchy and Britain coincided, for Disraeli was convinced that the survival of Turkey in Europe depended on cutting Bulgaria down to size. He therefore agreed that, in return for Austrian support on the Bulgarian question, Britain would propose in Berlin that the Monarchy should be given a mandate to occupy Bosnia Herzegovina and to garrison the Sanjak of Novi Bazar.

The Congress opened on June 18th, 1878, and was attended by a galaxy of leading statesmen. Andrassy represented the Monarchy, and when he appeared in his scarlet Hungarian general's uniform frogged with gold at the formal opening of the Congress, those who had not seen him before did not know what to make of him. It seemed incredible that this man, who by the Emperor's command had been hanged in effigy in Budapest twenty-seven years earlier, should now represent that Emperor wearing the highest Order in the Monarchy, the Golden Fleece. Junior members of the British delegation were reminded of the leader of a tzigane orchestra, or a gypsy on Epsom Downs. His exotic appearance hardly inspired confidence in his reliability, and Disraeli's first comment was reserved. The Count, he reported to Queen Victoria, was 'a picturesque looking person but apparently lacking calm'.[38]

The British Prime Minister's opinion of Andrassy, however, rapidly improved. Describing a four-hour argument with the Russians on the Bulgarian problem, 'the severest four hours I can well recall', he told the Queen that throughout it Austria had steadfastly supported him,[39] and noted a few days later 'I . . . find Count Andrassy a manageable man'.[40] The Imperial Foreign Minister's capacity for summing up people no doubt contributed to this. He realised that Disraeli, the old Jew with his sphinx-like impassivity, had a clear idea of what he wanted, was determined to get it, and that what he wanted was all that the Monarchy could wish. Andrassy therefore confined himself to playing the role of what the British Press described as 'the brilliant second', never thrusting himself forward, resolutely supporting Disraeli and the other British delegate Lord Salisbury and leaving them to make the running, which they did. The Congress ended with a treaty in which the greater Bulgaria of San Stefano was trisected into an autonomous principality under a Christian prince to be elected by the Bulgarians, East Rumelia, a semi-autonomous province under

Turkish administration, and Macedonia which was returned to Turkey. And, most important of all to Franz Joseph, the Monarchy was awarded a mandate to occupy and administer Bosnia Herzegovina and authorised to garrison the Sanjak of Novi Bazar. Andrassy returned to Vienna and announced to the Emperor 'the doors of the Orient are now open to your Majesty'.[41] Franz Joseph was delighted. At last he had been represented with distinction at a meeting of the leading statesmen of Europe and, for the first time since his accession, territory had been added to the Monarchy. The German Ambassador reported to Berlin that the Emperor's melancholy expression which had recently been so noticeable had disappeared, and his pleasure that his reign had been marked by a success was apparent to every one.

It was now necessary to advance through the doors of the Orient into Bosnia Herzegovina. These provinces, forming a wedge between the coastal strip of Dalmatia and the valley of the Save which marked the frontier of Hungary, were remote, little known, and thinly inhabited by one and a half million people, half of whom were Muslim and half Orthodox, most of them illiterate and miserably poor. Sarejevo which, with its domes and minarets, bazaars and veiled women, impressed at least one Western visitor as being more oriental than Cairo, was the only town of any size. Much of Bosnia consisted of mountains covered with thick forests and split up by deep gorges. Herzegovina was an arid plateau, large areas of which were devoid of vegetation, surrounded by a wall of mountains. Both provinces were isolated from the main Balkan trade routes, and communications within them were primitive. Apart from about three hundred and fifty miles of indifferent road traversing a series of ravines by means of collapsing bridges, there were only tracks which were impassable in bad weather. The Monarchy had been awarded a mandate to occupy a most unprepossessing area, generally regarded, with the possible exception of Albania, as the most backward of all the Sultan's European territories.

Andrassy is alleged to have maintained that the occupation of Bosnia Herzegovina would be no more than a 'parade march' carried out by 'a company of hussars and a band'. Certainly he was determined that the occupation force must in no circumstances give the impression of entering as a conquering army. When the advance guard crossed the frontier at the end of July 1878, they brought with them a proclamation informing the local inhabitants that 'the Sultan had entrusted his friend, the Emperor, with the protection of their lands' and that they came as friends to restore order, peace and prosperity.[42] The former statement was hardly true, and the latter unsupported by money or supplies with which to purchase local goodwill. Within five days the first opposition was encountered from bands of local Muslims and deserters from the Turkish garrisons which were still stationed in the two provinces. The operation soon showed every sign of developing into a campaign similar to that which the British were often compelled to fight (sometimes with signal disaster) on the North-West Frontier of India, a campaign in barren country against an enemy who sniped from the mountain side, constantly threatened the supply lines and could not be brought to battle. Andrassy observed that one could not make an omelette without breaking eggs. The Emperor after three weeks began to speak of the necessity of 'rescuing' his forces and insisted on the mobilisation of several more divisions for, as he told his ministers, 'to abandon the mandate which it is in our interest to retain, and with which we have been entrusted by Europe would mean the end of the Monarchy'.[43] When resistance finally ceased at the end of October more than 150,000 troops had been engaged and had suffered over 5,000 casualties. In an operation costing 85 million gulden a very large sledge-hammer had been used to crack a very small nut.

The performance of the army had not been distinguished. It demonstrated that the Monarchy alone could not hope to defeat Russia in the field, and that unless an ally was forthcoming the forward policy in the Balkans with the risks of war with Russia which this entailed must be halted. In the following year an ally appeared. Since the Congress of Berlin relations between Germany and Russia had deteriorated. Alexander II was reported to be under the influence of his Minister of War who was strongly anti-German. If France attacked in an attempt to recover Alsace Lorraine, Russia might strike at Germany from the east. This was the nightmare which haunted Bismarck, and which the rum and champagne which according to the British Ambassador he was now taking 'between dinner and bed time, frequently but copiously',[44] failed to dispel. The situation forced him to the decision that in view of the unpredictable attitude of Russia he must make sure of the Monarchy. Towards the end of August 1879, Andrassy received a proposal from the German Chancellor for a defensive alliance—the prize which he and the Emperor had worked for eight years to win. The Imperial Foreign Minister drove a hard bargain. In the treaty which was signed in Vienna on October 7th, each party contracted to go to war in aid of the other if either was attacked by Russia, but there was no commitment for the Monarchy to intervene on the side of Germany if the latter was attacked by France. After this crowning triumph of his career Andrassy resigned, claiming proudly that the Monarchy had now resumed its proper place amongst the Powers of Europe and that the Emperor now had a free hand in the East. At the beginning of 1880 Franz Joseph could feel that if he had not yet reached a safe haven, he was beginning to enter calmer waters. Abroad his position was transformed by the German alliance, now the pivot of his foreign policy. At home the Compromise was generally accepted.

After thirteen years experience of making the Compromise work the Emperor had developed a remarkable talent for stopping dead and changing direction when he was about to run his head up against a brick wall. He made full use of the powers reserved to him under the constitution to appoint whom he wished to a ministerial post, refusing to allow them to resign until they were no longer useful and then dismissing them out of hand. In selecting his ministers he was uninfluenced by considerations of birth but, as he once told Andrassy, he insisted on working with men whom he could trust. By this he meant men who because they subscribed to his ideas could be relied upon to carry out his orders and who were temperamentally congenial to him, thinking as he did in terms of black and white, eschewing those abstractions and theories which he suspected and disliked because he found them incomprehensible. He treated them as subordinate officers rather than advisers, in discussion would never permit a departure from the subject under review and, never a good listener, if this was attempted, terminated the conversation abruptly. On taking office a minister might expect to receive a terse note such as the Emperor addressed to Prince Auersperg in 1871: 'Concealment of nothing from me, no innovations, unity, strict adherence to the laid down programme which will receive my support, I will tolerate no departure from it.'[45] Pessimistic by nature, and inclined to expect the worst of people rather than the best, he was determined to retain full control of affairs and constantly preoccupied to see that no minister became too popular or acquired too much power. It has been aptly pointed out that under Franz Joseph it would have been impossible even for Bismarck to have attained to a position similar to that which he held in Prussia.[46]

Appointments to posts at Court were also personally made by the Emperor, and he continued the traditional practice of giving them to members of the high aristocracy, a section of the community of which it had once been said that it did not contain four men competent to sit in the Upper House of Parliament. The result was that generally he was surrounded by men of mediocre ability, accustomed to listen to his most commonplace remarks with awed reverence, and amongst whom there was the mutual understanding that disagreeable news must if possible be kept from him. Franz Joseph was therefore to a great extent shut off by a Chinese wall of his own making from the mass of his subjects, most of whom only saw him from a distance, driving through the streets of Vienna or Budapest, inspecting troops, or on some public ceremonial or state occasion. But they knew a good deal about him. His courtesy was proverbial, so was his integrity. The most humble citizen could present a petition to his sovereign and, if it was found worthy of consideration, would be received in audience by him—and alone—and would find that he was conversant with every detail of their case. The Emperor drove from the Hofburg to Schönbrunn, his immense palace on the outskirts of Vienna, without an escort, accompanied only by an A.D.C., secure in the knowledge that while the inhabitants of his multinational domain might grumble from time to time about some aspect of Imperial rule, they did not want to do away with it. Demonstrations of loyalty and affection touched him deeply, but he made no dramatic statements or gestures to obtain them and never played to the gallery. With his serene sense of majesty he looked like an Emperor and behaved like one. While he could be kindly, he always contrived to convey the impression that there was a point beyond which the onlooker must not trespass, and that he stood alone in Olympian detachment, high above personalities and races, the patriarch of his subjects who could not conceive of existence without a patriarch.

Napoleon III once remarked that the difference between himself and Franz Joseph was that the Emperor of Austria could lose a battle, a province, a war, and still wake up next morning as Emperor, whereas he, Napoleon, was dependent on success. By 1880 Franz Joseph had lost two wars, several battles, all his possessions in Italy, been finally excluded from Germany and compelled to agree to the Compromise. But he was still the Emperor and had never, even in his darkest moments, considered relinquishing his post as the self-appointed sentry unceasingly on watch for the welfare of what he referred to as 'my' people. He had carried on and managed to caulk the seams of that 'worm-eaten battleship Austria'[47] as Bismarck once derisively called the Monarchy, and even though part of her superstructure had been shot away, she was still seaworthy, and he was still unquestionably in sole command. The situation, if not ideal, was now reasonably satisfactory, and Franz Joseph was convinced that he and nobody else was competent to decide what measures were necessary to ensure that it remained so. 'Nobody else' meant not only his subjects but the entire Imperial Family. With the exception of Archduke Albrecht, the Inspector General of the Army to whom he turned for advice on military (but only on military) problems, the Emperor had never welcomed unsolicited comments on his policy from his relations, even if they were older than himself. As for the younger generation, he was unable to comprehend their point of view and therefore considered their ideas uninteresting.

CHAPTER 2

The Emperor and the Empress

Shooting was the only relaxation which the Emperor permitted himself, and the only time when he wore civilian clothes—the leather shorts and green jacket with horn buttons of his peasant subjects. Whenever possible he invited Albrecht, Crown Prince and later King of Saxony, to join him for the stalking at Bad Ischl. Albrecht was his only close friend; Franz Joseph's temperament did not enable him to make friends easily, neither did his conception of his position permit it. Exalted though that position might be, it was also very lonely, and this loneliness was not alleviated by a placid family life.

Although in the proclamation announcing the abdication of his uncle, Ferdinand I, Franz Joseph succeeded to the throne 'by God's grace', in fact the whole affair was, as one of the attendant ministers noted, 'an arrangement within the Imperial Family'[1] made after consultation with their closest advisers, but without the slightest reference to the wishes of the inhabitants of the Monarchy. In this 'arrangement' Franz Joseph's mother, Archduchess Sophie, played a decisive part. She was one of those women whose affections are concentrated on their children. She was therefore easily persuaded that her husband Archduke Franz Karl, the Heir Apparent, had neither the personality nor the ability which the situation demanded, and to induce him to waive his right to the throne in favour of their eldest son. But for Sophie Franz Joseph would not have become Emperor until he was nearly fifty, for his father did not die until 1878. He owed the throne to his mother, to whom he was in any case devoted. It was a fact which he never forgot, and of which she on occasions no doubt reminded him.

The Emperor and the Empress

The Archduchess was a Wittelsbach, daughter of King Maximilian I of Bavaria, her sisters were the Queens of Prussia and Saxony, and she would dearly have loved to become Empress of Austria. But her adoration for her eldest son, 'my dearest, my heart's blood' outweighed her ambition. She saw him as 'the new anchor of the realm given by the grace of God' and consoled herself with the thought that she had been able to ensure that he was surrounded by people who shared her ideas. These were founded on emotion, consisted of a series of ingrained prejudices, and were certainly not progressive. Order, the Archduchess was never tired of preaching, must be maintained, mankind must be improved, and all this could only be done by the Monarch in whom absolute power must therefore be vested. But, stubborn and opinionated though she was, Sophie was not a cold-blooded scheming woman. Sentimental rather than imaginative and liable to burst into tears in moments of crisis, her overriding preoccupation was that all should go well with Franz Joseph. When it did she was delighted, when it did not she wept, lamented that years had been taken off her life and implored God to take her to her eternal rest. She does not appear to have attempted to exert any direct influence on politics, confining herself to presiding over the details of Court life, battering the Almighty with prayers for her son's wellbeing, fussing continually over his health, and beseeching his ministers to stop him from working so hard. In an endeavour to distract him she gave small *thé dansants*, which the Emperor who was an excellent dancer and by no means averse to waltzing with the attractive *Contessen* carefully selected by his mother, greatly enjoyed.

Attractive *Contessen*, however, impeccable their lineage could not, however, be considered as anything more than dancing partners, and as time wore on the Archduchess became much preoccupied with a question which she considered fell entirely within her sphere—the selection of a suitable bride for her son. This was not easy for Franz Joseph was hard to please, and the field of eligible princesses was limited. Finally Sophie decided on Hélène, the daughter of her sister Luise and Duke Max in Bavaria, head of the cadet branch of the House of Wittelsbach. The two young people were first cousins, and their marriage would be the twenty-second between the Houses of Habsburg and Wittelsbach, but the possible disadvantages of this close relationship do not appear to have occurred to the Archduchess, who in August 1853 invited Hélène, her mother, and her younger sister Elisabeth to Bad Ischl for a visit which she fondly hoped would lead to the engagement on which she had set her heart. Within a few days of their arrival Franz Joseph announced his engagement, not however to Hélène as his mother had planned, but to Elisabeth with whom he had fallen in love from the moment he set eyes on her.

Elisabeth—or Sisi as she was called by her family—was only fifteen. Duke Max her father, a gay raffish bohemian who mixed freely with all classes of people, regarded his eight children with indulgent affection and paid no attention to their upbringing. The family spent most of the year on his country estate at Possenhofen where Elisabeth, surrounded by brothers and sisters to whom she was devoted, was allowed to run wild, neglect her lessons, and ride to her heart's content. Naturally shy and sensitive, she had never been trained to appear in public, and when she came to Bad Ischl was no more than an enchanting child just out of the dancing class. On being told that Franz Joseph wished to marry her she wept. He was an attractive young man and she found him so, but the idea of becoming Empress terrified her, 'I am so young, so insignificant. I would do everything to make the Emperor happy, but will it succeed?'² The Emperor was in no doubt at all and, when obliged to return to Vienna, left with the utmost reluctance what he described as 'heaven on earth'. Archduchess Sophie thwarted for the first time by her son, gave way as gracefully as she could, but could not refrain from one derogatory remark. 'You are right,' she told Franz Joseph, 'Sisi is very pretty, but she has yellow teeth.'³

On April 22nd, 1854, Elisabeth arrived in Vienna for her wedding. The Emperor, the Imperial Family and the highest dignitaries of the Monarchy were assembled to meet her, surrounded by thousands of the citizens of the capital eager to catch the first sight of their future Empress. As the flower-bedecked ship which had brought her down the Danube approached the landing stage, they saw a tall slim young girl wearing a dress of rose coloured silk. When, before it had tied up, Franz Joseph leapt on board and, in one of the few public emotional gestures of his life, embraced her before them all, a storm of cheering broke out and, as one newspaper reported, there was not a dry eye in the crowd.[4]

A year earlier Elisabeth had been a child of no particular interest to anyone; now the free and easy life at Possenhofen was over for ever, and as she stepped ashore she entered another world. On reaching Schönbrunn, although tired and over-wrought, she was obliged to appear on the balcony again and again to wave to the crowd which had gathered in front of the palace. Then she was presented with the first of a series of memoranda setting out in detail the programme for the next few days and the part which she must play in it—the State drive into Vienna in a golden coach adorned with paintings by Rubens and drawn by eight white horses, the arrival at the Hofburg, the procession from there to the Augustiner Kirche, the marriage ceremony, the receptions and festivities which would follow it. She went through it all as if in a dream, surrounded by strange faces, stared at by myriads of people, bearing herself with astonishing composure, but white and silent. There was no honeymoon for the Emperor had no time for one, and within a week of being married he was once again at work in his study in the Hofburg only returning in the evening to Laxenburg, his palace twelve miles outside Vienna, where Elisabeth was left in the care of Archduchess Sophie.

Almost immediately there was trouble. Most doting mothers resent their daughter-in-law. Sophie by now forty-nine, an age at which many women are prone to be difficult and intolerant, was an exceptionally doting mother, always conscious of the fact that until Franz Joseph's marriage she had been the first lady in the Monarchy. She therefore considered herself entitled to the utmost respect and uniquely qualified to instruct Sisi in her new duties and responsibilities. Tactless and always stubbornly convinced that she knew best, the Archduchess, though well intentioned, was one of those maddening women who believe in pointing out people's faults to them, because to do so is for their good. She never left Elisabeth alone, would come into her room at all hours, and was constantly lecturing, advising, interfering, criticising. Sophie had expected to find a docile child who would listen gratefully and do what she was told, but she was met by tears, sulks or cold silence. The fact was that Elisabeth too was stubborn, had never been accustomed to discipline, and saw no reason why she should conform to pointless etiquette about which she was certainly not prepared to learn from her mother-in-law. In addition she was homesick, surrounded by uncongenial middle-aged ladies-in-waiting selected by the Archduchess, and lonely, for Franz Joseph was away so much. Unable to do anything without her mother-in-law's knowledge, and stifled by the formality and ceremonial with which she was surrounded, she wrote a number of sad little poems, spent a great deal of time playing with the birds and pets which she had brought with her from Possenhofen, and rode as often as possible in order to escape from the presence of the Archduchess. Within a few months the situation was a matter of general gossip at Court where the general opinion was that 'there is no sympathy between the Archduchess Sophie and her daughter-in-law, the former makes criticisms and gives orders which displease the young Empress to the last degree'.[5]

The Archduchess, quite unable to understand why her efforts to instruct her daughter-in-law were so poorly received, complained about Elisabeth to Franz Joseph. Elisabeth did not attempt to conceal her dislike for her mother-in-law from her husband, and was incensed when he merely attempted to soothe her down instead of standing up for her. The Emperor, deeply in love with his wife but also devoted to his mother, was in a difficult position. Preoccupied with affairs of state, unimaginative and only twenty-four, he understandably refused to face up to the basic antipathy between the two women, hoping that in time their relationship might improve, and meanwhile ignoring their quarrels as far as possible. He made no objection when, after their first child, a daughter, was born, the Archduchess promptly removed the baby to her own apartments and made all the arrangements for its care. Elisabeth, never allowed to see her daughter alone, was much upset by this, and when Sophie also attempted to take over

Emperor Franz Joseph I, from a painting by Jozef Kiss

Empress Elisabeth, from a painting by Winterhalter

Gisela their second child, she at last prevailed on Franz Joseph to take her side. He wrote to his mother stating that he considered that his children's upbringing should be under his wife's control, and appealed to her not to judge Sisi too harshly. The Archduchess had to give in, but she did so with much ill grace, and thereafter a direct struggle developed between the two women for influence over the Emperor.

In August 1858 when a son, Rudolf, was born, it seemed that Elisabeth was gaining the upper hand. Now twenty-one, she had given her husband the heir for whom he longed and he adored her. But she still retained the caprices and wilfulness of a child, and in the following year these brought about a crisis in their relationship. It began when after the outbreak of war in Italy the Emperor left Vienna to place himself at the head of his army. Elisabeth was distraught, wept continually, neglected her children, refused to eat, rode for hours on end and in the opinion of the family physician an 'icy chasm' now existed between her and Sophie. She wrote a series of over-wrought letters to Franz Joseph who, when replying to them, implored Sisi to take care of her health, pull herself together and play her part by visiting the wounded in hospital. He assured her that his one comfort after that 'hard bitter day' of Solferino was 'the thought of returning to you my angel',[6] and again, after concluding peace with Napoleon III, that his one desire was to return to Vienna, and that the only joy which he would derive from it would be to embrace her again.[7] His pleas had no effect. When, desperately in need of consolation, he came back to his capital, he found Sisi whom he had 'so longed to embrace' a mass of nerves, wearing herself to a shadow with riding and walking, able apparently to think only of herself, and on worse terms than ever with his mother.

This unhappy situation dragged on for over a year. What occurred to the personal relationship of the Emperor and Empress during this time can only be surmised. Faced with the consequences of what he described as 'the robbery of Victor Emmanuel and the continuing villainy of the arch blackguard in Paris', with 'the critical situation in Hungary and the unending demands from all parts of the Monarchy', Franz Joseph had as he told his mother 'hardly a second' in which to think of his own affairs.[8] Possibly Elisabeth felt neglected because he had so little time to spare for her, possibly too he sought temporary consolation elsewhere and this wounded her pride. Whatever the cause or causes she became ill and appeared to be on the verge of a nervous breakdown. The idea that illness could have a psychosomatic origin had yet to be evolved; it was announced that because of her cough she must spend some time in a warmer climate. Meran or the Dalmatian coast were suggested, but the Empress insisted that she must get away from the Monarchy, and on October 17th, 1860, she departed to Madeira leaving Franz Joseph alone to struggle with his manifold problems, and abandoning her children to the care of her mother-in-law.

Elisabeth was away for over seven months. Towards the end of May 1861 she returned to Vienna and for a few days appeared at Court, apparently fully restored to health. Then all official functions were cancelled, and it was announced that she was seriously ill with some sort of lung trouble which once again made an immediate change of climate imperative. On June 23rd she sailed from Trieste for Corfu. She had been back in Vienna for under six weeks, and in the circumstances it was inevitable that every kind of rumour should circulate. Why had she left again so suddenly? And why, if her health had really deteriorated so rapidly, had she been sent to recover in Corfu of all places which at that time of year was hot and malaria ridden? When it became known that within a fortnight of leaving Austria the Empress already looked much better, speculation as to the real reason for her departure increased to a degree which was personally distressing and publicly embarrassing for the Emperor but, in spite of every effort to persuade her to return, the summer wore on and she refused to budge. Finally, Franz Joseph himself went to Corfu, and hammered out some sort of compromise with her. In October she moved to Venice where the children were sent to visit her and where he came to see her as often as his work allowed. From there, as varying accounts about the nature of her illness spread through the courts of Europe, she insisted on going to Bavaria, and it was not until August 14th, 1862, after having been away for the greater part of two years, that she suddenly returned to Schönbrunn. Archduchess Sophie was away, so that perennial source of friction was for the time being removed. Franz Joseph did not abandon his annual shooting trip, but apart from that spent all the time he could with his wife and endeavoured to gratify her every wish. Although there were still stories of differences between them, Elisabeth was beginning to laugh again, she appeared to be well, and it seemed that she was prepared to settle down.

For the next few years the Empress spent more time in Austria. Now a ravishingly beautiful young woman, she was becoming conscious of the power which she could exert over Franz Joseph who gradually realised that, protest though he might, she would do as she pleased. He began to give in to her over the selection of her household, and even raised no objection when at the end of 1864 Elisabeth appointed a nominee of Andrassy's, Ida Ferenczy, as one of her ladies-in-waiting to assist her to learn Hungarian.

Elisabeth began the study of this difficult language early in 1863 in order to make herself understood by Rudolf's nurse. One reason why she continued it may have been that it was an occupation bound to annoy her mother-in-law who detested anything to do with Hungary. Certainly, she was encouraged to do so by the attitude of the Hungarians who, aware of the strained relations between the Empress and Archduchess Sophie, calculated that they might exploit this situation to their advantage, for if they could enlist Elisabeth's sympathy for their cause she might influence the Emperor in their favour. They lost no opportunity of doing so. Flattering articles about her appeared in the Budapest press; Hungarian magnates who saw her in Vienna openly praised her beauty; all the insidious and by no means inconsiderable national charm was employed to win her over. It was not a difficult task. As she was implacable in her mistrust and dislike of those who were unfriendly to her, so Elisabeth was quick to respond to people who appeared to admire her. Her romantic love of liberty predisposed her to the Hungarian cause, and the easily aroused enthusiasm, gaiety and panache of the temperament of that nation attracted her. When, at the end of January 1866, she accompanied Franz Joseph on an official visit to Budapest and replied to an address of welcome in perfect Hungarian, the British Consul-General there reported that it was impossible to describe in the dry language of an official despatch the enthusiasm which this had evoked.[9] The Emperor was delighted. 'Sisi,' he wrote to his mother, 'is a great help to me here with her courtesy, tact and discretion'.[10]

Elisabeth's personal success in Budapest not only helped Franz Joseph, it also pulled her out of herself and gave her confidence, and so she was able to sustain and help her husband through the bitter blow which he suffered six months later over the Prussian victory at Königgrätz. She was at Bad Ischl when the war broke out, but at once returned to Vienna. During the dark days which followed she only left his side to visit the wounded in hospital, and otherwise was constantly with him, endeavouring to cheer and comfort him, watching over him, as the Archduchess Sophie (who to give her her due was always ready to praise her daughter-in-law when she approved of her actions) wrote to the eight-year-old Rudolf, 'like his good angel'.[11]

After Königgrätz the Empress left Vienna for Budapest ostensibly to visit hospitals there. When she arrived she was met at the station by Deak and Andrassy who escorted her to the royal palace. 'It would have been cowardly,' Deak said later, 'to have taken no notice of the Queen when she was in distress.'[12] Whatever the reasons for this gesture (they were probably a mixture of instinctive Hungarian chivalry towards a beautiful woman in need of help and enlightened self-interest), Elisabeth was warmed and touched by it, and listened with attention while they stressed the urgent need for the Emperor to give Hungary the internal autonomy for which they asked before more radical elements took over. They were in any case preaching to the converted, for the Empress who hitherto had depised and taken no interest in politics, had for some time been a passionate devotee of their cause.

The Empress already knew Andrassy who was dazzled by her beauty and altogether enchanted by her. She, fascinated by his brilliance and finding in him someone who did not hesitate to tell her the truth however unpalatable, soon came to see him both as a friend and the ideal person for effecting peace between Hungary and the Crown. When therefore she came to Vienna a few days later to fetch the children, she urged the Emperor to come to terms with Hungary, and to make Andrassy Minister of Foreign Affairs. This, however, was going altogether too far and too fast for Franz Joseph who explained that her suggestions required a great deal of consideration. Elisabeth was evidently still deeply concerned for her husband—it was noticed that when she was about to board the train for Budapest she suddenly stopped and with an infinitely touching gesture kissed the Emperor's hand— but she returned to the Hungarian capital dissatisfied and determined not to give way. She wrote imploring Franz Joseph to see the Count, telling him that if he did not do so:

> Nothing will remain to me but to console myself with the knowledge that, whatever may happen, I shall be able to say honestly to Rudolf one day 'I did everything in my power. Your misfortunes are not on my conscience.'[13]

When, after seeing both Andrassy and Deak, the Emperor still could not make up his mind, she became impatient, sulked, and at first refused to respond to his plea that she should rejoin him in Vienna, telling him coldly that Schönbrunn was too unhealthy for her and the children. Franz Joseph replied bitterly:

> My dear Sisi, it would be contrary to my duty to accept your exclusively Hungarian point of view. . . . If you find the air here unhealthy, so be it. . . . I must simply make the best of it and continue to bear patiently the lonely existence to which I have long become accustomed. In this connection I have already learnt to endure a great deal, and one becomes used to it.[14]

But this was only a passing outburst. He continued to write to her frequently, now signing his letter 'your Männchen' or 'Manekin' —'your little man'—telling her of that despondency about the situation which his absolute self-control never allowed him to show in public:

> I am very depressed and find my courage leaving me the nearer we get to the peace and as the internal difficulties against

which we have to struggle become more apparent. Only my
sense of duty keeps me going.[15]

He was exhausted and he needed her, but another fortnight
elapsed before she returned to Vienna.

When the Compromise was finally agreed one of Elisabeth's
dearest wishes was fulfilled. She had acted as a catalyst in achieving
it, breaking down the Emperor's prejudices about Hungary,
influencing him into thinking urgently about the problem, and
the Hungarians were in no doubt of their debt to her. The poet
Eötvös wrote:

> For three centuries we had tried faith, then again and again
> hope, until only one possibility remained: that the nation
> should be ready to love some member of the reigning family
> from the depths of its heart. Now we have succeeded in this I
> have no more fear for the future.[16]

He spoke for all his countrymen. They were aware of the trouble
which Elisabeth had taken to learn their language, and of her
interest in Hungary. Her grace, skill and courage as a rider excited
their imagination, her beauty and charm captured their hearts.
They adored her, and she knew it. When on June 8th, 1867, after
the coronation of Franz Joseph she knelt before the high altar of
the cathedral in Budapest and, in accordance with tradition, St.
Stephen's crown was held over her shoulders to make her Queen
of Hungary, she looked as one of the spectators afterwards wrote,
'quite supernaturally lovely . . . as moved and absorbed as a bride.
I rather felt, too, as if in one respect she did interpret it in this
sense.'[17]

Elisabeth had an intuitive understanding of the Hungarians and,
while after the Compromise she exerted no influence with the
Emperor on their behalf, their affection for her remained undimin-
ished. She was happy in Hungary as she never was in Vienna.
There is a description of her at a Court dinner in Budapest in 1868
wearing a necklace of rubies, emeralds and diamonds, the Hungarian national colours, talking with animation throughout the
evening to Andrassy,[18] which is in striking contrast with her

behaviour in Vienna, where she avoided Court functions whenever possible and, when obliged to hold receptions, was alleged to have only two conversational gambits, 'Do you ride?' and 'Have you any children?'[19] Her personal triumph in Hungary was bitterly resented by the Viennese aristocracy and when it was known that she was again pregnant and determined that her child should be born in Hungary, one of them went so far as to say in an unguarded moment that it would serve the Empress right if she had a miscarriage.[20] They resented the number of Hungarians whom she appointed to her household, and at Court the feeling against her had hardened into an atmosphere of icy dislike of which, sensitive as she was, Elisabeth was only too well aware, and which made her feel 'desperate' at the mere thought of having to go to Vienna. One situation had, however, eased with the passage of time—Archduchess Sophie, now an old lady, no longer attempted to criticise her daughter-in-law. Relations between the two of them could never be affectionate, but when Sophie was dying in 1872 Elisabeth sat with her for ten hours, saying later that although the Archduchess had made family life difficult by interfering in everything, she had always meant well. In view of past difficulties it was an extraordinarily restrained statement.

But now in any case there was no need to be so much in Vienna. Under the terms of the Compromise the Emperor had to spend part of each year in Hungary, where as a coronation present the nation had given him the house and estate of Gödöllö, about twenty miles outside Budapest. The shooting there was excellent, and the surrounding countryside ideal for riding. To Elisabeth's delight it was possible to escape there from the formality of Court life, and Franz Joseph, who now always addressed his wife in letters with the Hungarian salutation 'Edes Lelkem'—'my darling heart'—also came to find it, as he wrote to her, a place to which he could retreat when the politicians in Vienna were becoming too infuriating. Their youngest daughter Valerie was born at Gödöllö in 1868, and there during the next few years the Emperor and Empress spent some of their happiest times together.

Except for the children and a mutual pleasure in riding, by the time of their Silver Wedding in 1879 Franz Joseph and Elisabeth had few interests in common. Temperamentally they were poles apart. The Emperor unimaginative, generally uninterested in people except in so far as they affected affairs of State, conservative and mistrustful of new ideas, was incapable of dramatisation—it would never have occurred to him to use his wife's phrase 'the treadmill of life' to describe his apparently frequently unrewarding work for the Monarchy. It was the existence into which he was born, he had to get on with it, and that was that. He tended to reduce anything extraordinary or incomprehensible to the ordinary and day to day, and this, together with his iron self-control, often made him appear insensitive and almost de-personalised in public. In fact, as his letters to those nearest to him show, he was far from being without feeling, but even to them he had great difficulty in expressing it. With rare exceptions his letters to Elisabeth were an uninspired record of the state of the weather, the health of their relations, what he had shot and whom he had sat next to at dinner. He was quite incapable of following her into the dream world into which she escaped or of sharing her love of literature. When persuaded to see a performance at the Burgtheater of her favourite Shakespeare play, *A Midsummer Night's Dream*, he confessed afterwards to having found it 'indescribably stupid'. Her interest in new ideas was distasteful to him, but he tolerated it because there was no alternative, as he tolerated her foibles—her dieting and obsession with slimming, her large dogs (which he personally found extremely tiresome), her exaggerated passion for riding—and put up with her eccentricities such as the importation of a small negro boy to play with his youngest daughter, or her curious choice of birthday presents, a tiger, a medallion or a lunatic asylum. When she appeared to be ill he was anxiously concerned for her although quite unable to understand what was wrong for, himself blessed with exceptional physical and nervous stamina, illness was something quite outside his comprehension; one was, he considered, either alive or dead, there was nothing in between the two. But he bore with more patience than any of his courtiers her frequent refusals to make the ceremonial appearances which her position demanded, and her failure to understand the responsibilities incumbent on her as an Empress. 'You know me and my habits and my *extinction de roi*,' Elisabeth once wrote to him, 'but if you do not like me as I am, well I must be pensioned off.'[21] Franz Joseph never had any intention of doing anything of the sort. He had learnt through the years to accept her as she was with her moods, her depressions, her sudden change from tears to gaiety. He had learnt too to endure his loneliness during her many absences and to be grateful for the times when she was with him. Possibly it was her elusiveness, the fact that he could never wholly possess nor understand her, which bound him to her with such deep and enduring love.

Elisabeth reciprocated this love after her own fashion. Throughout her life she reacted strongly to personalities. Some evoked in her an incandescence which brought out all her charm, with others she remained so cold and withdrawn that someone who saw her at the Hofball was left with the impression of a person 'so closely limited by concentration on self as to be *nulle*. She had absolutely no atmosphere, no magnetism. The face, still beautiful in feature and colouring was as expressionless as a fashion photo. . . .'[22] It may be that Franz Joseph only rarely evoked this incandescence in her, but as time went on she became tenderly concerned for him, showing an almost maternal solicitude for his welfare. Real though this solicitude was, to conform to his dearest wish and to be with him more was, however, something of which she was temperamentally incapable. To do so involved putting up with an existence which was antipathetic to her and when confronted with something antipathetic while Elisabeth made no scenes, she also made no attempt to endure it, withdrew into herself, and whenever she could went away, moving from place to place, alone and beset by a restlessness best expressed in her own words:

The goal of a journey draws one on because the journey lies ahead. If I was somewhere and knew that I could never leave it, even though it were Paradise it would seem to me to be Hell.[23]

By 1880 she was not content to remain for long even in her beloved Hungary, but was constantly on the move—to Ischl,

Bavaria, Meran, hunting in England and in Ireland. In the years to come she would go farther—to France and the Mediterranean, back to Corfu. It seemed as though she was trying to get away from herself. But, frequent though her absences were, she always returned, always to be welcomed by Franz Joseph with the utmost affection. She could and did rise magnificently to the occasion in a crisis, and would play the role of Empress superbly at a great State function. But, unlike her husband, she was quite incapable of sustaining a long haul, and she would not remain for long in Vienna. It would have been possible for Franz Joseph to be with her more had his conception of his duty as Emperor been less rigid, but rigid it was and even his love for Elisabeth was subordinated to it. Because he could not change this, and she could not fit in with it, central to each other though they remained all their lives, they were both lonely.

Much apart though they were, by 1880 the Emperor and Empress had, however, settled down to a form of *modus vivendi*. Franz Joseph was quick to notice an attractive woman and Elisabeth knew it; she, he was well aware, had many admirers. Occasionally in their letters each reassured the other about this. Franz Joseph's eye may have roved from time to time, but never for long. It pleased Elisabeth to be admired, but no more than that, even Andrassy was kept at a distance. That there may have been speculation and gossip about her relationship with him is suggested by her assurance to Ida Ferenczy when the Count was coming to visit her in Bavaria in 1869: 'Don't worry, I won't fall on his neck.'[24] That such speculation and gossip was quite unfounded is confirmed by a letter from Andrassy himself to Frau Ferenczy. In it he told her that at the end of a day's hunting the Emperor asked him to escort the Empress in a carriage to the station. It was a long journey in the dark over a rough road, and with such a beautiful woman in such a situation even the most happily married man might be expected to lose his head. But, he he stressed, nobody—repeat nobody—would for a moment forget who had been entrusted to his care.[25] That Andrassy's friendship was the firmest Elisabeth ever had in her life was attested by her favourite daughter Valerie many years later when he died.[26] But friendship, and no more, it remained. Each had far too great a respect for the other to contemplate anything else, and there is no evidence that Franz Joseph ever thought they did. While he regretted his wife's absence he had no doubts as to her fidelity, and his love for her remained such that he always gave in to her.

In her capacity for getting her own way Elisabeth enjoyed a unique position amongst the Imperial Family, but she rarely used her great influence with Franz Joseph to promote the interests of others. With her unconcealed dislike of Court ceremonial, her imagination and active mind, she had much in common with those younger members of the family who questioned the value of rigid adherence to tradition and were convinced that change was essential to the survival of the Monarchy. But, aloof, temperamentally erratic and preoccupied with her own ideas, she does not appear to have been someone in whom the younger generation felt they could confide, or to whom they could turn to plead their cause with the Emperor. This inability to combine, and the loneliness which resulted from it, was a recurrent and tragic characteristic of the House of Habsburg.

CHAPTER 3

The Emperor and the Imperial Family

Franz Joseph was undisputed overlord not only of the Monarchy but of all his relations. His authority over them was codified in the Habsburg *Familien Statut* or Family Law promulgated in 1839 during the reign of his predecessor Ferdinand I. This defined the family as consisting of all the Archdukes (and their wives and widows) and Archduchesses descended in the male line from the Empress Maria Theresa, and was signed by Ferdinand and his Chancellor, Clemens Wenzel Lothar, Prince von Metternich-Winneburg who, since Ferdinand was somewhat dim-witted, exercised great influence over his sovereign. The Family Law reflected Metternich's ideas. As the Crown was the only link between the nationalities in the Monarchy, and it was vested in the House of Habsburg, it was imperative that all members of that House should present a united front in support of the Emperor, and that some unfortunate lapses from this in the past should not be repeated. Since Ferdinand was incapable of enforcing discipline within the family, a code of conduct for them must be laid down in a document which unequivocally defined the Emperor's power over his relations, and which could be invoked should circumstances so demand. Also, since the private finances of the House of Habsburg were now inadequate to enable its growing number of members to live in the style appropriate to their station, they must to some degree become a charge on the State, and it was necessary to clarify what this should be. It is not possible to establish who took the initative in drafting the Family Law, but it would seem likely that it was promulgated, not by Ferdinand's command but at his Chancellor's suggestion.

The final clause of the Family Law stipulated that an attested copy of it should be given to all Archdukes and Archduchesses, thus ensuring that they were left in no doubt whatsoever of where they stood. According to Clause (3b) they had a right to be maintained in a manner appropriate to their rank, and Section VI enumerated the appanages, dowries and widow's pensions due to them from the State. Clause (3a), however, stated that, although they were entitled to all the public honours and privileges appropriate to members of the Imperial House, the Emperor could command at any time that these should be suspended. The rest of the Law was framed with the same object, to make it clear to all Archdukes and Archduchesses that they were dependent on the favour of the head of the family, and that to enjoy it they must conform to his orders. What he could decree was fully set out. Described variously as 'the Emperor', 'the Sovereign' or 'the Head of the Family' (with various honorific adjectives attached), he was mentioned forty two times in sixty one clauses, and in such a manner as to make his position quite unequivocal giving him more power over the members of his family than the law of the land could exert over his subjects. Any member of the House of Habsburg who wished to marry had first to obtain his consent and, if they persisted in doing so without it, not only forfeited their rights and privileges for themselves and their children, but their marriage so far as the Emperor was concerned was 'null and void'. Their wills and marriage contracts were only valid if approved by him; he had the right of deciding the education of their children and of the nomination of members of their Households. He could banish, place under police surveillance, or take such action as he saw fit against any member of the family whose behaviour he considered warranted it, and in all disciplinary matters his decision was final. In addition the Emperor controlled the *'Familien Fond'* or family fortune of the House of Habsburg which had been set up by Maria Theresa in 1765, and since he had the power to distribute up to two-thirds of the substantial income of this fund amongst such members of the family as he might select, he was in a position to apply financial sanctions against any misbehaving Archduke. The State, obliged to make such alterations to the Archducal appanages as the Emperor might order, had no power to interfere with the Family Law. It was a document designed to safeguard the succession, to ensure the status of the House of Habsburg and to preserve its property, investing the Emperor with the power to be both judge and jury in all matters concerning his relations who under it enjoyed no rights, only privileges conferred by his grace. None of them ever dared suggest to Franz Joseph that it should in any way be modified.

Until 1880 the Emperor had on two occasions only found it necessary to take severe disciplinary action against members of the Imperial Family. The first was when his second cousin, Archduke Heinrich, married an opera singer. Franz Joseph dismissed the Archduke from the army, deprived him of his title and banished him for four years to Switzerland. The second was when his brother, Ferdinand Max, insisted on accepting the crown of Mexico.

Ferdinand Max was imaginative, romantic and impulsive, interested in art, natural history and literature, resembling Franz Joseph only in his Habsburg pride, ambition and desire to rule. As boys the two had been close friends, but as they grew up tension developed between them. Max wanted to have a share in running the Monarchy; Franz Joseph politely but firmly turned down his suggestions and, jealous of the fact that his brother's good looks and easy charm made him popular with the Viennese, sent him to Trieste to serve in the Navy. The Archduke who fell in love with the sea and the south, was eventually appointed Commander-in-Chief of the Navy and, for the year before Solferino, Governor of Lombardy and Venetia, but his relations with the Emperor did not improve. Max resented what he regarded as Franz Joseph's lack of support for and interference in naval affairs, chafed at the restrictions imposed on him from Vienna, criticised Imperial policy in Italy, and became restless and frustrated. After the loss of Lombardy he went on a voyage to Brazil, and found it the ideal place 'for those who have come to a resolution to break with the stormy past and to work their way to a blameless future.'[1] When, therefore, at the instigation of Napoleon III, he was asked if he would be prepared to accept the crown of Mexico, his first reaction was enthusiastic. 'For centuries,' he wrote, it has been the practice of all great dynasties to place their younger Princes in positions where they can bring political and diplomatic advantages to the Motherland. The former glories of our House have been tarnished by the circumstances of the present time. . . . Nobody sees more clearly than I that it is the duty of our House to redress this. [2]

The Emperor did not agree. On principle he was opposed to the idea of any member of the family carving out a position for himself, and he considered that once an Archduke became the ruler of another country, his unfailing support of the interests either of the Monarchy or the House of Habsburg could not be guaranteed. In addition, Max, after Rudolf who was still a child, was next in line for the throne, but it would be geographically impossible either for him to exercise a Regency should this become necessary, or to rule over the Monarchy from Mexico. Franz Joseph did not however at once exercise his full power as head of Family and forbid his brother to contemplate the Mexican venture, but he pointed out the hazards attached to it. The Archduke became doubtful about the project, but eventually allowed his mind to be made up for him by his wife Charlotte, the daughter of the Coburg King Leopold I of Belgium. A member of one of the most ambitious Royal Houses in Europe, Charlotte was determined to become Empress of Mexico and at that time she dominated her husband. At the end of 1863 Max, who believed that he had the support of Napoleon III, announced that he had finally decided to accept the Mexican crown, and so precipitated an open rift with the Emperor.

Franz Joseph wrote to Max telling him that if he went to Mexico he must renounce all claims to the throne of the Monarchy, his appanage and all other financial rights as an Archduke. There was a bitter argument between the two brothers. The Emperor finally relented in so far as to promise that if the Mexican venture was a failure, Max and Charlotte could return to the Monarchy where they would be given the privileges appropriate to their rank, but on the question of the succession he was immovable. Finally, he went down to Miramar and forced his brother to sign the act of renunciation. He wept when they finally said goodbye on the station at Trieste, but after that so far as he was concerned the matter was over and done with, and Max was out on his own.

The Mexican venture went badly. Max arrived to find that only a fraction of the population supported him, Napoleon III broke his word and the assistance on which he had counted from the French dwindled away. Franz Joseph unmoved, avoided Charlotte when she came to Europe to plead for support for her husband, and did no more than assure Max's envoy that if the Emperor of Mexico was forced to return to the Monarchy he would restore to him his rights to the family property. Max never returned. On June 19th, 1867, a few days after Franz Joseph had been crowned King of Hungary in Budapest, he was executed by a Mexican firing squad. He died bravely with all the dignity of the Habsburgs. When the news reached Vienna Archduchess Sophie was inconsolable and he was deeply mourned, not only by members of the Court, but also by many of the general public. The Emperor sent a warship to fetch the Archduke's body home for burial in the Habsburg family vault, and wrote to Albrecht of Saxony that he found it difficult to realise that Max would never again shoot with them at Bad Ischl, but on the whole he did not appear to be deeply moved. He knew that Napoleon III had been largely responsible for his brother's tragic end, but a fortnight after Max's death he replied warmly to the French Emperor's letter of condolence, assuring him that he was certain that Napoleon had done everything in his power to avert this, and adding 'this is fresh proof of your friendship which is very near to my heart'.[3] Six weeks later the two of them met in Salzburg. Franz Joseph needed Napoleon's support against Prussia, and the interests of the State took priority over any personal condierations.

Franz Joseph's action over Heinrich's marriage and Max's attempt to establish himself as Emperor of Mexico must be considered in the context of the age in which he lived. Throughout Europe in the nineteenth century it was accepted in most classes of society that the position of head of the family conferred upon its occupant exceptional authority which, in times of crisis, he would

Archduke Albrecht

Archduke Johann Salvator, from an engraving by A. Weger

exercise to safeguard the interest of the family as a whole, rather than to promote the wishes of any of its members. This consideration applied particularly to heads of Royal Houses, anxious to preserve their thrones not only for themselves but for their heirs. Franz Joseph's attitude was midway between that of Queen Victoria, who did not permit the private life of the Duke of Cambridge to affect her opinion of the Duke's military abilities, eventually consenting to his appointment as Commander-in-Chief of the British Army, and those Czars of Russia who banished any Grand Duke whose conduct displeased them to a remote part of the Caucasus or to Tashkent. Absolute though the power was which the Family Law conferred on Franz Joseph, and although he interpreted some clauses of it, particularly with regard to marriages, more severely than Queen Victoria would have done, he did not use it arbitrarily. When he took severe disciplinary action against any member of the Imperial Family he did so because he was convinced that this was necessary to protect Habsburg interests. But when those interests were not seriously threatened, although quick to show displeasure he was slow to punish, for he was not a vindictive man. He never, however, left the family in any doubt as to his position. Only his nearest relatives were permitted when talking to him to address him by the familiar second person singular '*Du*'—everyone else must call him 'Your Majesty'. His brothers and children when writing to him began their letters 'Your Majesty, dear Brother', or 'Your Majesty, dear Father'. One section of Queen Victoria's cousins referred to her amongst themselves as 'Aunt Queen'; it is inconceivable that any of his relations should have referred to Franz Joseph as 'Uncle Emperor'.

With the exception of his mother, Elisabeth and his children, the Emperor had no close personal relationship with any of his family, but he was courteous to them all, financially generous, would take pains to ensure that they had what he considered to be due to them in the way of houses, special trains, boxes at the opera, and would himself draft telegrams asking them to lunch or dine. On January 1st, and once a week throughout the winter, he gave a family dinner party at which no courtiers were present, and which every Archduke and Archduchess who was in Vienna was expected to attend. On these occasions the atmosphere, as at any large family gathering was usually strained, and Elisabeth, who disliked most of her Habsburg relations, avoided them whenever she could. Franz Joseph, no conversationalist at the best of times, tended to be more than usually monosyllabic, the number of subjects which could safely be discussed was limited and, since the Emperor was served first, ate rapidly and all the plates were removed as soon as he had finished a course, junior Archdukes at the bottom of the table were liable to go hungry. Nobody, including it may be suspected Franz Joseph, enjoyed the family dinners, but he insisted on them as a demonstration that, outwardly at least, the family was united.

By 1880 there were over sixty Archdukes and Archduchesses. Most of the latter seem to have been agreeable nonentities dutifully marrying whoever might be designated for them, bearing numbers of children, passing the time with innocent diversions such as painting water colours to be sold at bazaars for the benefit of the poor, and generally giving no trouble. Many of the Archdukes were uninspiring and, with a very few exceptions, Franz Joseph was neither fond of them nor had any great opinion of their capabilities. He held simple but definite views about their position and behaviour. They must conform to Court etiquette, conduct themselves with propriety, and appear on ceremonial occasions whenever ordered to do so. They must not attempt to interfere in any aspect of affairs of State, endeavour to conjure up popular support for themselves, or contract unsuitable marriages. Provided they complied with these rules they could lead an unexacting life with plenty of money, excellent shooting and a number of social privileges. If they wished to go into the army they were assured of rapid promotion. There was no objection to their mistresses provided they conducted these liaisons with discretion and that no question of marriage arose. All that the Emperor required of his family was that they should fall in and do what they were told, leaving him to make the decisions for the Monarchy and the dynasty. It seemed to him to be a very reasonable bargain which, because there had been no serious trouble since the disastrous Mexican venture of Ferdinand Max, he assumed they accepted. Confident of this, he did not envisage in 1880 that the rigid enforcement of the terms of this bargain would lead within the decade to an irreconcilable clash of opinion, the outcome of which would be to destroy the two outstandingly talented younger members of the House of Habsburg.

To the ordinary citizens of Vienna the Archdukes driving by in their carriages, the spokes of which were gilded in the degree appropriate to their rank (half gilt for the Emperor's brothers, a quarter gilt for his more distant realtions), were enviable and privileged beings. Court protocol emphasised their status, laying down for example that members of the families of other sovereigns must call on them when visiting Vienna—a chore which involved the Prince and Princess of Wales in 1869 in so many calls that the British Ambassador reported 'it was hard work to get through the lot'.[4] Each of them gathered around him a small coterie of deferential hangers-on, amongst whom his will reigned supreme. But when the Emperor appeared all Archdukes were equally subservient, each assumed the same kind of 'court face', and none of them were at ease in his presence.

Of all institutions in nineteenth-century Europe none were slower to move with the times than the courts of reigning sovereigns. Most of them continued the traditions of the previous age, and none more rigidly than the Court of Vienna, where the ceremonial laid down for every conceivable occasion—births, marriages, funerals, dinners, balls, religious processions—was observed as it had been for decades, and would it seemed be repeated for all eternity. The result was an atmosphere which obliterated personality, a quality for which the majority of the high aristocracy whose sixteen quarterings gave them the right of entrée to Court, and from whose ranks the Court officials were appointed, were not notable. Lord Frederick Hamilton a young attaché at the British Embassy summed them up as:

genial, friendly, hospitable incompetents[5] who had all intermarried for centuries, and if they did not trouble their intellect much there may have been physical difficulties connected with this process for which they were not responsible.[6]

As a foreigner he found it 'illogical' that Countess Karolyi, the charming and vivacious wife of the Austrian Ambassador in Berlin, should not be invited to Court in Vienna because she lacked the necessary quarterings. A good many other people agreed with Lord Frederick about the Austrian high aristocracy or 'First Society'. When members of this 'society of cousins' met one another politics, literature, or art were seldom discussed, but there was a great deal of gossip about family affairs such as Aunt Rosa's recurrent migraine, Cousin Fritz's latest shooting achievement, who was likely to marry whom which, since everyone was referred to by a nickname, was dull and bewildering to the uninitiated. All of them had large country estates, to which they retired to destroy very large quantities of game during the shooting season: when in Vienna their main amusements were dancing, gambling and racing. Generally they were decorative, took life lightly and had a certain idle charm.

The amusements of the First Society of the Monarchy were those of their day and shared by their equivalents elsewhere. Many of the British aristocracy spent a good deal of time shooting, gambling and racing. In a censorious moment Queen Victoria described them as 'profligate and worthless', but later she qualified that sweeping pronouncement. 'In any Country a great proportion of the Aristocracy will be idle and fond of amusement . . . but I think that in no country more than ours do the Higher Classes occupy themselves.'[7] This was certainly true so far as politics were concerned—an average of over fifty per cent of all British Cabinet Ministers were men with hereditary titles, moulded by the same education (which in many instances was Eton and Balliol), and so linked together by shared memories rather than inter-relationship. By 1880 their Austrian contemporaries, while still closely grouped around their sovereign, with a few exceptions played no important part in affairs of State, were no longer prominent in diplomacy, a sphere of activity which had once been their exclusive preserve, and the day was fast approaching when three-quarters of the generals in the army would be commoners. Many of them, however, were constantly short of money and so, while they made a relatively small contribution to the service of the State, had turned their attention to a new field which would have been unthinkable a quarter of a century earlier—commerce. Some dozen Princes and many more Counts sat on the boards of various companies. There was thus some restricted contact between the high aristocracy and members of the 'Second Society'.

The 'Second Society', which included the lesser aristocracy, senior civil servants and officers, prominent intellectuals and members of the professional classes, was led by financiers and industrialists, many of them Jewish. The latter had come to the fore in the economic expansion which began in the second half of the century and which continued in inverse ratio to all political difficulties. Their taste dominated Vienna, by 1880 a rapidly growing capital. In 1857, by Imperial decree, the bastions surrounding the old city had been pulled down and during the next few years replaced by the Ringstrasse, a magnificent broad tree-lined avenue, over half of the large new houses along which belonged to commercial magnates. The renaissance style façades of these mansions aped the palaces of Florentine merchant princes. Each had a series of reception rooms decorated in the style of Makart, the painter who at that time was much in vogue, with rich dark crimson brocade on the walls, bouquets of dried flowers, immense mirrors, heavy plush curtains of old gold; crammed with sofas, tables covered with velvet cloths with long tassels, innumerable occasional tables, stools inlaid with mother-of-pearl and screens plastered with photographs, on the general principle that the more furniture which could be got into a room the better. There the financiers and industrialists, their wives loaded with jewellery and dressed in opulent colours, entertained not only their business colleagues, but also the leading writers, actors and painters of the day for, if not always faultless in taste, they were keenly interested in the arts.

The new rich of the Second Society were connoisseurs of beautiful women, believed that economic progress was the panacea for all ills and were determined to rise socially. The height of their ambition was to be received at Court, but in 1880 this was quite unattainable. The Emperor was prepared to reward a financier who helped to raise a loan or contributed to some public cause with the Order of the Iron Crown (which automatically entitled the recipient to place 'von' before his name) and, after a further large loan or two, to make him what the First Society derisively described as a 'Finanz Baron'. He appointed Anselm Rothschild a member of the Upper House of Parliament in recognition for the part which that banker had played in extricating the State from a most awkward financial predicament after Solferino. But this was an exceptional mark of favour and the limit to which Franz Joseph was prepared to go. The Rothschilds financed many of the major industrial ventures in the Monarchy, and he knew that he could not do without them, but not even for them was he prepared to relax the rule that nobody with less than sixteen quarterings had the entrée at Court.

If it was impossible to be received at Court, the next best thing was to cultivate those who were. Racing was an aristocratic sport. A Finanz Baron who spent enough on his horses could hope eventually to be elected to the exclusive Jockey Club where some of the aristocracy who were making money through the Jews could not wholly avoid meeting them socially. The aristocracy accepted invitations from financiers and industrialists to dine, but seldom invited them back, and if, as occasionally happened, an impecunious young Count married a Finanz Baron's daughter, he was despised by the rest of his class who refused to receive his wife. With a few exceptions there was no question of the aristocracy throwing open their doors to members of the Second Society. Princess Pauline Metternich was one of these exceptions. Renowned for her wit, vivacity and outstanding chic, she had known the Paris Rothschilds when her husband was the Emperor's Ambassador to Napoleon III, and on returning to the Monarchy received the Vienna branch of the family, as she received leading actors and anyone else who happened to interest or amuse her. Princess Hohenlohe the wife of the Emperor's Lord Chamberlain, was another. Before her marriage she had known many of the leading German intellectuals, and in Vienna invited artists, writers and dramatists to soirées at the Augarten Palais where, by contrast with similar evenings in the houses of most of the aristocracy:

> the men did not talk about nothing but their last shoot and the forthcoming races, and the ladies did not confine themselves to criticising each other's clothes and discussing family trees.[8]

But these Princesses were almost in a minority of two. However financially obliging they might find some of its members, the majority of aristocracy looked down on the Second Society.

Neither the First nor the Second Societies provided much entertainment for the Archdukes. One of the main amusements of the aristocracy, gambling, was forbidden to them by the Emperor who did not allow them to join the exclusive clubs where it took place. Any close social contact with financiers and industrialists incurred Franz Joseph's displeasure, for he considered them ostentatious and vulgar. There was therefore no question of an Archduke forming the equivalent of the Marlborough House set which in London surrounded the Prince of Wales. One form of diversion was, however, permitted. Provided there was no scandal, the Emperor had no objection to a member of the Imperial Family spending an occasional evening incognito with a pretty actress or ballet dancer, thus escaping for a few hours into the world of the ordinary Viennese and an atmosphere which, in refreshing contrast to his normal surroundings, was gay, easy going and above all *gemütlich*.

The adjective *gemütlich* is untranslatable. It is a compound of agreeable, cosy, tolerant, warm hearted, and there is a hint of kindly laughter in it; it conjures up pictures of golden autumn days, light shining on a glass of wine, the comforting warmth of a tiled stove; it conveys an impression of live and let live and immediate pleasure in simple things. This sense of well being was not to be found amidst the ceremonial and formality of the Court, nor amongst the aristocracy and the Finanz Barons, the former absorbed in their own affairs and the latter jockeying for position —but it pervaded the city of Vienna, and it was engendered by the ordinary Viennese.

Most of the citizens of the capital were not seriously concerned about politics, for in their view there was no point in being concerned about something in which one could play no part. Parliament was elected on a limited franchise and, since political meetings were banned and the press liable to censorship, they had not much chance of political self-expression. After their bid to achieve it in 1848 failed they became conditioned to the dogma that the Emperor, assisted by such ministers and generals as he saw fit to appoint, ran the Monarchy. Foreign observers found their attitude astonishing:

> There is no Eastern city as oriental as Vienna, as regards outward public apathy about great events . . . the most important rumours are discussed with an amiable fatalism and dismissed after a moment with one of those *gemütlich* smiles, which are quite as impressive as the Frenchman's shrug in conveying the opinion that nothing matters much.[9]

The Times correspondent wrote this in 1887, but it was equally applicable to the previous three decades. 'Happy is he who forgets what cannot be altered' had become a fundamental tenet of the Viennese. It did not prevent them from grumbling like any other community about matters which directly affected them, such as taxes and the price of food, but they also complained equally loudly if someone took their usual seat in the café which they frequented. Grumbling was a Viennese pastime, a rhetorical exercise which was an enjoyable means of letting off steam. It could give the impression that life in Vienna was hell on earth. In fact it was nothing of the sort as the Viennese, to whom existence anywhere else was unthinkable, were well aware.

To the casual observer walking through the streets, the city appeared to be always *en fête*. If most of its inhabitants were denied the right to vote they still had their places of amusement—the Wienerwald in which to wander in the spring and picnic in the summer; the Prater with its fun fair to which on the first of May the Viennese came in their thousands to watch the Imperial Family, the blue blooded and the rich, drive in their carriages along the Haupt Allee; the Volksgarten where everyone of all ages came to listen to the band; cafés where wine was cheap, the head waiter an adviser and confidant, and a clerk felt as much at home as a Count in the Jockey Club. And the authorities could not deprive them of music to which to listen, to sing, and above all to dance. Dancing was a passion shared by all classes. During Carnival week balls were given not only by the Emperor, the aristocracy and the Finanz Barons, but also by the City Council and every guild and profession—artists, journalists, the *'Club pour l'étude des langues française et anglais'*, the Fiaker (cab) drivers, even the washerwomen, and at them everyone danced to the music of Johann Strauss. He was in universal demand, to conduct and to compose waltzes for special occasions, to provide people with the escapism for which they craved. Strauss was the uncrowned King of Vienna, and every Viennese his devoted slave. Billroth, the brilliant founder of the Vienna school of surgery spoke for them all: 'We sing and make music, go to Strauss, and with him bury our heads in the sand of our *gemütlichkeit*.'[10]

'It is asked "Of what use is Romance?" Ask me rather "Of what use is salt?" without which, in the end no food is palatable.'[11] Prince Friedrich Schwarzenberg's aphorism was enthusiastically endorsed by the Viennese, but they took their love affairs lightly and conducted them in a manner which left few broken hearts. The girl of the people, the actress or the dancer at the Opera might be prodigal of her favours, but her natural gaiety saved her from being sentimental and, while she did not dissimulate over what she wanted, she knew how to stop at the limit of what was permitted to her. To hold things lightly, to enjoy them while one had them but not to try to cling to them, to consider that it did not matter if one had nothing to eat on Monday provided one had had a good time on Sunday, such was the temperament of the Viennese. It was this attitude to life which made the city what one gay young foreign Prince described as 'heavenly', and of which another delighted visitor wrote 'I doubt that one could amuse oneself more in Paradise'.[12] In this Paradise an Archduke could for a while forget one of his main afflictions—boredom.

CHAPTER 4

Archduke Albrecht and the Army

The doyen of the Imperial Family, and keenly aware of it, was the Emperor's cousin Archduke Albrecht born in 1817, the eldest son of Archduke Karl who had secured for himself a place in the history of the Monarchy by beating Napoleon Bonaparte at the battle of Aspern. He entered the army when he was thirteen determined to emulate his father, and although less able than Archduke Karl, succeeded thanks to an excellent memory and a capacity for hard work, in acquiring a thorough knowledge of his profession. Extremely ambitious, he was determined to rise on his own merits. It was said that when he was made a Commander of the Order of Maria Theresa after the battle of Novara in 1839, he protested that he did not feel that he had earned this distinction and would have preferred a lower grade of the Order. But whatever the Archduke's personal view of this achievement, thereafter he was steadily promoted, reaching the rank of Field-Marshal after twenty-three years' service. When the war broke out in 1866 he was appointed Commander-in-Chief in Italy, and distinguished himself by defeating the Italians at Custozza.

Albrecht rose to the highest rank in the army against a background of personal tragedy. His only son died in infancy, and his wife, to whom he was devoted, when he was forty-seven. Of his two daughters one, caught by her father smoking, set her dress on fire while trying to hide her cigarette and was burnt to death; the other married Prince Philip of Wurtemberg, an incorrigible gambler. It is likely that this series of disasters embittered a man who was temperamentally difficult, and in every way a far less attractive character than his younger brother Wilhelm, who by 1880 was the only other Archduke to hold any position of public importance. Wilhelm was Inspector of Artillery and also Grand Master of the Teutonic Order with the sonorous title of *Hoch und Deutschmeister*, an office which brought him in a very large income, but carried with it the disadvantage that the rules of the Order forbade the Grand Master to marry. The Archduke did not allow this to worry him unduly, and many stories circulated in Vienna of his assignations and love affairs. None of them, however, were malicious for Wilhelm was generous, easy going and universally popular, not only with the Viennese but in the Imperial Family. The Emperor found his cousin entertaining, Wilhelm was one of the few members of the family who had a kindly word for the Empress, and to his younger relatives he was the prototype of an amiable jolly uncle.

Albrecht was by no stretch of imagination to be described as amiable. Austere, deeply religious, with an impeccable private life, the Archduke was hard on himself and hard on others. No one was more insistent that the position of the Emperor and the honour of the House of Habsburg must at all costs be safeguarded. Habsburgs, he was never tired of proclaiming, were born into a position exalted above that of all other mortals. The title of Arch-duke he asserted was older and therefore superior to that of any Grand Duke or Kurfürst, the bearer of it took precedence over reigning Princes, and the mere idea of considering that the eldest son of such a Prince was of equal rank with the Crown Prince of Austria was ludicrous. And high above all Archdukes stood the Emperor who, he maintained:

> is the head of the family, their judge, their Sovereign whom all members of the family must honour and obey, and be his most loyal servants always, thereby setting an example to his subjects.[1]

It must, Albrecht considered, be made clear that there was a quite unbridgeable gap between the Emperor and his subjects, and that within the family Franz Joseph must insist on the precedence con-ferred by seniority and degree of relationship with him being strictly enforced. No Archduke must be allowed to get out of step, for if any one of them was praised too much and became too popular, invidious comparisons would be made, and this could only ultimately damage the Emperor; therefore they 'must be ridden on a tight rein'. These views were also those of the Emperor, but Albrecht held to them with a rigidity and expounded them with a vehemence which made Franz Joseph appear benevolent. The Emperor's ideas on how the Imperial Family should behave were strict, but the Archduke's were set in concrete. He expected everyone to live up to his standards and preached about this incessantly for, always conscious of his position, he considered that he had a right to say what he thought. Unfortunately, he had little of Franz Joseph's natural courtesy, was deficient in both humour and charm, and tended to be the Cassandra of the family. Albrecht could never have been anyone's favourite uncle, and it is alarming to think what would have occurred if he had had to deal with Elisabeth.

As a Field-Marshal and senior member of the Imperial Family, Albrecht (many people resented this) had constant access to Franz Joseph, but their relationship was one of mutual respect rather than affection, and the Emperor had no great opinion of his cousin's political judgement. The Archduke, who in the course of his career had been entrusted with several diplomatic missions in which he had not been outstandingly successful, described himself as 'a soldier and thank Heaven only a soldier', and disliked what he referred to as 'the slippery paths of diplomacy'. [2] Nevertheless he was not backward in offering advice about political matters, which Franz Joseph did not hesitate to reject if he saw fit, and sometimes abruptly. When in 1866 Albrecht exhorted him to cut short his stay in Budapest because his prolonged absence in Hungary was causing resentment in Vienna, he replied curtly:

The Emperor knows very well what he wants. . . . Furthermore he is not the Emperor of Vienna, but regards himself as ruling equally in each of his Kingdoms and provinces. [3]

It was as well that Franz Joseph did not often listen to the Archduke's view on affairs of State for Albrecht was one of the most conservative figures in the Monarchy, detesting what he once described as present-day democratic tendencies dragging everything down to one level'. [4] His instinctive reaction to any mention of a political change was that it was undesirable.

Throughout his career the Archduke had to overcome severe physical handicaps, for he was born short sighted and suffered from recurrent bouts of fever. With his grey beard, protruding lower lip and thick steel-rimmed spectacles, he looked more like a German professor than a Field-Marshal. Yet Albrecht's whole life was bound up with the army, dedicated to ensuring that it remained supranational as the dynasty of which it was the instrument was supranational, there to serve the Emperor (not the State) in absolute obedience and loyalty. Any member of it who failed in his duty was therefore in the Archduke's opinion guilty of a personal crime against his sovereign.

Disagree though they did over politics, Franz Joseph's and Albrecht's view of the army was identical. The Emperor who from the time he was a child had been fascinated by everything to do with soldiers, and except when out shooting always wore uniform, never forgot the part which the army had played in putting down the revolt in 1848–49, considering it the guardian of his throne and his dynastic bodyguard. Like Albrecht he held the soldierly virtues of obedience and discipline to be superior to all others. To both of them Field-Marshal Radetsky, the paladin who proudly asserted that day and night he was ready to defend the House of Habsburg, and who as an octogenarian did so in 1849 by thrashing the Italians and, for the time being, saving Italy for the dynasty, was the epitome of military virtue. When the old man died in Milan in 1858 and his body was brought home for burial on his family estate in Bohemia, by Franz Joseph's command a guard of honour was mounted at every station through which the train bearing the coffin passed. On the morning after its arrival in Vienna the entire garrison were drawn up on parade. When the funeral cortège arrived the massed bands crashed into Strauss's Radetsky march, and the young Emperor and Field-Marshal rode forward, halted in front of the coffin, drew his sword and lowered it in a final salute to the old Field-Marshal 'my most loyal servant'. Then he placed himself at the head of the procession and led it to the gate of the city. It was a unique tribute, never to be repeated for any other of his subjects.

To maintain the spirit of Radetsky in the officers' corps was Franz Joseph's enduring aim, and one with which Albrecht entirely agreed. Unfortunately, the Emperor failed to realise that Radetsky's success had been achieved because he was not only a gallant and loyal commander, but also a master of his profession. Assuming that the former two qualities made the best officers, and suspicious of 'intellectuals' versed in military science, he therefore appointed to high rank a number of men whose ideas of warfare were outmoded, and who did not make the best use of the very large sums of money which, to the despair of successive Ministers of Finance, Franz Joseph insisted should be spent upon the army. All over Europe new weapons and tactics were being evolved, and in this evolution the Monarchy lagged sadly behind. The traditional spirit with which the Imperial army went into battle, determined 'heroically to storm a position whatever the opportunity offered' was out of date. The time was past when the bayonet charge—described by one Austrian officer as 'the poetry of war'—was decisive. The army had excelled, as the British excelled in far-flung corners of the Empire, in situations where:

> The gatling's jammed and the Colonel's dead
> And the regiment blinded in dust and smoke. [5]

But at both Solferino and at Königgrätz it had been sent into battle with the gatling already jammed, in other words with inadequate supplies, out-of-date weapons, and led by incompetent generals.

At Königgrätz the Prussians had brutally demonstrated to the Emperor that major reforms in the army must be made. His cousin Albrecht seemed to him to possess outstanding qualifications to carry out this task. He was the only successful general in the recent war, worked in a way which Franz Joseph understood, insisting that everything should be minutely recorded in writing, and last but by no means least was a Habsburg. It was appropriate that the dynastic bodyguard should be commanded by a member of the Imperial Family. After peace had been concluded with

Prussia the Emperor therefore appointed the Archduke Inspector General of the army, and Commander-in-Chief designate in time of war. He continued personally to attend all important manœuvres and to adjudicate on all senior appointments, but on questions of organisation, strategy and tactics he now regarded Albrecht as his military oracle.

In the reorganisation of the army the Archduke faced a gigantic task, several aspects of which were not made easier by the peculiar circumstances pertaining to the Monarchy. Three years' compulsory military service was introduced increasing the strength of regular units and reserves to a total, on paper, of 800,000 men, all of whom had to be fitted out with uniform and weapons at a time when both were still in such short supply that one reserve battalion appeared on manœuvres attired in shirts and underpants. The infantry had to be equipped with breech-loading rifles, and the artillery with the latest guns. All this required a great deal of money, and as public opinion was opposed to any additional military expenditure the army estimates, which had to be fought through both the Austrian and the Hungarian Parliaments, were the subject of annual and bitter controversy. All ranks must be trained in the use of up-to-date weapons and modern methods of warfare, and this was difficult because some parts of the Monarchy were very much more backward than others. N.C.O.s and troops, therefore, varied considerably in education and calibre. In training there were considerable linguistic problems to be overcome, and the Hungarians lost no opportunity of protesting about German being the universal language of command. Every effort must be made to speed up mobilisation—which in the Monarchy took eight weeks as opposed to Prussia's four and a half—but to do this was not easy because in order to prevent the troops from forming too close affiliations with the local inhabitants, regiments were stationed as far away as possible from the districts in which they were recruited, and in the event of a call-up reservists might have to travel for days to join their units. Every effort too, must be made to ensure that in the event of war as many men as possible were actually engaged in fighting: at Solferino and Königgrätz Napoleon and von Moltke respectively had managed to get a quarter of their armies on to the battlefield, compared to one-sixth of the Imperial troops. To solve these problems required improved staff work, planning and leadership. There was no longer any place for dilettantes on the staff, nor for the old-fashioned type of general who before Solferino made his newly-arrived Chief of Staff drink two glasses of brandy in rapid succession and then said: 'We do not need to discuss anything further. What you plan and write I will carry out, but I will assume personal leadership in battle.'[6] But whatever stress might be laid on the necessity for officers to be able and well qualified, and whatever the attempt to ensure that aristocratic birth was no longer the passport to promotion, all senior appointments had to be approved by the Emperor who was liable to be swayed by his personal likes and dislikes. Albrecht himself admitted within two years of being appointed Inspector General that 'A perfectly organised army does not exist, for it has to fit in with the conditions prevailing in the State.'[7]

On one thing, however, the Archduke, with the Emperor's full backing, was insistent: the old spirit of the army must be preserved. In spite of the splitting in two of the Monarchy by the Compromise it must remain the Imperial and Royal army, the force which bound together all nationalities, each member of which was faithful to the oath which he took to serve the Emperor in the spirit of 'all for one and one for all'.[8] This spirit did endure thanks to the career officers who remained an a-national caste. Many of them came of service families and had been born and brought up in the atmosphere of the regiment. A two-way mystique existed between them and their sovereign. To Franz Joseph they were 'his' officers; to them he was 'their' supreme commander and warlord on whose favour they depended. Loyal, humble and unpretentious, these officers were the backbone of the army. Their behaviour was dominated by that conception of honour which the Emperor himself held, and which demanded unquestioning obedience and absolute fidelity to their oath of service to him. In serious cases of a breach of honour the culprit was visited by two of his fellow officers who handed him a letter summarising his offence together with a revolver, and then withdrew leaving him to decide what to do next. The decision was almost always the same: suicide. The mystique which bound the army to the Emperor was enforced by spartan means, but on the whole it worked, producing devotion like that of the N.C.O. who through lack of education had never succeeded in passing the necessary examination to obtain a commission, and who on his retirement asked for one recognition only of his fifty years of service, the gilded sword-sling of an officer, in order that when he died it might be laid on his coffin.

This devotion was, however, due to the aura in which by 1880 the Emperor had finally managed to envelop himself, not to Albrecht. The Archduke had never been popular in the army. Jealous of his colleagues, quick to imagine criticism and to resent it, as a junior officer he had been an awkward subordinate—a harassed Minister of War once said of him that of all the Archdukes in the army Albrecht was the most trying because he was always remonstrating about something.[9] When he reached high rank he was hard on those who served under him, and at the battle of Custozza in 1866 reduced John, his Chief of Staff, to the verge of a nervous breakdown. There were two schools of thought about Custozza. Officially the victory was ascribed to the Archduke, but some officers considered that a great deal of credit should go to John who had drawn up the operational plans for it, and noted with disgust that Albrecht did not demur when he was thereafter referred to as 'the victor of Custozza', paying no tribute whatsoever to his Chief of Staff. Some of them too, may have known that after John's death in 1876 the Archduke took steps to obtain all his personal papers, and have drawn their own conclusions from this.[10] And, to a great many officers, the Archduke's behaviour over Benedek was even more equivocal. Benedek was arraigned before a Court of Inquiry after he had lost the battle of Königgrätz. He had given a written undertaking to Albrecht that he would never under any circumstances attempt to defend his conduct, and he kept his promise until he died. On December 4th, 1866, the Emperor ordered that no further proceedings were to be taken against Benedek, and this order appeared in the official gazette published in the *Wiener Zeitung* on December 8th. The same issue of the paper also, however, contained an article asserting that the General had irrevocably ruined his military career, and placed the whole blame on him for the disaster. It was a vicious attack on the personal honour of a gallant and loyal officer, which could not have been published without the authorisation of Archduke Albrecht (who had in fact seen the proofs and corrected them), and it did not pass unnoticed. Decades of devoted service could, it appeared, be ignored if the interests of the Monarchy demanded a scapegoat or, to put it more bluntly, to maintain a grandiose conception a human sacrifice must be made. Benedek permitted himself only one comment on the affair, in his will, when he wrote bitterly that this attack confounded all his ideas of justice and decency. He asked to be buried in civilian clothes and without military honours, but when he died in Graz most of the garrison wearing full uniform voluntarily attended his funeral—a clear demonstration of the army's opinion of the treatment meted out by higher authority to Benedek.

The treatment of Benedek and John apart, there was a good deal of complaint amongst junior officers about the fact that in Albrecht's reorganisation of the army the loyalty of the average officer was not rewarded by improved conditions of service. The highest rank to which most of them could hope to attain was that of major or, if they were exceptionally lucky, colonel, and there were cases of men who were still lieutenants at the age of forty-two. They served for most of their careers in provincial garrison towns where the only places of amusement were a couple of cafés, a hotel and a third rate music hall, which they could seldom afford to patronise, for most of them were in debt and had to lead an austere existence to keep up appearances. Loyal to the Emperor's person they remained, but by 1880 their morale in general was poor. Archduke Albrecht, himself a very rich man, seemed unable to understand that improved conditions of service would do more to raise the morale of officers without private means than the smart uniforms and military bands on which he insisted for this purpose, the cost of which they were compelled to meet out of their inadequate pay.

By 1880 Albrecht had been Inspector General for over thirteen years. At the time when he took up the post the Emperor made two other important appointments to assist with the reorganisation of the army, nominating Colonel Count Friedrich Beck-Rzikowsky head of his personal Military Chancery and General Baron Kuhn von Kuhnenfeld Minister of War. Of the two of them Beck had survived in his post, Kuhn had not. The Minister of War was the son of a career officer, who had risen to high rank through sheer ability, enjoyed an excellent reputation both for integrity and gallantry in the field, had a range of interests which extended far beyond military subjects and was one of the best read men in the army. But although cultured he was not polished, outspoken to the point of rudeness and at loggerheads with Albrecht. Kuhn, impulsive with a tendency to liberal free-thinking, was convinced that as Minister of War he was responsible to the people for the army. The Archduke, for whom the army existed to serve the Monarch and the Monarch only, flatly disagreed with Kuhn, considered his methods slapdash and superficial, and bitterly resented his criticism of the aristocracy and the Church. Kuhn heartily reciprocated Albrecht's dislike. He considered the Archduke to be stodgy, smug, self-important, incapable of large-scale thinking and did not hesitate to tell him so, adding on one occasion that, sick as he was of being frustrated, he would infinitely rather be Minister of War in Abyssinia than in the Monarchy. Eventually Kuhn was sacked from his post and relegated to a provincial command. In fairness to Albrecht it must be pointed out that his attitude was similar to that of many other military commanders of his time and for some years to come—Lord Kitchener for example told the Viceroy of India that in the interests of discipline he could tolerate no criticism of his plans from his subordinates. But it was an attitude that discouraged initiative and original thinking, and Kuhn's fate convinced many of the Emperor's senior officers that the way to promotion lay in obeying orders from above efficiently and without question, raising no controversial points, and generally emulating Beck.

Beck as the head of the Emperor's Military Chancery was the link between Franz Joseph and Albrecht, and thoroughly approved of by both of them. He was hardworking, ambitious, a smooth, clever staff officer, aware that the way to get on was to please his superiors, which he did. Beck excelled at paper work and his files were always in order. To Franz Joseph the efficiency with which he ran the Chancery meant that he was a competent soldier, to whose opinion when questions of personnel and senior appointments arose he paid great attention. Albrecht considered him a thoroughly sound officer. The Emperor found both of them highly satisfactory. The position by 1880 was therefore that, although Albrecht was now so blind that he could barely recognise anyone at a distance of more than five yards and had to dictate all his letters to his Adjutant, there was not the slightest indication that a younger man would replace him as Inspector General at any time in the foreseeable future, and Beck, through whose office every paper concerning military matters passed before it reached the Emperor, was firmly entrenched and exercised to some extent the influence of an *éminence grise*. Anyone therefore who wished to raise some point concerning the army with the Emperor had first to win over Albrecht or Beck or both, and as those who attempted it learnt, frequently to their cost, the chances of doing so were slight.

The result was to convince junior officers that, if they valued their careers, it was wiser not to campaign for the adoption of modern weapons and methods of training by the Imperial Army. One young officer, however, refused to remain silent. By 1880 Archduke Johann Salvator had already made himself notorious for his forward thinking and disregard for established authority.

PART TWO

Youth and Impatience

CHAPTER 5

Archduke Johann Salvator

According to Albrecht all Archdukes must be made 'to feel at home at Court, so that they should never forget . . . the duties of their exalted rank with all its advantages and disadvantages'.[1] Those Archdukes who were members of the Grand Ducal family of Tuscany—'Die Toskaner' as they were known to their relatives— were, however, notably reluctant to appear at Court at all. They were descended from Maria Theresa's second son, a cadet branch of the Habsburgs which had ruled Tuscany since the middle of the eighteenth century where they were expected, although their State was autonomous, to conform to the Emperor's policy and generally to provide a useful adjunct to his influence south of the Alps. The Family Law awarded the Grand Duke of Tuscany the same powers with regard to his branch of the family as were exercised by Franz Joseph over the rest of the House of Habsburg, but stipulated that he must refer all important decisions to the Emperor for approval.

Successive Grand Dukes made Tuscany into a model state. Cobden who visited it in 1847 found the standard of living of its inhabitants higher than that of any country in southern Europe; Lamartine described it as 'a haven of peace', and it was said of Grand Duke Leopold II who reigned from 1824 until 1859: 'It is the habit of the good Prince Leopold to wander through Florence nearly always on foot and move among the crowd without molestation.'[2] Tuscany looked outwards to the Mediterranean and all 'Die Toskaner' loved the sea. Brought up in the warmth, light and colour of the south at an easy-going Court, they attached no importance to formality and ceremonial, and there was a streak of fantasy and originality about them utterly foreign to

Franz Joseph. They had become, in fact, Latinised Habsburgs; when the triumph of Italian nationalism after the Emperor's defeat at Solferino in 1859 forced 'the good Prince Leopold' and his family to leave Florence and take refuge in the Monarchy, a collection of exotic cuckoos entered the family nest.

Leopold who had abdicated, a few weeks before the family fled, in favour of his eldest son Ferdinand, bought Schloss Schlackenwerth in Bohemia where he lived in retirement until his death in 1870, apparently making no effort to influence his children or to direct their lives. For all practical purposes Ferdinand, now in the terminology of the *Almanach de Gotha* a '*ci-devant régnant*', was the head of the family. 'Nando', a handsome amiable man, made his headquarters in excessively uncomfortable grace and favour apartments provided by the Emperor in Salzburg, and built himself a small villa at Lindau on Lake Constance. At first he refused to renounce his claim to Tuscany, an attitude which caused the Emperor, forced after Königgrätz to improve his relations with the King of Italy, considerable embarrassment. Finally, in 1870 Ferdinand yielded and signed an act of renunciation, whereby he retained the title of Grand Duke for his lifetime but promised never to return to Italy. Having given his word he kept it, but he remained a Florentine at heart and always spoke Italian to members of his immediate family. He detested Court and appeared there as little as possible, but he got on well with Franz Joseph for he was cheerful and good tempered, never betrayed a confidence or attempted to exert influence, and shared the Emperor's passion for shooting.

Archduke Karl Salvator, Ferdinand's brother, also disliked Court life. An excellent craftsman and a first class locksmith, in Vienna his favourite amusement was to travel incognito on buses and trams, a pastime which the Emperor deprecated, but found harmlessly eccentric compared with the behaviour of the third Toskaner brother Archduke Ludwig Salvator. Ferdinand and Karl Salvator avoided Court as much as possible: Ludwig Salvator simply went away from it. Known as 'the learned Archduke' he wrote and spoke fourteen languages, and when not voyaging round the Mediterranean, spent most of his time in

Majorca writing books about the geology and natural history of North Africa and the Balearic Islands. Many stories about his strange behaviour filtered back to Vienna. He was alleged to be a sun worshipper, and it was said that when in Majorca he dressed like a peasant in linen trousers and sandals, his shirt cuffs tied together with string. He appeared to have some curious companions, amongst them an exquisite young man with curly hair and a small moustache who died at the age of twenty-three, and to whom Ludwig Salvator dedicated a very large marble memorial showing his friend wearing a species of toga falling off his shoulders, leaning on one arm and gazing up at a beckoning angel. On the other hand there were also rumours that some of the crew of the Archduke's yacht, whose meals and sleeping quarters he shared, were beautiful girls in disguise. On his rare visits to the Monarchy Ludwig Salvator occasionally appeared at Ischl, where his dishevelled appearance caused some dismay. He possessed only one uniform tunic which he wore on the Emperor's birthday, and, although at times a witty and brilliant conversationalist was, with the exception of the Empress who had a penchant for eccentrics, regarded as odd by the Imperial Family.

Altogether from Franz Joseph's point of view the return of 'Die Toskaner' to the Monarchy was not an unmixed blessing. Having lost Tuscany they were short of money, their appanages had to be paid for by the State, they were an additional charge on the Family Fund, but neither Ferdinand nor his next two brothers were prepared to earn their keep by swelling the ranks of the Archdukes on ceremonial occasions. However, they did not attempt to meddle in politics and if (to the Emperor's annoyance) Ludwig Salvator failed to conform to the family rules and keep Franz Joseph informed of his whereabouts, at least he indulged in his curious, and it must be feared scandalous, behaviour outside the frontiers of the Monarchy. Albrecht's views on the failure of the three elder Toskaner brothers to conform to their status may be imagined, but he agreed with the Emperor that much might be expected from the youngest member of the family, Johann Salvator,[3] the responsibility for whose upbringing had been assumed by Franz Joseph. By the time he was twenty it was evident that this young man had a great deal of talent and both the Emperor and the Archduke hoped that, under their direction, this might be canalised to the service of the dynasty.

Johann Salvator, born in November 1852, was seventeen years younger than his eldest brother Ferdinand. His mother Maria Antonia, a daughter of Francis I, King of the Two Sicilies, was a strong-minded woman with a profound belief in the Catholic faith. She disapproved of Ludwig's behaviour and regarded Ferdinand and Karl Salvator as uninteresting ciphers. All her affection and hopes were centred on her youngest child Johann Salvator, or Gianni as he was known in the family.

Johann Salvator's letters to his mother, in which he addressed her always in the formal third person, as opposed to the intimate second person singular used by his brothers, show him to have been a devoted son, unfailingly courteous and concerned for her welfare. He wrote to her in Italian, for Maria Antonia spoke practically no German, a language which Johann Salvator himself only started to learn after his family left Florence, and which he at first found difficult, reporting to his mother that his tutor was not pleased with him, for he was still making a lot of mistakes, 'but I am trying hard to improve'. [4] More assurances as to his application to his lessons (which by then included arithmetic, French, history, German, military subjects and music) followed, 'I will try to give you pleasure by carrying out my duties and by diligent studies' [5] and, three weeks later, 'of course I will do all I can to justify your expectations by diligent studies and good behaviour'. [6]

Two such letters to his mother within three weeks suggest that a complaint of some kind had reached her. Possibly while upset she was not altogether surprised. Although Gianni was highly intelligent and blessed with a facility for the rapid assimilation of any subject to which he applied himself, he had not been an easy child to control, for he was impetuous and apt to fly into rages disregarding the adjurations of his elders and betters, whom he delighted to tease. An old-fashioned Nanny would have described him as 'sharp'. However whatever incident occasioned these letters was smoothed over, and on August 16th, 1865, three months before his thirteenth birthday, Johann Salvator entered the army.

Although nominally gazetted to a regiment, the young Arch-duke continued to live at Court for the next six years while he continued his military studies. Although still a boy he was expected to play some part in the monotonous ceremonial round. The Emperor evidently was kind to him, allowed him, accom-panied by his tutor, to visit the Paris Exhibition, to make several journeys to Western Europe, and made no objection to the variety of interests which Johann Salvator was developing. These included photography, music (he began to compose songs), paint-ing, 'I am about to start painting in oils which will be very enter-taining but very difficult'.[7] an attempt to design a new lock for a gun of which he sent his mother an excellent drawing[8] and, in 1868, the beginnings of a project which was to be an interest and joy to him for the rest of his life, the purchase and renovation of Schloss Orth, an old castle superbly situated on the Traunsee near Gmunden. At the beginning of 1870 Grand Duke Leopold II died in Rome. Relations between the Monarchy and the Kingdom of Italy were strained, and Franz Joseph would not allow Johann Salvator to attend his father's funeral. 'No doubt he had good reasons for this,' he wrote to Grand Duchess Maria Antonia, 'but you will understand how much I minded not being able to be present at the funeral of beloved Papa.'[9] From then on he appears to have felt that it was more than ever incumbent on him to look after his mother, and to press on with his plans for Schloss Orth in order to provide a home for her.

Unlike his contemporaries, Johann Salvator was uninterested in shooting, and at the age of sixteen commented sardonically on the boredom of being compelled to admire twenty-one pairs of antlers recently bagged by his eldest brother. Neither, it seems, did he much care for fashionable balls. 'Carnival week is over and thank Heaven I have not had to show my paces during it!'[10] His letters to his mother until he came of age give the impression that he led a solitary life in the midst of the Court, pursuing his own interests and developing his own ideas. The latter, by 1868, gave Maria Antonia cause for anxiety; it seems that Gianni was abandoning the faith in which she had brought him up and was becoming a free thinker. He wrote assuring her that he had fulfilled his religious duties in Holy Week, adding a few days later that, if not orthodox in all his beliefs, 'I can say that I am not a bad Christian'.[11] With this she was apparently for the time being content; her favourite son could usually win her over and persuade her to let him do what he wanted. When he was seventeen she vetoed his proposal that he should take a holiday in Western Europe. He replied that he certainly would not do so if she did not wish it, but pointed out that the alternative proposed for him—a tour of Croatia, Dalmatia, Hungary and Transylvania—while it would enlarge his sphere of knowledge, would not provide the recreation which he needed after a strenuous summer of work and manœuvres, that to be honest the 'uncivilised Danubian countries' did not attract him, and therefore he would far rather go to northern Italy, Switzerland and the Riviera.[12] Maria Antonia gave in.

Shortly before this the Grand Duchess received a letter from one of the architects with whom Gianni was dealing on her behalf over Schloss Orth warmly praising His Imperial and Royal Highness's 'zeal and perseverence . . . qualities which will undoubtedly develop still more in the future'.[13] Johann Salvator's handling of the problems attached to the purchase and renovation of the Schloss, and the thoroughness with which he went into every detail was astonishing in view of the fact that he was not yet twenty. He had the ability to succeed in any one of a number of professions, but as an Archduke the army was the only career open to him. There was no need for him to exert himself over his military studies, for as a member of the Imperial Family he was automatically assured of rapid promotion. However in addition to being a hard worker he had a fierce desire to excel, and as he grew up the ambition of a clever boy to be top of the class hardened into the determination of a young man to rise to the highest rank of his profession. He chose to serve, not in a smart cavalry regiment, but in the artillery, a branch of the army which attracted keen young men with progressive ideas many of whom were of middle class origin. At the beginning of 1872, when he was not yet twenty, he passed an exam for accelerated promotion with outstanding distinction. His army record adds that he had wide general knowledge, was a first-class horseman, swimmer, gymnast and fencer, knew a great deal about building, and that his special interests included architecture, painting, drawing, turnery, photography, sculpture and music.

Johann Salvator was now a major. He had grown up to be a short, sturdy man who, like many short men, made up in personality for what he lacked in height. A portrait of him at that time, before he grew a beard, shows a young officer, the ribbon and badge of the Order of the Golden Fleece threaded through the top buttonholes of his tunic, striking rather than handsome, with a broad forehead, a full determined mouth and (his best feature) large deepset eyes. The three-quarter face pose, emphasising the line of the jaw and the aggressive thrust of the chin, conveys the impression of someone prepared to accept any challenge. An obstinate determination to succeed in whatever he set out to do was perhaps the dominant feature of the Archduke's character. But there were others: he also had boundless energy, a great deal of youthful exuberance and a strong streak of romanticism. When he smiled his face lit up, and as he began to talk in his soft baritone voice—he was a good conversationalist and when he wished could be highly entertaining—he must have been extraordinarily attractive to any woman.

Within a few weeks of passing his promotion examination Johann Salvator left Vienna for a tour of the eastern Mediterranean visiting Egypt, Turkey, Greece and Sicily. He was fascinated by Egypt the first Oriental country he had seen, looked at every classical site which could be reached in the time available, and in Rome was received in audience by King Victor Emmanuel. He returned reluctantly to Vienna where he increasingly disliked living at Court, and the attendance at State functions which this entailed. On the one hand his natural love of liberty and independence inclined him to liberal ideas, and the formality and ceremonial which surrounded the Emperor seemed to him archaic and suffocating. On the other, unable to forget that he had been born a Prince of Tuscany and that in Florence his branch of the House of Habsburg had ruled in their own right, he bitterly resented the fact that in the Monarchy this now counted for nothing and that, as distant relations of the Emperor, he and his brothers were relegated to the lower ranks of the hierarchy of Archdukes. This made him all the more determined to achieve a position in the army which would give him freedom of action and a chance to command, and his attitude to the Court and the aristocracy who had the entrée to it was therefore one of 'very well, I'll show them', accompanied by a desire to show them up. He teased the ladies-in-waiting, was delighted if he succeeded in disconcerting them, and did not seem to mind what he said, shocking Prince Hohenlohe, the Emperor's Lord Chamberlain, by referring to some aspect of ceremonial as 'degrading', and scandalising someone who was deploring the loss of Tuscany with the retort:

> I do not agree with you at all. The Tuscans are Italians, the Italians wanted unity and the existence of the Grand Duchy was an obstacle to this; it was necessary for the Grand Duchy to be abolished. The people are not made for Princes.[14]

When he chose, Johann Salvator could be charming, courteous and altogether delightful, but at Court, while invariably respectful to the Emperor, he rarely chose to be anything of the sort. People either liked or disliked him very much indeed. While his ability was generally acknowledged, he was not popular in Court circles, the members of which had neither the tolerance nor the imagination to understand the point of view of a clever and angry young man with a very large chip on his shoulder.

However, after his return to Vienna in May 1872, Johann Salvator only spent a few weeks penned up at Court. His interview in Rome with Victor Emmanuel displeased the Emperor, always hypersensitive about any action taken by a member of the Imperial Family which might be construed as touching on affairs of State. Johann Salvator he decided must be brought to heel. The problem of how to discipline members of their family who misbehaved was common to all nineteenth-century monarchs, and in the case of the British usually solved by despatching the offending Prince on a prolonged tour of the remoter parts of the Empire. Franz Joseph had no overseas possessions, but there were in the Monarchy a number of dull provincial garrison towns to which a recalcitrant Archduke could be sent until (hopefully) he had seen the error of his ways. In June Johann Salvator was therefore posted to Lemberg. It was not an enjoyable experience. The heat he complained was killing; his working day started at 5 a.m. and ended at 8 p.m. except on Sundays, and this was no day of recreation. After church one had to receive some sixteen to twenty callers, then one dined with the G.O.C. and nothing could be more boring, 'after dinner, which lasts for an eternity, I am condemned to listen to the so-called funny stories of the General and some of his guests'.[15] But he continued to work hard, 'in order to please you and be a credit to the family',[16] with the aim of passing the exacting examination for the *Kriegschule* or War College, qualification for which would enable him to become a staff officer. In December 1872 the Archduke was declared of age and became entitled to an appanage and a 'household' which, since he was a junior member of the Imperial Family, consisted of Baron Mensshengen, appointed by the Emperor to be his Adjutant and also, Johann Salvator evidently suspected, his watch dog. 'I am certain I shall want to get rid of him, but we will see.'[17] Some months however passed without incident. It seemed that he was fulfilling his promise to his mother to devote himself to his military duties 'and to behave well both in public and private'.[18]

Johann Salvator was now beginning to form his own opinion of the progress of the much talked of reorganisation of the army which had been inaugurated after Königgrätz. He was a fourteen-year-old cadet at the time of that battle, and during his military studies had learnt a great deal about it. He knew of the final charge of the Austrian I Corps who, towards the end of the day when all hope was lost, obeyed the order to attack and advanced with colours flying and drums beating to lose 279 officers and 10,000 men in just over twenty minutes;[19] of the magnificent performance of the artillery to which von Moltke himself had paid tribute; of innumerable acts of heroism which had saved the honour of the Imperial army. But nevertheless the Prussians had won, proving that courage alone could not prevail against superior equipment, planning and training, and this Johann Salvator like many of his contemporaries bitterly resented. The defeat left him with a lasting hatred of Prussia, and a determination that such a humiliation must never occur again. He did not perhaps know that the Prussian military attaché in Vienna considered that no State possessed better raw material for her soldiers than the Monarchy, but it was an opinion that he certainly held, convinced that the Emperor's troops, if their training and equipment were brought up to date, could beat any army in Europe. But in his judgement this was happening far too slowly. There was still far too much emphasis on pointless drill and regulations, the artillery were not being supplied with up-to-date equipment, the morale of junior officers was low because they were barely able to exist on their pay, amongst the senior officers there was a great deal of dead wood to be cut out.

The young, inclined to underestimate the difficulties with which the older generation have to contend, are quick to criticise what they have failed to do rather than to appreciate what they have achieved. Johann Salvator, by nature impatient, was no exception to this rule. He considered that the senior officers responsible for the organisation of the army were not getting on with the job, and it seems possible that, always outspoken, he eventually said so. According to his army record he was sentenced in October 1873 to eight days house arrest, for insulting his Commanding Officer and for conduct detrimental to regimental discipline. No further details of the offence are given, but it was followed by further retribution—transfer from Lemberg to Temesvar.

Lemberg was a metropolis compared to Temesvar on the outer confines of the Monarchy, situated in that uncivilised area to which the Archduke felt 'so little drawn'. Johann Salvator's first impressions of it were unfavourable. The town was small and ugly, the surrounding countryside flat and monotonous, the climate vile. It was impossible to find any decent accommodation, the barracks were filthy, the 13th Artillery Regiment to which he had been posted was composed of the dregs of the rest of the Corps, and the calibre of the officers, with the possible exception of the Colonel, deplorable. Gradually, however, things improved. He managed to buy a house, his work in the regiment began to show results and this was so satisfactory that 'I would not have believed that my prison or institute of correction could be so agreeable'.[20] Archduke Wilhelm arrived on a tour of inspection and praised his work. There was a mention of promotion.

Then, when everything seemed to be going well, Johann Salvator once again fell out with his Commanding Officer whom he alleged had behaved offensively towards him on various public occasions and, in an exceedingly bad temper, went to Vienna to put his case to Archduke Albrecht the Inspector General of the army. The result of this expedition was not all that he had hoped for. Franz Joseph received him, agreed that he was right to seek advice, and said vaguely that no doubt everything would be put right. Albrecht expressed astonishment at what had occurred, but ordered his turbulent young relative to go back to his regiment and advised him to keep calm. Johann Salvator returned to Temesvar, continued to work hard, was praised by the Emperor at the September manœuvres, and in November promoted Lieutenant-Colonel. His annual report described him as an outstandingly able, highly qualified and keen staff officer, of whom great things were expected once his knowledge was supplemented by more experience.

Unfortunately, calmness was a quality which the Archduke did not possess. His failure to obtain redress for what he considered to be a legitimate grievance rankled. It seemed to him symptomatic of the attitude of senior officers to much that was wrong with the army, and he published an anonymous article in a military journal which he admitted contained 'observations which were somewhat outspken'.[21] Officers had never been forbidden to write articles on military subjects, but were liable to incur punishment if they were so unwise as to criticise their superiors. Johann Salvator managed to escape detection and, rendered overconfident by this, proceeded to develop his ideas in a pamphlet of some 140 pages entitled 'Reflections on the Organisation of the Austrian Artillery' which appeared in Vienna at the beginning of 1875.[22]

Although he had no difficulty in expressing himself on paper, at the age of twenty-two the Archduke had not yet learnt the art (which he never fully mastered) of dealing tactfully with controversial subjects. His 'Reflections' included a slashing attack on out-of-date regulations, wastage of manpower, the inadequacy of pay and uniform allowances and blocked promotion. He calculated that unless the estimates were increased it would take 146 years, 5 months and 5 days to bring the equipment of the artillery up to date, and was acid about the manning of the fortress artillery, a dumping ground for inefficient officers in which anyone serving was left for years to rot in some outlandish place such as an island fortress off the Dalmatian coast, 'that southern Siberia'. Finally and disastrously he aired his views on foreign policy, urging that the highest priority be given to the fortification of Prague and Olmütz to protect Bohemia against further aggression by Prussia, for 'in spite of all assurances of friendship we must face up to the fact that the expansionist aims of Prussia threaten the Monarchy'. [23] He asserted that the only guarantee for the future lay in an alliance with Russia.

Within weeks Johann Salvator's authorship of the pamphlet was discovered. The open advocacy by an Archduke of an alliance with Russia did not pass unnoticed abroad. The Austrian envoy in Belgrade reported that suggestions were being made in Russian circles there that the Archduke should replace King Milan on the throne of Serbia. Andrassy was informed that while Bismarck would probably not make a formal protest, the whole episode had given rise to the most unfortunate reactions in Berlin. Franz Joseph, enraged, took immediate action. An announcement appeared in the military gazette that Archduke Johann Salvator had been transferred from the artillery to the 12th Infantry Regiment in Cracow, and he was ordered to report to the Emperor at once. He later wrote to his mother:

In Vienna I found the exalted personages in a great state of agitation. The Emperor, Albrecht and Wilhelm gave me a tremendous scolding. The gist of the long dissertation was that though my facts were correct, for political and disciplinary reasons I should not have written the pamphlet. The Emperor was very angry indeed. After this lecture I left Vienna within twenty-four hours and came to Cracow. I am not eligible for leave, and I am no longer an artilleryman because certain creatures do not want to have me in that branch of the army which I know best.[24]

The Archduke's reference to the Emperor's anger was no doubt an understatement. The Crown Prince and every Archduke received a copy of the following letter:

A brochure entitled, 'Reflections on the Austrian Artillery' of which Archduke Johann Salvator has acknowledged himself to be the author has recently been published. In it he discusses circumstances relating to official and personnel matters in that branch of the service to which he belongs, in a manner incompatible with and severely damaging to order and discipline, the foundations of the army.

I have therefore found myself compelled to transfer this Archduke from the Artillery which he has denigrated to Infantry Regiment Wilhelm No. 12 and personally to punish him with a severe reprimand.

I draw your attention to this incident,[25]

Franz Joseph.
Vienna,
17th February, 1875.

It was the equivalent of an announcement posted on the school notice board giving the reasons for the demotion of a prefect as a warning to the rest of the community.

While Johann Salvator privately admitted that his brochure was 'imprudent', he was not prepared to concede that anything which he had written in it was wrong: 'At least I have the satisfaction of having told the truth.'[26] Within weeks of arriving in Cracow he wrote a series of articles attacking the proposed fortification of that city as being pointless and unnecessary, by implication a restatement of his thesis that there was nothing to fear from Russia, and he also accused Kuhn, the Minister of War, of being incapable of standing up to Andrassy in defence of the true interests of the Monarchy. This provoked a reply from the Minister who observed sarcastically that it was regrettable that people should meddle with subjects which they had neither the talent nor the experience to judge. To have incurred the anger of the

Emperor and alienated Albrecht, Wilhelm and Kuhn did not augur well for the Archduke's future career. He realised this, telling his mother when he undertook to write the history of the Infantry Regiment Erzherzog Wilhelm No. 12 with which he was serving, 'this will preserve me from the temptation of writing on other subjects. It will be an innocuous book.'[27] For some time he was careful to keep out of trouble, and in the spring of 1876 was reinstated in the artillery and promoted to command a regiment in Komorn, 'a dreary fortress' but at least near Vienna. When at the beginning of 1878 Franz Joseph received him in audience, was affable and full of praise nominating him Colonel Proprietor of an artillery regiment, it seemed to Johann Salvator that he was back in favour. An appointment a few months later to command a Mountain Brigade in the force which was being assembled to occupy Bosnia Herzegovina then gave him his first chance of seeing active service.

When mobilisation began the Archduke went into strict training, gave up tea, coffee, and all forms of alcohol, and ate very little meat. It was traditional for members of the Imperial Family when in the field to be attended by a large number of servants, and to take with them a great deal of impedimenta in order to make themselves as comfortable as possible. Johann Salvator brought with him his charger and one mounted groom: his personal possessions were slung in packs on these two horses. Such austerity in a Habsburg Prince was so unprecedented as to be shocking, and caused a great deal of comment amongst his staff. They were dismayed when they discovered that their Brigadier expected them to follow his example, and insisted that they had the same rations as the troops, but the Archduke paid no attention to their protests. On July 29th he crossed the Save and led the advance guard into Bosnia. The so-called roads were appalling, and the weather abnormally bad, for there was great heat by day and torrential rain at night. The sickness rate rose sharply, and the divisional supply column, a train of waggons 24 kilometres long, fell further and further behind the main body of the troops. It took over a fortnight to reach Travnik, sixty miles from Sarajevo.

Within ten days Johann Salvator had his first experience of

action, firstly in a skirmish with a strong enemy force, and then at Jajce, a fortress which was stormed after a battle fought under a murderous sun in which the guns had to be manhandled up the mountains. His officers, while admiring his courage under fire, found him impatient and short tempered. By the time the brigade reached Travnik Johann Salvator was in fact feeling very ill, but managed to take part in several mopping-up operations and reconnaissances before collapsing with what was thought to be acute dysentery—later it was discovered to be typhoid. It was decided that he must be evacuated back to Brod in Croatia. There a fortnight later he recovered sufficiently to write to his mother:

Half dead from dysentery like many of the troops I arrived at Brod after an exhausting and not undangerous journey ... I had the luck not to be molested by the many bands of robbers who render the road precarious. It is a real mercy, a blessing of providence that I have emerged so well from this appalling country ... a sick man can easily die at the hands of these beasts who are not fit to be called men; if you are fit and with your troops it is not dangerous, or at least the danger is small. The journey did me no harm, and at least as a result of swallowing opium powders the dysentery has stopped. I am very weak and dispirited, but thank Heaven am already beginning to feel much better, and as I telegraphed you am sure I will be able to resume command of my Brigade within the next fifteen days. . . . You in Vienna will have realised partly at any rate the numerous blunders which have been committed by our having been forced to enter Bosnia. [28]

Altogether it was as the Archduke told his mother an 'unfortunate' campaign. The unexpected ferocity of the opposition which they encountered seriously undermined the morale of the Imperial forces. When their line of communication was in danger of being cut and the main base at Banjaluka was threatened, the doctors in the hospital there prepared to poison themselves rather than be captured alive by the enemy. The 'mountain brigade' which Johann Salvator commanded was neither trained nor equipped for mountain warfare. In addition to the supply chaos (which drove a number of officers to the verge of suicide) there were far too many instances of units getting lost, troops firing on one another in mistake for the enemy, and unjustifiably harsh action against the local peasantry. The state of the Archduke's health when he reached Brod gave him an excuse for taking no further part in the fighting. But he was a keen and determined soldier and a fortnight later resumed command of his brigade at Travnik. Within a few days of his return he was appointed acting Divisional Commander and captured Livno, remaining there as military commandant of the district.

Livno, which commanded the main road into Bosnia from Dalmatia, was dirty, windswept and bleak. In addition to wrestling with the eternal supply problem, rebuilding the fortifications and defence lines and generally attending to all aspects of the duties of the garrison, Johann Salvator was engaged with what he described to his mother as 'political affairs'.

> These include setting up a judicial system and a body to represent the community . . . adjudicating in innumerable disputes . . . putting the civil and military administration in order, distributing an indemnity of 10,000 florins levied on the guilty to those who have suffered loss, in short a host of things which take time to study, prudence to decide, and energy to carry out. . . . You can imagine the difficulty of the language, of having to deal with anyone who speaks nothing but Turkish through two interpreters, one who translates what I say in German or Italian into Bosnian, the other who translates the Bosnian into Turkish and vice versa! However, I have succeeded in establishing the necessary order, public safety and in enforcing the law. [29]

Towards the end of November the Archduke returned to Vienna, ill and disillusioned. He had hoped that the occupation of Bosnia Herzegovina would be the first step on the road to Salonica, the outlet on the Aegean which he believed to be vital to the Monarchy, but the campaign had demonstrated that until the army was drastically reorganised any further expansion in the Balkans was out of the question. Johann Salvator considered that even Bosnia was going to be 'not only a difficult mouthful to digest, but evocative of other complications'.[30] A catastrophe could occur there and with this he was determined not to be associated. When he heard of a proposal that 'for political reasons' he should be posted to Mostar the capital of Herzegovina, coupled with a hint of greater things, 'the ridiculous idea of making me Sovereign Prince of Bosnia and Herzegovina', he pleaded that his health would not stand a return to the Balkans. 'Only an imbecile would accept such a throne.'[31] He was prepared to do anything not to get mixed up in this disastrous venture:

> I know that it is a decisive moment in my life. . . . In time the Emperor's eyes will be opened and I am sure that one day he will be glad not to have compromised an Archduke. I am only one amongst many Archdukes. Why not send one of the others?[32]

Several months hammering at the 'omniscient Beck' resulted in appointment to a divisional command in Komorn, a place which Johann Salvator did not care for, but it was better than Bosnia:

> I am absolutely opposed to any new appointment in that country for I consider that the position of an Archduke there now would not only be difficult and compromising but absolutely useless.[33]

But, in spite of the fact that the Military Cross of Merit which the Archduke was awarded after the Bosnian campaign, was accompanied by a citation paying tribute to his administrative ability, by the beginning of 1880 it did not seem that Komorn would be, as he hoped, a stepping stone to a position in Vienna where he could influence the reorganisation of the army. At the beginning of 1880 the only alternative position offered to him was a posting as Military Governor to Temesvar.

CHAPTER 6

Crown Prince Rudolf

Crown Prince Rudolf, born in 1858, was six years younger than his cousin Archduke Johann Salvator. As a child he was a source of anxiety as well as pride to his parents for he was frequently ill, accident prone, and when at the age of six he left the nursery to begin his education, highly strung and nervy. Great attention was paid to the selection of his tutors, Franz Joseph stipulating that while they must on no account be free thinkers, they must be conversant with the problems and circumstances of the times—an enlightened directive in view of his personal dislike of many of the current liberal progressive trends.

The Emperor's choice (thoroughly approved by the Archduchess Sophie) of the man to supervise his son's upbringing was less happy. Count Gondrecourt was a soldier of the old school who believed that boys must be strictly disciplined in order to toughen them, and his methods were far too severe for a sensitive child. Elisabeth, erratic, capricious and frequently abroad, was no more capable of consistently sustaining the role of a mother than she was of undertaking the conventional duties of a wife. But in her own way she was devoted to Rudolf, and when she saw that after a year of Gondrecourt's supervision the boy was becoming a nervous wreck, decided that the Count must be dismissed. The Empress perhaps already sensed, as she said years later, that on the rare occasions when the Emperor, accustomed to deferential requests, was confronted with a flat demand, he was so astonished that he gave in; in other words that the only way of dealing with him was to stand up to him. This she now proceeded to do, telling Franz Joseph that he must in effect choose between her and Gondrecourt, and following this up with a letter in which, without any form of affectionate preamble, she demanded power to decide everything which concerned the children until they came of age.[1] This ultimatum had an immediate effect. The Emperor replaced Gondrecourt with Count Joseph Latour von Thurnberg who gradually succeeded in winning both the Crown Prince's confidence and his friendship. Had Elisabeth insisted, Franz Joseph would probably also have permitted her a greater say in the detail of her son's upbringing. She did not so insist because this would have involved a sustained effort of which she was temperamentally incapable, but her intervention over Gondrecourt was decisive for Rudolf's happiness throughout the rigorous years of his education.

The Crown Prince was compelled to work far harder and to learn far more than any of his contemporaries, for like Queen Victoria and the Prince Consort, Franz Joseph was determined that no effort should be spared to fit the heir to the throne for the great position to which he would one day succeed. A curriculum was therefore drawn up which was even more formidable than that inflicted on the Prince of Wales. In addition to all the usual subjects, Rudolf was required to learn Hungarian, Polish, Czech, the history of every nation in the Monarchy, the rudiments of military science and, in accordance with Habsburg tradition, he received intensive instruction in the Catholic faith. Latour submitted frequent and detailed reports on every aspect of his charge's progress to the Emperor. Inevitably these contained some criticism. Rudolf like most boys was careless about subjects which bored him. Latour also noted that he was inclined to evade anything which he found disagreeable, telling people what he thought they wished to hear rather than the truth. The Crown Prince's apparent aversion to any form of religious instruction also gave the Count cause for concern. Rudolf's philosophy tutor bore this out, reporting that his pupil constantly asked questions, would not be content with conventional answers, and had a habit of working out those answers for himself in terms of natural science. There was, however, general agreement that the heir to the throne was exceptionally talented and that (in contrast to his father a self-confessed 'deplorable stylist') he had a quite outstanding gift for expressing himself both in writing and in speech—an overall verdict which, for all the Prince Consort's efforts, could scarcely have been applied to the Prince of Wales.

Academic prowess apart, Rudolf appeared to the world in general to be developing into everything which could be hoped for in a Crown Prince. By the age of ten His Imperial Highness had excellent manners. Von Arneth, the great historian, described how he went to the Hofburg in 1869 to be present at Rudolf's history examination. A small boy advanced and shook him by the hand saying solemnly, 'I hear that you exercise yourself with history, history is my favourite subject too, but I have not got further than Servius Tullius.' [2] Von Arneth found him charming, so did the diplomatic corps in Budapest when Rudolf was presented to them at the age of fourteen. The Prince of Wales, when on a visit to Vienna, wrote to Queen Victoria saying that the Crown Prince was 'a very nice young man', but added that he was sorry to observe the way in which he was 'treated almost like a boy by his parents'. [3]

This was a penetrating remark. During Rudolf's childhood his parents had not seen enough of him to realise how fast he was developing. The Empress was away a great deal; the Emperor had little time to spare for his son. At this time the Crown Prince appears however to have been devoted to his father who, to his delight, taught him to shoot at a very early age. Franz Joseph was determined that his heir should become a first-class shot. 'I greatly regret,' he wrote to Rudolf then aged eleven, 'that in spite of some excellent chances you missed everything. . . . The important thing is not to lose heart, and every time you go out to be determined that you are going to be successful.' [4] This exhortation was unnecessary. The Crown Prince practised his marksmanship by killing bullfinches or any other kind of wild life which came in sight. He had inherited his father's passion for shooting. But he also had all his mother's love for nature and was already a keen ornithologist. It seemed—and this emerged even more clearly in the future—that the traits which he had inherited from each parent often conflicted, and that he was unable to reconcile them within himself.

When at the age of six Rudolf was allowed his first glass of champagne, he drank a toast to the ravishing portrait of Elisabeth by Winterhalter. As he grew older he loved riding with his mother and was delighted when she was admired—he probably felt more at ease with her than with his father. But she was away a great deal, when there often absorbed in her horses and her adored youngest child Valerie, and so to her son, although an enchanting apparition, loving, indulgent, sometimes gay, whose return was eagerly to be awaited, she was not a consistent thread running through his life. Her intervention on his behalf over Gondrecourt, perhaps the most important thing she ever did for him, was one of the rare occasions when Rudolf was the main object of her attention.

Of the Crown Prince's two surviving sisters Valerie was too young to confide in, and Gisela married when he was fourteen. Amongst his contemporaries with whom he had not much in common, he had some companions but no friends. He led a solitary existence and, reading a great deal, evolved ideas which he felt a compulsive need to express. To satisfy this he began to attempt to summarise them for Latour, the one person in whom he had complete confidence, and who at that time formed a stable background to his life. 'My mind seethes with thoughts,' he wrote at the end of 1873, and went on to say that while realising he could never hope to learn all that he wanted, he was sure that the thing which mattered more than position, titles, riches or anything else was to strive to acquire more knowledge. [5] During the next few years the notes which reached Latour showed that the Crown Prince was acquiring some views which were hardly compatible with his position as heir to the throne of the oldest Catholic dynasty in Europe. Priests, he wrote, were deliberately fostering superstition in order to dominate the mass of the people.

The Government has changed and moved a step nearer to becoming a republic. Kingship has lost its former power . . . the whole conception of rulers is no longer valid in these days. [6]

The nations of Europe have emerged . . . from the times of revolution and the struggle for freedom on to a higher plane, rejuvenated, strengthened and exalted. [7]

Such views must have made startling and disconcerting reading. Possibly Latour kept Rudolf's notes to himself and did not show them to the Emperor, in the hope that if he did not betray the Crown Prince's confidence he might be able to influence him in the right direction. If he did show them to Franz Joseph possibly the latter dismissed them as the foolish fantasies of an adolescent. Certainly the Emperor did not attempt to change Rudolf's tutors, and wrote to Latour when the Crown Prince attained his majority in July 1877: 'You have in every way brilliantly justified the trust I placed in you.'[8]

Rudolf was about to be nineteen and at an age when the Prince of Wales still had a governor and was labouring at the university, was given his own household the head of which was Count Karl Bombelles, a naval officer who had been seconded to accompany Ferdinand Max to Mexico. His record of service there commended him to the Emperor, and he was personally acceptable to Rudolf, who according to his grandmother Archduchess Sophie in many ways resembled Ferdinand Max. Bombelles has been variously described as a typical courtier, a bigoted Catholic, and a sophisticated man of the world. It has been hinted that he acted as *maître de plaisir* to the Crown Prince. Certainly he was a different stamp of man from Latour, but whereas Latour had power to supervise, Bombelles had no authority to do any more than attempt to guide Rudolf, a task of which he wrote a month after his appointment: 'May God help me always to give the right advice, and see that when I make a mistake no harm results from it.'[9] Evidently he already realised that his position might not be easy.

The Crown Prince who as a boy was weedy, pale, and according to the Prince of Wales 'not at all good looking', had grown up into a slim elegant young man with that air of insouciance of one who is so perfectly aware of his position that he has no need to stress it. He had brown hair and hazel eyes and, although not handsome, possessed an easy charm which was to make him, when he chose, irresistible. According to his future sister-in-law, who if in many respects an unreliable witness, was nevertheless a connoisseur of attractive men:

He was more than handsome, he was fascinating. . . . His nervous force equalled his sensitiveness. His pale face reflected his thoughts. . . . Rudolf's smile . . . was the smile of an angelic sphinx, a smile peculiar to the Empress. He also had her manner of speaking, and these traits, added to his winning and mysterious personality, charmed all with whom Rudolf came in contact.[10]

Before this young man the world with all the pleasures which were his to command now lay open.

It was decided that the Crown Prince should see something of foreign countries, for with the exception of a few visits to Germany he had not travelled outside the Monarchy. During the next twelve months he went to Dalmatia, Corfu (where he stayed with his mother), Switzerland, Bavaria and England. In Dalmatia and Corfu he had his first sight of the sea and the south both of which thereafter held a lasting fascination for him. In Bavaria he stayed with the Empress's cousin King Ludwig II. Ludwig was Wagner's patron, an eccentric monarch who would have nothing to do with Court ceremonial, and lived in one or other of the castles which he had built at vast expense in a strange world of fantasy. He adored Elisabeth who, although she had been fond of him, had come to find his behaviour so eerie that she could scarcely bear to be in the same room with him. So far as the King of Bavaria was concerned the visit was a great success, and he was extravagant in his praise of the Crown Prince. Rudolf was more reserved, but in Ludwig's attitude to religion he evidently found a kindred spirit, telling him:

I must admit that I am reluctant to express my ideas on religion . . . but to you I can say everything which I think and feel for I know that you too are very enlightened in your views.[11]

He added that he found the restrictions on religious thinking imposed by the Catholic Church 'impossible'.[11] His discussions with Ludwig strengthened those early ideas which had so disconcerted Latour.

On the visit to England which lasted eight weeks, Rudolf was accompanied by Bombelles and one of his former tutors, Karl Menger, the brilliant professor of political science at the University of Vienna and a prominent liberal freethinker. He was taken to see military establishments, the Houses of Parliament, the Bank of England and the British Museum, toured factories and visited Edinburgh, Dublin and some of the larger provincial cities. The Prince of Wales went out of his way to entertain him and gave a dinner in his honour at which Disraeli was present. Queen Victoria invited him to Osborne, a severe test which he passed with flying colours. 'The young C. Pce left . . . today' the Queen reported to her son, 'and I am much pleased with him. He, as *all* Austrians, is most easy to get on with.'[12]

On the way back from this successful visit to England Rudolf spent a few days in Paris and Berlin, and then shortly after his return to Vienna set out on an ornithological expedition down the Danube to shoot birds for skins and specimens. Later in 'Notes on Sport and Ornithology', the Crown Prince described fifteen of the happiest days of his life. The journey by steamer down the Danube was a revelation to him. 'Not until one travels in this way does one understand that fanatical enthusiasm for a sailor's life to which I myself openly confess.'[13] As they left behind them 'the stereotyped uniformity of Western Europe'.[14] he delighted in the immense arc of the sky and the view to infinity of the Hungarian plain, 'for which I have such an admiration that I am blind to all its monotony'.[15] Of the lower reaches of the river he wrote, 'I felt immensely drawn towards those dark forests with their oaks centuries old and their rich fauna'.[16] He did not, however, allow his pleasure in his surroundings to distract him from the object of the expedition, kept exact ornithological notes, and although there was a great deal of rough walking and wading through marshes, contributed his full share to the 211 specimens of different kinds of birds shot by the party, one of the members of which was Alfred Brehm, Professor of Zoology at the University of Vienna. Brehm had a European reputation and fascinated Rudolf:

He has a gift of speech such as I have never before met with in any scientific man, and an especially wonderful talent of recalling striking experiences and observations on nature and making others realise them.[17]

Their journey down the Danube together was the beginning of a friendship between the Crown Prince and the scientist, a convinced supporter of Darwin's theory of evolution, which lasted until the latter's death.

In the year after he was declared of age Rudolf had increased his knowledge of the world. But, in the opinion of some members of the Court, this had not improved his character. He appeared to be obsessed by a determination to slaughter in or out of season any bird or beast which came within range. As Beck, who did not care for him, had prophesied a year earlier, chasing after girls had become one of his main preoccupations. He was voicing a number of deplorably liberal ideas. Rudolf's misfortune was that on the Emperor's express instructions he had received a far more 'modern' as well as a better education than most young men of his own age. But he was now expected to take his place in the Imperial Family and at Court, an intellectual in a hierarchy rooted in tradition, to most of the members of which these new ideas which he considered important were not only uninteresting but often suspect. This apart, Court functions were dull. It is not surprising that the Crown Prince like many of the other young Archdukes sought his amusements elsewhere, expended his surplus energy on shooting and, endowed as one of his tutors had said, with an active mind and the ability and desire to use it, turned for intellectual stimulus to men like Menger and Brehm.

What—or who—started Rudolf thinking along the liberal progressive lines which Menger and others later assiduously fostered? The background against which the Crown Prince grew up probably had something to do with it. The first years of his life coincided with a series of disasters in Franz Joseph's reign— Solferino, the reluctant retreat from autocracy which culminated in the Compromise, Königgrätz—a time during which he was surrounded by grown ups with anxious faces. When the German Liberals came to power, a period of economic prosperity began, the grip of the Church on the people weakened, and there was a general relaxation of tension. That those liberal ideas dominant outside the Court, with their belief in progress through the advancement of science, that all problems could be solved by rational thinking, appeared to have produced successful results, cannot have escaped the notice of a boy with an active questioning mind. This he had inherited from Elisabeth, to whom no subject which aroused her interest was taboo, and who was not the sort of mother who edited her thoughts when talking to her children. While it is improbable that the Empress actively tried to influence her son, it is also unlikely that she attempted to argue him out of his views and her freely expressed opinions may have affected him.

The attitude of Archduke Johann Salvator may also not have escaped the Crown Prince's attention. The Archduke got on well with the young, was uninhibited, outspoken and never dull. The cousins probably did not see a great deal of each other while the Crown Prince was growing up, for the Archduke was stationed in the provinces and only intermittently visited Vienna. But Rudolf undoubtedly knew of Johann Salvator's ideas, for they were the subject of much discussion and criticism at Court. He kept (it was found amongst his papers after his death), his copy of Franz Joseph's circular letter to members of the Imperial Family informing them of the Archduke's punishment after the anonymous publication of his artillery pamphlet in 1875. This warning against venturing into print was however lost on Rudolf, and may have had the opposite effect of suggesting to him a method by which he could make his opinions known. On his return from England, the Crown Prince collaborated with Karl Menger in writing a pamphlet entitled 'The Austrian Aristocracy and its Constitutional Function. A Warning to Aristocratic Youth'.[18] This was published anonymously in Munich towards the end of 1878. It accused the aristocracy of the Monarchy of opting out of responsibility, of unwillingness to compete with the bourgeoisie for positions in the army and the civil service, and of failing to play the part in Parliament prescribed for them in the constitution, not because they were unpatriotic, but because they were badly educated and idle. The part which the Crown Prince played in writing this denunciation cannot be established, but it certainly reflected the views which he held at the time. This anonymous venture into print was the first of a long series to come.

If some of the courtiers disapproved of Rudolf, there is no evidence of any serious friction between the Emperor and his son in 1878. Franz Joseph shared the Crown Prince's enthusiasm for shooting. Game laws at that time were not as strict as they are today, and therefore, while he may have deprecated Rudolf's addiction to wholesale slaughter, he probably did not consider it a flagrant infringement of sporting etiquette. So far as women were concerned, love affairs were accepted as part of the pattern of society. Even Queen Victoria, much as she disapproved of it, put up with the Prince of Wales's liaison with Lily Langtry. It is improbable that Franz Joseph objected to his son having his fling, provided he avoided any embarrassing entanglement. Moreover, both father and son had the Habsburg urge to rule over a powerful Monarchy, and in 1878 they were united in their enthusiasm over the prospects for this which had been opened up by Andrassy's achievement in Berlin. The Crown Prince summed up the Emperor's reception of the news that Austria had been awarded a mandate to occupy Bosnia Herzegovina in a letter to Latour:

> The joining of two provinces to the Monarchy has as we all knew it would overjoyed Papa. . . . I believe that in Bosnia Herzegovina he is aiming at compensation for Lombardy and Venetia.[19]

To Rudolf, who considered Andrassy 'an outstanding man', the Count's success in Berlin meant even more than this. He saw it as the first step towards the fulfilment of a vision which he had attempted to outline when he was seventeen in an essay which he called 'The position of Vienna and our future'.[20] In this essay he described the Danube as the artery linking together the Monarchy and all the inhabitants of south-eastern Europe, arguing that whoever controlled the latter would be a great power and that to do so was now the mission of Austria, a mission to be carried out not by force of arms but by peaceful means, bringing civilisation and culture to the backward races of the Balkans and so becoming their leader. 'We must look to the East. . . . The Slavs are the

H

people who will count in time to come. Once Austrian genius has them in its thrall the Monarchy has a great future there.'[21]

The Crown Prince also appreciated far better than his father the importance of new markets in the Balkans, and the urgent need of obtaining another port in addition to Trieste 'the lung of the Empire', the only larger commercial harbour left after the loss of Italy. He had inherited his mother's interest in strange and exotic countries and her love of the sea, both of which were incomprehensible to Franz Joseph. To the Emperor nothing could compare in beauty with the pine forests of the Monarchy, and he wrote to Elisabeth when on his journey to the opening of the Suez Canal, 'I long for snow'.[22] He was a bad sailor, understood nothing of the importance of maritime communications and did not even possess a naval uniform, explaining that as he did not even understand how to sail a paper boat he saw no point in dressing up as an admiral. Rudolf by contrast was keenly interested in the navy and irresistibly drawn to the south:

> To me the mountains of the south are far more attractive than the Alps of Central Europe. Their form, the warmer light, the contrast between snow, deep blue sky and southern vegetation are far more interesting than the uniformity of pine woods with the dull leaden lightless sky above.[23]

Andrassy's success therefore excited him because it fulfilled a psychological need. It was a breakout from the landlocked Monarchy to the sea, the first step on the road to the Aegean. While Franz Joseph thought without any claustrophobia of the Monarchy as a central European state, Rudolf was already beginning to envisage his inheritance as a Danubian Empire.

Surrounded by people who edited what he was told, Franz Joseph may not have been aware of the full extent of Rudolf's liberal views, or if so have dismissed them as a phase which service in the army would correct. At the end of July 1878 he nominated the Crown Prince supernumerary colonel of the 36th Infantry Regiment which was then stationed in Prague, a gesture of reconciliation to the Czechs, who ever since the Compromise had been pressing for increased recognition of what they considered to be their historic privileges. Rudolf welcomed the appointment, both as a task to which he could devote his energies and a means of escape from Vienna. He was warmed by the enthusiasm with which he was welcomed in Prague, and at the end of the year announced that he did not propose to come to the Hofball because 'I very much prefer to be where my duty lies, rather than to amuse myself in Vienna'. [24]

A regimental group photograph of the Crown Prince with his brother officers shows that there was nothing flashy about the men with whom he now worked. Several of them have paunches and thinning hair, few of them have many medals. They look like what they were, members of an ordinary decent line regiment, but they appear to be perfectly at ease with the fair, slim young man standing in their midst, and he with them. He was happy, enjoyed working 'from 7.00 a.m. to 6.00 p.m. with only half an hour off for lunch'. [25] and in Colonel Hotze he evidently had the best type of old-fashioned fatherly Commanding Officer. Hotze found the Crown Prince personally likeable describing him as:

Most interesting . . . highly intelligent, full of energy and determination to get on, warm hearted and . . . far more mature than his age.

After a year he recommended that Rudolf should be given sole command of the regiment, pointing out that this would give him invaluable experience of handling and leading men, and encourage his interest in the army which was at present his overriding enthusiasm. This, he stressed with some insight, was most desirable because the possessor of such an active mind must have an objective to work for, otherwise he would merely dissipate his talents and waste his time. [26] Franz Joseph agreed to this recommendation, and on August 18th, 1879, appointed the Crown Prince Commanding Officer of the 36th Infantry Regiment. Rudolf was delighted. He had been the subject of some unfavourable comment from Archduke Albrecht; this was proof that 'Papa is now entirely on my side . . . my dearest wish is now fulfilled.' [27]

Life in 1879, was however by no means all work and no play. The Crown Prince had an opportunity of continuing his study of natural history during a two months journey to Spain and Portugal on which, in addition to Brehm, he was accompanied by Count Hans Wilczek, a philanthropist and explorer, the model of everything which Rudolf considered a member of the aristocracy should be, and with whom he formed a lasting friendship. During the autumn at Gödöllö he rode and shot all day, never going to bed before two in the morning. Elisabeth's lady-in-waiting Countess Festetics noted in her diary:

> He is so nice, but incapable of moderation, however it is a good thing when he enjoys innocent and normal pleasures, for otherwise he gets up to so many escapades that one becomes rather anxious. [28]

But, whatever the Countess's reservations, at Gödöllö that autumn Rudolf charmed everyone by his gaiety and high spirits. He told his sister Valerie, 'If only I could live to be a hundred. It is terrible to think that in the end one must die', [29] and looked forward to 1880 with high hope and confidence.

CHAPTER 7

The Young Men and Love

Most of the Habsburgs had an eye for a pretty woman, and Rudolf and Johann Salvator in this at least resembled the rest of their family. At the age of twenty the Archduke first thought of marriage. He fell in love with an English girl whom he met on board ship on the way back from his first journey to the eastern Mediterranean and, after they parted, wrote offering to give up a very great deal for her.

Most darlingest of angel girls.

I must lavish on you terms of endearment. You are my loveliest love, *mia cara carissima, ma petite chérie*, my own sweet rose of Kent. I thought myself often in love before I had the happiness to meet you, but was mistaken. You fill my soul as nobody else has ever done. I am in despair at being told that I may not pay you further attention. My Imperial rank stands in the way, say you and your honoured mother, of courtship *pour le bon motif*. It should, did I not realise the utter vanity of being penned up with 70 relatives on an isolated peak. I hate my position, am determined to live like a man should, and not like a poor creature who must be spoon-fed from the cradle to the grave. It depends on you whether I shall go on as 'archduckling' or not. . . . My courage is equal to emigrating to Australia, where I am sure I would fall on my feet. I would be a manager of a theatre, a teacher of French, German or Italian or the curator of a zoo or a botanical garden, or I could be a riding master or a stock rider. Without going so far as Australia, I might get married in Italy to the girl of my choice. I was born a Tuscan, and the statutes of the Grand Ducal family are dead letters there. As you can never be an Archduchess, I should be only too happy to cease to be an Archduke, but hope ever to be counted your darling Arch-duckling.

Johann.

—or, since you like my soft Italian name, Giovanni—but not on any account (Don) Juan.[1]

Nothing evidently came of this shipboard romance and the Archduke remained on his 'isolated peak'. In 1875 when his mother suggested that a suitable bride might be found in the Orléans family, he replied firmly, 'For the present I have no intention of marrying'.[2] Three years later, still a bachelor, he made a will a few days before the start of the Bosnian campaign. One clause of this provided for the setting up of a trust fund of 40,000 gulden, the income from which was to be paid to Fräulein Ludmilla Stubel.

Ludmilla, or 'Milli' Stubel as she was generally known, came of a lower middle-class family and was the third of four sisters. Their father's early death made it necessary for them to earn their living, and their mother made no objection when one after another they went on the stage—it was a reasonably certain means of acquiring a rich lover or (hopefully) eventually a husband. At the age of fifteen Milli became a ballet dancer at the opera. Although her talent was negligible she moved gracefully, had a lovely figure, thick blonde hair and large blue eyes, and soon attracted Johann Salvator's attention. The start of the affair was reminiscent of a Viennese operetta—the young Archduke seated in his box searching through the programme for the name of the young dancer, the contrived meeting with her and the bribing of the aunt who was supposed to chaperone her home after the performance, supper in a private room, assignations in the fourth gallery of the Opera House during rehearsals. It was the accepted pattern for a passing adventure, and provided it was ahered to no damage was done, no hearts broken, and no adverse comments made.

Johann Salvator however behaved most unconventionally. Within a few weeks of meeting Milli he called on her mother, formally declared his feelings for her daughter, arranged for her to have lessons in deportment, languages and singing, and made a point of meeting the entire Stubel family. Time went by and he showed no signs of tiring of Milli, to whom he began to confide his hopes, fears and ambitions. Much of what he said must have been incomprehensible to her, for she was uneducated and except for her love of music she had nothing in common with the Archduke. But her good humour was unfailing, and with her warmth and capacity for soothing him he found in her someone with whom he could relax and escape into the world of Viennese *gemütlichkeit* to which she belonged.

The affair, which Johann Salvator made no attempt to conceal seemed, to the disapproval of the Court and the distress of his mother, to be developing into more than a short-term liaison. Opinions differ as to when it began, but by the time the Archduke made his will in 1878 it had certainly been in progress for several years. Hopes that it might come to an end if he was kept away from Vienna by his army duties failed to materialise. On one posting at least Johann Salvator took Milli with him, registering her with the local authorities as his housekeeper, a flouting of convention which gave rise to a great deal of acid criticism. In so far as this was directed at himself the Archduke appeared not to care in the least. He was enchanted by his mistress, and delighted by her success at the parties which he gave for his brother officers. 'Everyone admires her . . . she makes me forget all the troubles which I have to endure in Vienna.'[3] He maintained that she was fit to take her place in any company and the innuendoes and sneers directed at her enraged and embittered him:

It is incomprehensible to me why she is so persecuted. People should be angry with *me* because I behave indiscreetly, carelessly, in a manner which deserves censure . . . why do they go for her saying things about her which are absolutely untrue; why do they slander her in such a damaging way?[4]

He returned to this theme again and again as more pressure from which he could not protect her was brought to bear on both of them:

In the course of time I have learnt to bear the many injuries which they have done me, but the wrongs which they do my innocent Miltschi embitter my whole life.[5]

It was open to Johann Salvator to defy everyone and marry Milli, but this would mean dismissal from the army and probable exile from the Monarchy, which in 1880 when he was still determined to succeed in his military career was more than he was prepared to sacrifice. But the more he was adjured to give her up, the more obstinately he clung to her. In 1881 his commanding general while praising his efficiency, noted that he was 'apt to be sarcastic'. The strain of the situation was by now affecting his temper.

In 1883 a way appeared out of this apparently hopeless impasse. The Archduke at last found someone more acceptable whom he felt he could marry—a widowed Countess Attems. As she was not of royal blood the marriage would have to be morganatic, but this was possible under clause 19 of the Family Law if the Emperor gave his permission, and Johann Salvator was hopeful of obtaining it, since the Countess belonged to the high aristocracy and held a position at Court. He proposed and she accepted him, with the proviso that nothing was done clandestinely. The Archduke took the plunge and asked Franz Joseph for an audience. A few days later Grand Duchess Maria Antonia received a letter from her son marked as being for her eyes only, containing an urgent appeal for help.

'After having asked the Emperor to consider a *petition*', Johann Salvator wrote to his mother,

> I said to him: 'For some time I have been keenly and seriously interested in Countess Attems, and having come to know her I want to marry her'. . . .
>
> 'Oho, that is what you have in mind,' interrupted the Emperor. Then, recovering from his surprise and adopting a benevolent expression, he said to me, 'If this affair is not very dear to your heart I wish you to abandon this idea.'
>
> *Me:* 'Your Majesty, if the affair was not very dear to my heart I would not have dared to tell Your Majesty of it.'

The Emperor: 'Yes, but nevertheless I would prefer you to give it up, there are already quite enough marriages like this in the family.'

Me: 'Your Majesty sees that I do not permit myself to take this favour for granted, for I have believed it to be my duty first to find out from Your Majesty whether my request would be contrary to your august wishes, and Your Majesty can be certain that these will always be sacred to me.'

The Emperor: 'My dear Johann, I thank you for the loyalty and frankness with which you have come to me, and I thank you for wanting to respect my wishes.'

He said this at once, and with the utmost benevolence.

Me: 'Your Majesty will deign to keep to yourself the request which I have permitted myself to make?'

The Emperor (agitatedly): 'I swear to you that nobody will know anything of what you have told me.'

That was the end of the audience, the Emperor being pressed by affairs of State, but he gave me his hand most affectionately and I saw that he was not upset, and that his disagreement was not concerned with the person but was a matter of principle. In my haste and—to tell the truth—great agitation, I omitted to say that it was solely a question of a *morganatic* marriage *provided for under clause 19* of the Family Law. . . . I believe that if I had said that the Emperor would have been more receptive.

It is very difficult for me, indeed practically impossible, to renew the request which I have just made, dear Mamma. Would you feel able to intervene with the Emperor simply to inform him of what I omitted to tell him, and to stress to him how happy he could make me. . . . Tell me, dear Mamma, whether you will take any action or not. If not I must try to forget all that I have hoped for . . . I request you once again not to talk about this to anyone. . . .[6]

If Maria Antonia tried to help her son she was unsuccessful— Franz Joseph remained adamant. As Johann Salvator said, principles mattered to the Emperor more than people, and in the interests of what he believed to be right he was prepared to grind down individuals, regardless of the effect on them. By forbidding the Archduke to marry Countess Attems he destroyed the former's attempt to put his personal life in order, and drove him back to Milli Stubel.

At the age when Johann Salvator, swept off his feet by his shipboard romance, first contemplated marriage, Rudolf did not want to marry anyone. In April 1879 he made a will which ended with a number of farewell messages one of which was 'a last kiss to all the pretty women of Vienna whom I have loved so much'.[7] At the beginning of that year he wrote to Latour, 'I am not yet betrothed and will not be so for some time.'[8] He was enjoying himself a great deal with 'the pretty women of Vienna', and similar diversion was easily obtainable in Prague. But there was the perpetuation of the dynasty to be considered, and by the end of the year the Emperor decided that the time had come for the Crown Prince to marry. Eighteen years earlier Queen Victoria had reached a similar decision about the Prince of Wales, but for a different reason. An end must be put to Bertie's 'scrapes' and 'miserable escapades', and the only 'forlorn hope' for correcting his deplorable weakness where women was concerned was, the Queen was convinced, a good wife. The problem was to find one. A similar problem confronted Franz Joseph at the end of 1879.

It is illuminating to compare the premises and difficulties of the Queen and the Emperor in their selection of a bride for their respective heirs. While Queen Victoria admitted that great alliances are desirable for various members of the family, she was doubtful of their political value. 'I attach little importance to them, for they can no longer affect the actions of governments and are only a source of worry and difficulty for the princely family.'[9] Nor—and here she differed from all continental royalties—did she object to morganatic blood, explaining to her eldest daughter the Crown Princess of Prussia:

I can't help thinking what dear Papa said—that it was in fact a blessing when there was some little *imperfection* in the *pure* Royal descent and that some fresh blood was infused . . .

darling Papa *often* with vehemence said '*We must have some strong dark blood*'.[10]

She was on the other hand exacting in the attributes which the future Princess of Wales must possess—education, character, a good disposition and looks.

In one sense Franz Joseph's problem was easier than Queen Victoria's, in another a great deal more difficult. While anxious that the Crown Prince should settle down, he did not envisage the main object of the marriage to be Rudolf's salvation from moral perdition. Therefore, while he did not wish to force his son into marrying a princess who was antipathetic to him, he was not particularly concerned about the looks and temperament of his future daughter-in-law. He was, however, very concerned indeed about her status. She must be a member of a reigning family with no trace of morganatic blood in her ancestry, and she must be a Catholic. No Bavarian princess could be considered for there had already been too much intermarriage between the Habsburgs and the Wittelsbachs. Fresh blood was needed but where was it to be found? Luther, as someone pointed out, had done untold damage; there were fewer Catholic than Protestant reigning families in Europe, and Catholic princesses were in very short supply. Rudolf was uninterested in such eligible daughters of the German Princes as were available, and during his journey to Spain had not found a Spanish princess who attracted him. The Italian royal family were upstarts, and the Bourbons and Orléans were no longer reigning dynasties. There remained the Belgians. The Emperor instructed Count Chotek his Ambassador in Brussels to ascertain whether King Leopold II would agree to the marriage of his second daughter Stephanie to the Crown Prince, and received a reply that the King consented with alacrity.

In some ways this was a case of scraping the bottom of the barrel. Stephanie was a Coburg, and by comparison with the Habsburgs the Coburgs, originally minor German princelings, were very small beer indeed. They had only achieved royal status in 1831, when Stephanie's grandfather Leopold accepted the crown of the new kingdom of Belgium. But they had important relatives. Leopold, Queen Victoria's 'dearest uncle', exploited the dynastic principles of the nineteenth century to his considerable advantage by arranging marriages between members of his family and a number of ruling families. Bismarck referred to the Coburgs as 'the stud farm of Europe'. Some of them had great ambitions and powerful lusts. To promote the former they married the very best people they could induce to accept them; to satisfy the latter they took mistresses, in the choice of whom they were not fastidious, and with whom they associated without any regard for decorum. They were generous neither with their affections nor their money. Their heads ruled their hearts with much profit to themselves, for they were clever, calculating, never took unnecessary risks, and once they had achieved an advantageous position clung to it like leeches. Coburg blood was not very blue, but it was extremely sticky.

Stephanie's father, King Leopold II, embodied most of the unattractive characteristics of a not very attractive family. Tall, with a long beard and a very large nose, sensuous lips and cold heavy lidded eyes, he had a knowledge of economics and finance unequalled by any of his fellow monarchs. By 1880 he was engaged in drumming up support for a vast project, the ostensible object of which to abolish the slave trade, but which he intended to manipulate not only to further Belgian commercial interests in Africa, but also to grab a colony there for himself. He was skilful at concealing his intentions, and only once exhibited emotion, on the death of his eleven-year-old son, a blow from which he did not recover. He never forgave his wife for her failure to bear him another heir, and regarded his daughters with something approaching hatred because they had survived their brother. Queen Victoria found him 'very odd' and complained of his habit of saying disagreeable things to people. Elisabeth, who detested all the Coburgs and considered them intriguing ambitious upstarts, referred to him coldly as a financier on a throne, and was opposed to the idea that Rudolf should marry his daughter. The Empress was frequently exaggerated in her likes and dislikes, but in this case there was a good deal to be said for her attitude.

Charlotte, Leopold II's sister, had driven her husband Ferdinand Max into the disastrous Mexican adventure, lost her reason when it failed, and was shut up in a castle in Belgium, hopelessly insane. Leopold's behaviour to his wife, Archduchess Maria Henrietta, was such that within a few weeks of her marriage she lamented, 'If God hears my prayers I shall not go on living much longer.'[11] The Habsburgs' previous experience of marrying into the Coburg family had not, as Elisabeth pointed out, been happy, but this consideration appeared to carry no weight with Franz Joseph. He had never seen Stephanie, but she conformed to his basic requirements and was related to the ruling houses of England, Prussia, Russia, Portugal and Brazil as well as to the Orléans. Dynastically it was a useful match.

At the beginning of February 1880 Rudolf wrote from Prague to Latour:

A new existence is beginning for me, and I cannot deny that in some ways I still find the prospect of it rather unpalatable.

And, eleven days later:

Please say nothing to anyone about Chotek's mission or anything connected with it, for I want to keep the whole affair secret until I have gone to Brussels and seen for myself.[12]

The Crown Prince left for Brussels at the beginning of March. He knew Stephanie's elder sister Louise, who had lived in Vienna since her marriage to her cousin Prince Philip of Coburg-Kohary, and Louise, a flamboyant vivacious beauty, was very attractive. Possibly Stephanie might be like her. On arrival in the Belgian capital he found however a girl of sixteen, tall for her age, with large hands and feet, who did not in the least resemble her sister. Stephanie had a good complexion (it was her only asset), but she was plump, ungraceful and seemed to be almost indecently self-possessed. By no stretch of imagination could she be called attractive. But the Emperor had made it clear that he wished for this marriage; the King of Belgium was evidently delighted at the prospect of his daughter becoming Crown Princess of Austria; nobody else of suitable rank was offering so Stephanie would have to do. Rudolf proposed to her, well primed by her parents she said 'yes' without a second's hesitation, he placed the ring which he had brought with him on her finger, and they were formally betrothed. They had known each other for twenty-four hours.

Writing from Brussels Rudolf assured Latour that he was happy and had found what he was looking for:

> Stephanie is pretty, good, sensible, very distinguished and will be a loyal daughter and subject of her Emperor and a good Austrian. [13]

As a panegyric of his fiancée this sounds lukewarm compared to the letter which the Prince of Wales wrote to Queen Victoria when he got engaged to Princess Alexandra:

> I cannot tell you with what feelings my head is filled and how happy I feel. I only hope it may be for her happiness and that I may do my duty towards her. Love her and cherish her you may be sure I will to the end of my life. [14]

However, four days later, although without mentioning Stephanie by name, the Crown Prince reaffirmed that he was happy, adding that he was getting on admirably with his future parents-in-law, and in the course of a number of conversations with the King of Belgium found him one of the most sensible and clever men and one of the best talkers he had ever met 'from whom one can learn a great deal'. [15] Evidently King Leopold had exerted himself to charm Rudolf and succeeded in giving him the impression that he was the paragon of a modern ruler. It no doubt helped the Crown Prince to believe that the Emperor had chosen a bride for him worth marrying for her relations if not for herself.

The Empress was in London on her way back from hunting in Ireland when she heard of Rudolf's engagement. It seemed to her the height of folly, but it had to be accepted as a *fait accompli* and she arranged to go to Brussels on her way back to Vienna to meet her future daughter-in-law. This meant an overnight journey from England arriving in Brussels at 8 a.m. Brussels station on a cold March day is a desolate place, and eight in the morning a forbidding hour for a trying encounter. The Belgian

Royal Family on home ground, and with the advantage that they had not spent most of the previous twenty-four hours travelling, were assembled on the station when Elisabeth's train drew in. A salute was fired, the guard of honour stood to attention, the band struck up the Imperial Anthem, the carriage door opened and the Empress appeared wearing a dark blue dress trimmed with sable, immaculate, poised, beautiful. Rudolf rushed towards her and flung both arms round her—so far as he was concerned his mother had swept everyone else off the stage, and beside her his fiancée looked like a lumpy, badly dressed schoolgirl. Elisabeth took one look at Stephanie and was horrified. It was not her habit when displeased to say so, but her manner left the onlooker in no doubt of what she felt, and on this occasion it was icy. The visit was not a success.

His mother's disapproval of Stephanie notwithstanding, Rudolf continued to put a bold face on the situation. He was now publicly committed to this match, and managed to convince himself that after a fashion he was in love. There could however be no question of an early marriage, for Stephanie had not yet started to menstruate, and the Crown Prince returned to his regiment in Prague. In the autumn when he visited his parents at Gödöllö, the ever-observant Countess Festetics noticed that he often fell silent and seemed to have something on his mind. If Elisabeth noticed that her son was unhappy she said nothing. She had been overruled about his engagement and there was nothing left to say. Franz Joseph, cheerful and relaxed, apparently did not notice that anything was wrong.

A long engagement with the time which it gives for doubts and invidious comparisons is notoriously trying. By the end of the year Rudolf confided to Latour that he was suffering from a fit of black depression:

> I am in a very bad frame of mind as you see. This is because I come in contact with very few people and sit for hours at my desk reading and studying. When one is alone one is even more astonished at the stupidity of humanity than when one is in the midst of what is going on.[16]

Carnival failed to raise his spirits, 'I am not dancing any more. I feel too old and too solemn'. [17] In this gloomy mood the Crown Prince was despatched for the second time to Brussels. On this visit all he could find to say about Stephanie was that she looked well and had grown, but the hoped for 'symptoms' had not yet appeared. His enthusiasm for her parents had evaporated. They did not, he told Latour, want to give the impression of marrying off their daughter 'at any price'. 'I reflected that that was precisely the impression which they were giving, but as a polished courtier did not say so.' [18]

In the circumstances it was still impossible to fix a date for the wedding and something had to be done to fill in the time. A few days after returning to Vienna Rudolf set out on a journey to Egypt and the Holy Land, accompanied by Ferdinand of Tuscany who was the same age as the Emperor, Count Josef Hoyos who was not much younger, and the Court Chaplain. Franz Joseph was determined that his son's behaviour should be carefully supervised. Nevertheless, as the ship steamed south under blue skies Rudolf's spirits rose. Egypt was a revelation to him:

> I heard the song of the birds . . . and drank up with delight the balmy air of heavenly Egypt, thinking of the hardships of the European winter which I had for once escaped . . . one must have known the delicious magic of these happy lands to understand their indescribable charm and boundless attraction. [19]

He visited the bazaars, bought old weapons and Arab ornaments, contrived in spite of the Court Chaplain to have an evening out watching Egyptian dancing girls, and looked at a number of antiquities. But the main object of the expedition was to shoot. In the desert round Cairo, in the Fayoum, and on an expedition up the Nile by steamer the Crown Prince shot everything in sight—lynx, wolves, lizards, hares, kestrels, pelicans, herons, eagles, falcons, buzzards, and a great many smaller birds. The same pattern was repeated in Palestine. Rudolf dutifully toured Jerusalem ('we had of course to kiss many sacred rocks and stones'), [20] but was far more enthusiastic about the prospect of shooting a hyena near Bethlehem. He left 'the glorious golden sunlit East' with much regret. There was now no longer any reason for delaying his wedding and it was to take place on May 10th.

Meanwhile in Brussels much attention had been paid to training and grooming Stephanie for the position which she would occupy as wife of the future head of the oldest dynasty in Europe. It had been rewarded with no more than medium success. While she was less plump than at the time of her engagement, the end product of a considerable expenditure of effort and money still walked badly, and had red arms, tow-coloured hair with no lights in it, small eyes set too close together, no eyebrows or eyelashes to speak of, and a pursed sulky mouth. Her expensive clothes were in atrocious taste. Stephanie herself however was perfectly satisfied with her appearance and, when she arrived in Vienna, not in the least overawed by her innumerable future in-laws or by the functions and public appearances which preceded her wedding.

Rudolf by contrast was tense and nervous. On the morning of the wedding Countess Festetics had a strange encounter with him in the Hofburg. She was leaving her room, having dressed for the ceremony, when a footman passed her carrying the bouquet which by tradition the Crown Prince had to present personally to his bride. She heard Rudolf's voice behind her asking her to stop for a moment and, turning round, was shocked to see how white and miserable he looked. He seemed to be unable to make up his mind to go through the door leading to Stephanie's apartments and, clutching the Countess by the hand burst out 'For God's sake say something cheering to me'. Deeply moved she replied, 'God bless your dear Imperial Highness and may you be happy'. He managed to choke out the one word 'Thanks' and went on his way. 'That,' the Countess noted in her diary, 'was the prologue to the marriage.'[21]

The ceremony took place an hour later in the Augustinerkirche, the Emperor playing his part with effortless majesty, the Empress superbly regal and graceful and, in lamentable contrast to her, Stephanie in a dress, quite unsuitable for a girl of seventeen, of heavy silver brocade with a train trimmed with garlands of roses.

She advanced up the aisle with what Archduke Wilhelm described as 'all the daintiness of a dragoon'.[22] 'Marriage,' said Cardinal Prince Schwarzenberg in his address to the bridal pair, 'is the mystery which binds two souls together for all eternity.'[23] It was to be hoped that he was right, for the two souls to which he referred had not a great deal in common.

In spite of the Crown Prince's misgivings his marriage at first went well—possibly because for the first time it gave him a family background of his own. When after two months there was a question of sending Stephanie to the country because she could not stand the heat of Prague, he was in despair at the thought of the separation which this would entail. At the end of the year he told Latour that she was the only person who could influence him, stressing that he was very much in love with her. In 1883 when she became pregnant he was overjoyed, when the child was born not in the least upset that it was a girl and delighted to be a father. In the following month he cut short a shooting trip to hurry back to his wife and daughter.

It seems likely that Stephanie too, whatever she may have said many years later in her memoirs, was at first content. She had a good deal of the Coburg conceit and was extremely position conscious. To be the first lady in the Monarchy after the Empress suited her admirably. She was more than ready to appear at any Court function, and to deputise for her mother-in-law during the latter's frequent absences. Elisabeth who disliked the Crown Princess and considered her a lout of a girl, possibly remembering the damage done to her own marriage by Archduchess Sophie, deliberately left her son and daughter-in-law to themselves, and there was no question of any struggle for influence over Rudolf between the two women. For several years, whatever his other discontents the Crown Prince appeared to be reasonably happy with Stephanie.

CHAPTER 8

Conflict of Ideas

In August 1880 the Emperor was fifty. His birthday was cele-
brated with loyal demonstrations throughout the Monarchy, and
at Gödöllö in the following autumn he was almost gay. Elisabeth
seemed to be well and was with him rather more; his youngest
daughter Valerie, the only one of the children still at home, was
old enough to be a companion. His private life was happier than
it had been for some time. Affairs of state too, gave him less cause
for anxiety. Abroad the position was transformed by the German
alliance. At home the Hungarians were relatively quiescent, and
in Count Taaffe Franz Joseph at last possessed a Minister President of the Austrian half of the Monarchy whose government
above party, supported by an 'Iron Ring' of Slav, clerical and
aristocratic deputies, met with his approval.

Taaffe himself in every way suited the Emperor. Descended
from an Irish family which settled in Bohemia in the seventeenth
century, and the same age as Franz Joseph, with whom he had
played as a boy, the Count, a former civil servant, proclaimed that
he belonged to no party and was an Imperial minister, appointed
by the Crown to do as the Monarch wished. He shared the
Emperor's mistrust of ideas and abstract theories, his empirical
approach to problems, and his belief that these could best be
solved by time and the application of orderly routine. In temperament and outlook the two of them had much in common.

Taaffe avoided wearing uniform, and was to be seen wandering
about Vienna in a grey overcoat with his hat on the back of his
head—an unimpressive, red-faced man with a drooping black
moustache and a receding chin. He was a poor speaker and often
accused of frivolity, for he had a habit of dismissing serious

matters with a joke which many people found irritating. But he knew exactly how to manage the Emperor, echoing his wishes, refraining from upsetting him with suggestions for sweeping reforms, concealing any disagreeable subject from him whenever possible or, if this was unavoidable, presenting it as being no more than somewhat tiresome. He removed worries from Franz Joseph, and in return enjoyed the latter's unwavering support for his policy of *fortwürsteln*, muddling through and inching along. His position was strengthened by the fact that he was a favourite of Archduke Albrecht's, got on with Beck, and was approved of by Freiherr von Braun, the cold, discreet civil servant who occupied the key position of head of the Emperor's personal secretariat. Andrassy, a man of broad vision and grand designs, had been able to persuade the Emperor to be bold, to forget the losses of the earlier part of his reign and to plan ahead. After the Hungarian resigned Taaffe became the minister who influenced Franz Joseph. His method of working reawakened the latter's ingrained caution and encouraged his natural tendency to think in terms of bureaucratic detail. The result was that in a matter of months the Emperor moved a long step forward into staid middle age.

In middle age convictions often harden into dogma. Franz Joseph's conviction that he bore the sole responsibility for the preservation and welfare of the Monarchy was now a dogma, and to it was added a clause that he had no obligation to provide an explanation of his policy to anyone whatsoever, including the Crown Prince. Had he wished to take Rudolf into his confidence the Emperor would have found it difficult to do so, for he was a man to whom the art of communication either in speech or writing had been denied. But the difficulty did not arise for he saw no reason to do anything of the sort. Rudolf to him was an inexperienced young man whose radical and unpractical views were not to be taken seriously. It did not occur to Franz Joseph to consider whether he himself, had he not succeeded to the throne at the age of eighteen, would have been content with an army career and a series of representational duties. Nor did he realise that his son was endowed with exceptionally active if unco-ordinated intelligence, needed scope to exercise it, was a Habsburg with all the family desire to rule, and troubled about the state of the Monarchy.

When he was first posted to Prague in 1879 Rudolf prided himself that he would be able to make a major contribution to the reconciliation between the Czechs and the dynasty and that, with this achievement behind him, his father would pay attention to his ideas. He told Latour:

> Later on, when I have more influence and experience, and can advise the Emperor against the present errors in political and military affairs and persuade him to adopt new policies, I shall return to Vienna and be happy to live there.[1]

These hope rapidly evaporated. Taaffe's policy of reconciliation with the Czechs was bitterly resented by the Germans throughout the Monarchy, and in June 1881 rioting broke out between them and the Czechs in Bohemia. For the Emperor this was merely another riot amongst a number which he had experienced during his reign. He was confident that Taaffe and the army could deal with the situation (which they did) and saw no reason for a change of policy. He decreed, however, that the Crown Prince must keep clear of local involvements in Prague.

The events of the summer of 1881 had a profound effect on Rudolf. No longer happy in Prague now that his freedom of action there was restricted, he was convinced that Taaffe's policy promoted strife and must be abandoned. In the autumn he went to Gödöllö determined to convince his father of this, only to discover that the Emperor would not listen to him. The interview was stormy. The Crown Prince prepared a short memorandum advocating amongst other things a Ministry of progressive civil servants to encourage the growth of Liberal and Conservative parties combining the various nationalities. But he then lost his nerve, did not submit it to Franz Joseph and, as on many other occasions wrote to Latour for advice. He had drafted the memorandum, he told the Count, not of any desire to put himself forward, but because he saw only too clearly 'the steep slope down which we are sliding'. He felt the Emperor must be made aware of it, and there seemed to be no other means of doing so. Talking was useless: 'I am never allowed to speak up and say what I feel and believe', and there was nobody else bold enough to speak the truth.

> Our Emperor has no friend . . . he stands alone on his pinnacle . . . he knows little of what people think and feel. . . . Those now in power are the only ones who get a hearing, and of course they present things as best suits them. He believes that Austria is now in one of its happiest epochs: this is what he is told officially, and he only reads the paragraphs which are marked for him in the newspapers.

Formerly the Empress had often talked to his father about politics and not hesitated to express her liberal views, but now she was only interested in riding. Rudolf asked Latour if the Emperor would consider his memorandum impertinent and an indication that he was a trouble maker—which God knows he was not and did not wish to be? There was he pointed out a real danger of this:

> The Emperor three or four years ago was to some extent liberal in outlook and had come to terms with the nineteenth century, now he is as he used to be in Grandmamma's time, reactionary, abrupt and mistrustful.

Would his father glance at the memorandum and dismiss it, as he had done everything Rudolf had ever thought or written, as the work of an unrealistic idealist? Or would he show it to people like Archduke Albrecht and Taaffe who would undoubtedly advise him to take no notice of it? Should he let the Empress read it? 'She is a highly intelligent woman.'[2] There is no record of Latour's reply, neither is there any evidence that Rudolf showed this summary of his ideas to his mother. Possibly Elisabeth never saw it, for since the Crown Prince's marriage she and her son had drifted apart. Certainly she would not have disagreed with it, for she too was worried about the position, telling Countess Festetics a few days after Rudolf wrote to Latour: 'The Emperor was popular as few Monarchs have been . . . but now he is merely being used as a balancing pole by that acrobat Taaffe.'[3]

Franz Joseph failed to appreciate the Crown Prince's point of view. Rudolf misinterpreted the Emperor's attitude towards him, exaggerating his father's apparent lack of interest in anything he had to say into antagonism. He was impatient, and he had neither the strength of nerve nor the staying power of his father. Franz Joseph had discovered through years of experience that time will ease out a great many problems. To Rudolf time was running out, and a setback tended to appear as the forerunner of a disaster which drastic measures must be taken to avert. He was unable to appreciate his father's achievement in holding the Monarchy together during thirty-three difficult and dangerous years, and saw only the defects of the system which had been evolved. Franz Joseph himself was aware of these defects, but he did not expound them to his son nor explain why they could not be remedied overnight; nor had he any comprehension of Rudolf's sense of urgency.

By the end of 1881 therefore father and son had taken up their positions on opposite sides of a chasm, and across it there was no dialogue between them. Franz Joseph saw no reason to initiate one, and Rudolf, so it would appear from his letter to Latour, was now too alienated and to some degree too frightened of the Emperor to attempt it. Neither did there seem to him to be any prospect of doing so successfully as long as Braun, Beck, Taaffe and Archduke Albrecht retained their influence with his father. The Crown Prince was convinced that Braun who had no use for new ideas could not abide him. He disliked Beck, now Chief of the General Staff whom he regarded as ultra-Conservative, a dislike which was heartily reciprocated, for Beck considered the heir to the throne to be far too quick to criticise, incapable of thinking seriously, and altogether unstable. No support could be expected from Taaffe. Rudolf detested both the Count's policy of maintaining, through a collection of bureaucratic mandarins enmeshed in red tape, a balance between the various nationalities of the Monarchy by keeping them all in a state of moderate dissatisfaction, and his Irish-Viennese attitude to life, a compound of 'Sure it'll do' and *'Ich kann nichts dafür'*—'I can do nothing about it'. Finally since he entered the army the Crown Prince had been at loggerheads with Archduke Albrecht whom he described in 1879 as:

> A pernicious influence in every way. . . . It is a pity, for in spite of the fact that he is my enemy and I will never forgive him for what he has done to me, he was once great, and it is sad to see him end up as a childish old man. [4]

At this time Rudolf was confident that Albrecht would soon be ousted, but the 'childish old man' remained Inspector General, as influential as ever, disapproving, lecturing, criticising his young relation, and losing no chance of making a derogatory remark about his friends. This quartet of Braun, Beck, Taaffe and Albrecht formed their own 'Iron Ring' around the Emperor through which no progressive ideas could penetrate. By the end of 1881 the Crown Prince, denied a hearing for his views, excluded from seeing State papers, was thoroughly frustrated.

Rudolf was not the only frustrated heir to a throne. In Berlin Crown Prince Friedrich Wilhelm, also a man of progressive views, was at the age of fifty ignored by his father, with whom he was barely on speaking terms. In England the Prince of Wales, seventeen years older than Rudolf, was still battling with Queen Victoria for permission to see official documents. The German Crown Prince could, however, console himself with the thought that, although apparently quite indestructible, his father was over eighty, and therefore this unsatisfactory state of affairs should not last much longer. The Prince of Wales with three houses of his own, an annual income of over £100,000, and frequently abroad, had so arranged his life that he rarely saw his mother, and the greater part of his interchange of views with her was conducted by correspondence, a method of communication which gave both of them time to reflect and eliminated a number of points of friction. When the Prince got into serious trouble he did not attempt to conceal it from the Queen: whatever her disapproval of his conduct she never failed to support him, and communication between them did not break down. Rudolf was in a less happy position than the heirs to the throne of either Germany or

England. Unlike Friedrich Wilhelm, he could not look forward to succeeding his father in the near future, for Franz Joseph was fifty-one and in excellent health. Without a house of his own, kept short of money and not allowed to travel outside the Monarchy without the Emperor's express permission, it was not possible for him to take evasive action like the Prince of Wales and, far less temperamentally robust, he was incapable of standing up to his father as the Prince did to the Queen. But he was not prepared to sit back and wait until some unpredictable date when he succeeded to the throne. Determined at least to acquire information, he turned to a section of the community of which Franz Joseph totally disapproved—the Press.

The Emperor considered the profession of journalism to be beneath contempt, and the people who practised it unreliable and potential trouble-makers. Moreover many of them were Jews and, in common with most of his family and the greater part of the aristocracy, Franz Joseph did not care for the Jews, essential though they were to him as a source of finance. His attitude towards them, while not anti-Semitic in the modern sense of the word, resembled that of many people in bygone days to their lawyer or doctor: one called them in when their professional services were needed, but did not ask them to dine. In the Emperor's opinion the Monarchy would suffer no loss if the only newspaper to appear in it was the *Wiener Zeitung,* the information in which consisted mainly of accounts of public functions and official announcements, and he endorsed Taaffe's endeavours to ensure that journalistic comment did not get out of hand. The Count did not hesitate to invoke the Press Law which empowered the confiscation of any publication containing an offending article, and in 1880 there were 635 cases of confiscation, for a number of German Liberal papers were sharply critical of the government. One of the most widely read of these was the *Neues Wiener Tagblatt.* Rudolf contrived to meet its editor Moritz Szeps in the autumn of 1881.

Szeps, a Jew, was an able journalist with excellent contacts, particularly in France. The *Neues Wiener Tagblatt* was noted for its reporting and interesting leading articles which Szeps, although his object was to reform the Monarchy, not to break it up, wrote from a standpoint which brought him into continual conflict with Taaffe. For the journalist this contact with the heir to the throne was a major professional coup. The latter found in Szeps a man with an optimistic view of life, a brilliant conversationalist from whom it was possible to learn a great deal, and a good listener who understood his misgivings about the state of the Monarchy. A relationship developed from their first meeting which lasted until Rudolf's death, and by the middle of 1882 the Crown Prince had begun to write anonymous articles for the *Neues Wiener Tagblatt*.

Rudolf soon became something closely approximating to one of Szeps's reporters, telling the journalist almost everything he knew and making no attempt to conceal his opinion from him. Much of their correspondence has been destroyed, together with many of the Crown Prince's original drafts for his articles. Much too of what passed between them when they met was recorded by neither in writing. But enough evidence remains to show that, given his position, Rudolf's indiscretion was staggering, and that the views which he expressed to Szeps on home and foreign affairs—and so by implication on his father's policy—astonishing. Towards the end of 1882 for example writing to Szeps about foreign affairs he said:

> We are indebted to France as the source of all the liberal ideas and constitutions in Europe, and whenever great ideas begin to ferment France will be looked to for an example. What is Germany compared to her? Nothing but an enormously enlarged Prussian regimental barbarism, a purely military State.[5]

The Crown Prince's opinion of the situation at home was equally trenchant:

> The rubbish which Taaffe produces. He after all is only the tool of the allied parties . . . they are playing with fire leading people astray, fanaticism, stupidity, unending low cunning, lack of character, lack of patriotism and of a desire for a greater Austria. . . . We are moving into dark and evil times, one could

almost think that the old Europe had outlived its days and was going to its doom. There must be a powerful reaction, great social changes.[6]

Possibly Szeps would have preferred not to have been the recipient of some of these communications; they were unusable as copy and if discovered could lead to serious trouble both for himself and Rudolf. But the Crown Prince was too valuable a source of information to be discarded and therefore, although under no illusions about the dangers of the contact, the journalist fostered it.

Although the Monarchy was not a police state, it was not a country in which there was complete freedom of speech. Taaffe employed a number of agents and informants and there was some censorship of letters from which, as in other European countries, the correspondence of royal personages was not exempt. The Crown Prince was a conspicuous figure and it was difficult for him to meet people without being observed. Even after his marriage, unlike the other Archdukes, he had no house of his own in Vienna but lived in a wing of the Schweizerhof, part of his father's palace, the Hofburg, where a special corps of guards were liable to report to higher authority any unusual comings and goings. Rudolf, extremely nervous of the possible discovery of his interchanges with Szeps, constantly impressed on the latter the need for discretion, stressing that every care must be taken to safeguard his anonymity, sending his letters and the articles which he wrote for the *Neues Wiener Tagblatt,* by special messenger or his valet Nehammer, and frequently saying that there was much which he would tell Szeps when they met which he could not put on paper:

> You will probably laugh at all my precautions, but I have got to be very careful indeed because unfortunately I have several times been indiscreet in what I have said, and therefore have gained the reputation in high conservative circles of being unreliable.[7]

This was in June 1882. Early in 1883 he wrote from Prague on the same theme:

They are becoming very watchful and suspicious of me, and I see more and more clearly every day with what a narrow circle of espionage, denunciations and suspicions I am surrounded. Be very careful if you are asked about your relations with me. Even if you speak to Nehammer, or give him messages or letters, don't omit the slightest precaution. Watch him too to see if he commits any error.[8]

Szeps took every precaution within his power, editing the articles where necessary to conceal the author's identity, personally making copies of them and returning the originals to the Crown Prince. In spite of his anxieties Rudolf's sense of security was very much more erratic. He was prepared to take extraordinary risks to meet Szeps, including asking the latter to come and see him in his former bachelor apartment in the Hofburg which he had kept on after his marriage. This consisted of a suite of rooms on the second floor looking out on one side over the Schweizerhof, a small courtyard approached through an arch from the Franzensplatz round which the main part of the palace was built, and on the other across an open space to the Ring and the wooded hills of the Wienerwald on the outskirts of Vienna. The main approach to these rooms led out of the Schweizerhof, and any visitor using it was certain to be noticed by the guard on duty. There were however several back entrances, one through a maze of corridors from the buildings on the far side of the courtyard which ended in a steep narrow unlit wooden staircase leading into one of the antechambers of the Crown Prince's suite, and another through the Augustinergang. This was a series of rooms housing the Imperial Coin and other collections which formed, ironically enough, a connecting link with Archduke Albrecht's palace. It could be entered by a small iron door set in the outer wall of the Hofburg, from where there was a choice of proceeding along the ground floor and reaching Rudolf's rooms by a side staircase, or of climbing a flight of steps on to the flat roof of the Augustinergang, and from there clambering through a window into the Crown Prince's apartment. Rudolf himself used one or other of these routes when he wished to enter or leave the

Hofburg incognito, and they provided a means of enabling people to visit him to whom he did not wish to call attention. Although not wholly secure, they offered a better chance of evading detection than the main entrance from the Schweizerhof.

Late in the evening of January 30th, 1883, Szeps was guided by Nehammer through the maze of corridors and down the steep narrow unlit staircase to an interview with the Crown Prince. Both of them were under pressure. Two days earlier Taaffe had banned the sale of the *Neues Wiener Tagblatt* in State-owned tobacconist's shops, a measure which cut its circulation by eighty per cent and threatened it with financial extinction. Rudolf was convinced that Archduke Albrecht suspected something and that his movements were closely watched. He came straight from the Hofball to meet Szeps, arriving a few minutes after midnight to find the journalist waiting for him. It was a strange situation. At the foot of the great ceremonial staircase Count Taaffe with the rest of the Emperor's guests was waiting for his carriage to leave the Hofburg. A few hundred yards away, in a room hung with portraits of his ancestors the Crown Prince, still wearing his general's uniform with the Order of the Golden Fleece, received the editor of the newspaper at which Taaffe had struck forty-eight hours earlier.

Nehammer served supper. Szeps ate nothing. Rudolf ate very little but drank four or five large glasses of champagne. The journalist, who later made a note of what he described as 'this extraordinary interview'9 had never seen the Crown Prince so agitated. He said at once: 'These are appalling times; tell me everything which they have done to you', and went on to stress that at the ball he had told various officials what he thought of the action taken against the *Neues Wiener Tagblatt,* but feared this would not help. Nothing he felt could now alter the evil turn that the situation was taking, and for this he blamed the Jesuits who were closely allied to 'the most influential Archdukes'. He now mistrusted everyone, even his old servants. After an hour's discussion of the plight of the *Neues Wiener Tagblatt,* Szeps made a move to go. Rudolf saying that he could never sleep in Vienna detained him. He then poured out a number of astonishing confidences saying that two years earlier he had been accused of being a Freemason or a member of some other secret anti-religious revolutionary society, and had only settled this by demanding a court martial; that Archduke Albrecht and the Jesuits were engaged in a conspiracy to convert the Orthodox in Bosnia to Catholicism which gravely endangered the interests of the Monarchy in the Balkans; that the Hungarians were now the sole supporters of liberal and constitutional ideas. Finally the Crown Prince told Szeps a curious story according to which in the previous summer Tisza the Hungarian Minister President, two of his ministerial colleagues, and a third important personage had proposed that he should be crowned King of Hungary. Archduke Albrecht had heard about this, solemnly warned him against accepting any such proposal, and as a result of the Archduke's interference it had been dropped. It is difficult to know what to make of this story. Since Franz Joseph was the crowned and annointed King of Hungary, a formal act of State, to which he would never have agreed, would have been necessary to enable his son to take his place. Was it a figment of Rudolf's imagination? Whatever the explanation the Crown Prince appears to have felt that he could command support in Hungary, the nation to which he was now beginning to turn as the one hope of the Monarchy.

The interview ended in the small hours of the morning. Rudolf returned to Prague, Szeps fought on to save the *Neues Wiener Tagblatt*. They remained in touch, and when the Crown Prince and Princess moved to Vienna a few months later, met frequently. In August rioting in Zagreb dealt a severe blow to Rudolf's faith in the Hungarians.

Poor Hungary [he wrote to Szeps] we are facing an epoch-making crisis. Things can't go on like this much longer. . . . Hungary will drift towards complete disintegration and a time will come when they find it necessary to interfere from Vienna but here, where there is the sound basis for the establishment of a modern state, political power is being systematically destroyed by all this 'Slavonifying' . . . here, however, in addition there is a reactionary tendency and personally I prefer the crumbling Hungarian Liberalism to Taaffe's Austria. [10]

As this letter shows, Rudolf's attitude towards the internal structure of the Monarchy was ambivalent and fluctuating. He still clung to the idea that it should be possible for all nationalities to become enlightened, so that if given more local autonomy they would not misuse it but work together as loyal subjects of the Crown. But when any instance arose of one race attempting to seek advantages for itself at the expense of the others, the Habsburg side of his nature asserted itself, and he came out in favour of a strong central government supported by the army. It was an example of the two-way pull which beset him throughout his life, and which he never succeeded in resolving.

The Crown Prince was faced with a similar two-way pull in foreign affairs. On the one hand, as he told Szeps soon after they met, France seemed to him to be the source of all progressive ideas and Germany by contrast nothing but an 'enormously enlarged Prussian regimental barbarism'. On the other he was enough of a Habsburg dynast to realise the importance to the Monarchy of the German alliance and, until the last years of his life, did all he could to foster it when he visited Berlin. The German capital was not an attractive city. Its straight streets bordered with houses ornamented with ornate stucco, porcelain plaques and glass mosaics, could not compare with the Baroque splendour, grace and aura of the centuries of tradition of Vienna. A Court, at which the sole table decorations when the German Emperor gave a State Banquet, consisted of a row of gigantic silver dish covers each surmounted by the Prussian eagle and with nothing underneath them, could not emulate the colour and poised ceremonial of a similar banquet in the Hofburg or Schönbrunn. There was no pleasure to be derived from going to Berlin, but whatever his inward feelings Rudolf could when the occasion demanded, and particularly when abroad, make an excellent impression. He did so on the occasion of his second official visit to the German capital in 1883, not only on the German Crown Prince and Princess with whom he got on well for, although a good deal older than himself they shared his progressive ideas, but also on Bismarck who, while finding Franz Joseph's heir rather timid, was nevertheless astonished by his grasp of affairs and the clarity with which he expressed himself.

Rudolf wrote for the Emperor a clear, concise report of his Berlin visit. That he got the chance of discussing it with his father seems unlikely. Franz Joseph still considered his son's views uninteresting and unimportant, an attitude which may explain why he took no steps to forbid the Crown Prince's contact with Szeps. By 1883 a number of people knew that it existed. Albrecht certainly suspected that something was going on, and Taaffe had information about a number of meetings between the journalist and Rudolf although not about what was said at them. The Archduke, never backward in finding fault with the younger generation, no doubt told the Emperor of his suspicions but was unable to support them with definite evidence. Taaffe with his policy of keeping anything upsetting from his sovereign may have said nothing until asked, and then adopted the attitude that eventually Rudolf would become less irresponsible; meanwhile provided he was given no information of any importance no harm would be done. Such advice would have been acceptable to the Emperor. He had a great many other things to think about and tried if possible to avoid the disagreeable. To summon Rudolf and lecture him would not only be disagreeable but might make difficulties with Elisabeth. In any case, confident as the Emperor was of his own power and authority, Rudolf's impact on affairs seemed to him to be no more effective than the futile efforts of a butterfly endeavouring to get out of a room by fluttering its wings in vain against the window.

Rudolf's frustration in the autumn of 1883 was shared, if for somewhat different reasons, by his cousin Archduke Johann Salvator. The latter, promoted Feldmarschall-Lieutenant (Lieutenant-General), was now commanding the 25th Division in the Vienna garrison, an appointment which, while it brought him back to the centre of power, had the drawback of attendance at Court and a number of social obligations all of which he disliked. In the second and final volume of his regimental history which appeared while he was still at Komorn, he had written of the revolt in 1848 in terms which were considered to be too sympathetic to the demands of the rebels. Conservatives in both civilian and military circles predicted that 'the worst was to be feared' of a man with such a 'revolutionary spirit',[11] and considered that the Archduke's attitude since his return to the capital confirmed this verdict. Johann Salvator made no attempt to endear himself to his detractors. Critical to the point of sarcasm about anything or anyone he disliked, he stigmatised as 'uneducated men' aristocratic officers who in his opinion did not take their profession seriously, went out of his way to be charming to their colleagues of humbler origin, made no attempt to conceal his contact with the Press, and generally refused to conform to conventional behaviour. He was in consequence accused of inverted snobbery, of showing off, and mocked at Court as wishing to draw attention to himself 'in order to be made a Baron'.[12]

The Archduke's outstanding competence could not, however, be denied. In 1882 after there had been a revolt in Bosnia, Andrassy suggested that he should be sent there as Governor. At the end of the year his annual report described him as 'a most gifted General, who is keenly interested in his profession and entitled to expect to rise to the highest rank. Time and experience will mature his judgement.'

Until the beginning of 1883 Johann Salvator managed to keep out of trouble with the Emperor. Then, while at Schloss Orth dealing with the annual accounts, he received a peremptory telegram summoning him to Vienna, where on appearing before Franz Joseph, he was sharply reprimanded by the latter for his failure to be present in the capital at the celebration of the six hundredth anniversary of the founding of the House of Habsburg, and for having gone on leave without permission. The Archduke did not take this well, writing to his mother:

Although the first reprimand may be merited, I believe that by spending the day in Gmunden going to church and hoisting flags to celebrate this happy (?) anniversary I may have served

K

the cause better than by being in Vienna adding to the swarm of Archdukes. The second rebuke was unjust. Mendel did not read Mensshengen's notification in his daily report book, and so made no mention of it to His Majesty. Even Albrecht told me I was innocent, and merely advised me to take less leave, especially when the Emperor is in Vienna. This means dear Mamma that I do not dare to come to Cannes because it would certainly get me into fresh trouble.[13]

This bad start to the year was followed a few months later by the Emperor's veto of the Archduke's proposed marriage to Countess Attems. By now too Johann Salvator was chafing at the apparent impossibility of getting a hearing for his views on army reforms. He had been unable even to obtain the reinstatement for a victimised officer for which he had been fighting for eight years.

The case of Major Menrad Laaba von Rosenfeld epitomised to the Archduke the worst aspects of the High Command of the Army. In 1875 it was discovered that the Major was the author of an article[14] defending official policy against the criticisms of it made by Johann Salvator in his 'Reflections on the Organisation of the Austrian Artillery', and under interrogation he admitted to having written another anonymous pamphlet[15] drawing attention to injustices and matters which needed remedying in the army. This could be considered insubordinate which the article rebutting the Archduke's thesis could not, but it was for the latter that Laaba was court martialled. The Higher Military Court found the Major guilty of a gross breach of discipline and sentenced him to be deprived of his rank and cashiered without a pension. Beck, summing up the case for the Emperor, conceded that on legal grounds there might be some doubt about this sentence, but emphasised that from the military point of view it was correct and that no appeal could be made against it. He ended by suggesting that the Emperor should in no way be associated with the affair—a suggestion which Franz Joseph annotated with the comment 'absolutely right'.[16] The implication was plain. Laaba had committed the unpardonable sin of attacking a member of the Imperial Family and therefore the dynasty which, in the interests of the Monarchy must be protected at all costs. His case had, therefore, soared into a realm where this consideration took priority over any question of justice to an individual, and the treatment meted out to him was a variation on a small scale of that received by Benedek. The reasoning in both cases was the same: there was one law for the House of Habsburg and another for lesser mortals.

Johann Salvator was disgusted by the sentence:

> This man who after all only tried to defend the army against my youthful attack, has suffered a far too hard not to mention unjust fate.[17]

He kept in touch with Laaba, endeavoured to help him find work, employed him from time to time as a confidential secretary, and fought for his reinstatement. In 1877 he persuaded the Emperor 'as an act of clemency' to restore to the former Major the pension to which he was entitled for thirty years' service, and in 1880 induced the Minister of War to appoint a Court of Enquiry to review the case. The Court recommended that Laaba's rank should be restored to him. The Minister of War when forwarding this finding to the Emperor for confirmation, pointed out that the sentence of the original court martial had no legal justification 'but was necessary at that time in order to make an example'.[18] Franz Joseph passed the recommendation on to Archduke Albrecht, and the latter, making it clear that whatever the rights or wrongs of the case he was determined that the original sentence should not be altered, turned it down.[19] By 1883 Laaba had still not been reinstated in his rank, an injustice which added to the long list of grievances which Johann Salvator harboured against Albrecht.

Towards the end of the year the Archduke, by then extremely frustrated, gave a lecture which he entitled 'Drill or Education'[20] to the Association for Military Studies at the Officers' Club in Vienna. In this he did not conceal his opinion of the system which Albrecht upheld, expounding the thesis that many of the concepts for military training drawn up fifty years earlier were hopelessly out of date, and that modern weapons and developments in warfare demanded that the object of such training should no longer be to instil into the troops blind obedience, but to teach them to think for themselves. Parade ground exercises, he maintained, destroyed the will, which in battle was crucial to victory. Men must understand the orders which they received, and be encouraged in that 'sense of duty, resolution and endurance' which had made the Prussians so successful. Discipline must be enforced, but with the object of producing competent intelligent soldiers, not marionettes: 'No lunatic is cured by being put into a strait jacket, the mind cannot be disciplined through the body.' Johann Salvator's theme was the same as von Moltke's: 'Superiority is no longer to be found in the weapon but in the hand that carries it',[21] and he enlarged on it with great care, attacking the system without naming its perpetrators. He did, however, pose one query:

> How can it be that people persist in their error when they have enough experience in war to know that success depends on factors other than drill? Is it conviction or opportunism, or a curious reflex of that desire to dominate which exists in most men and makes them want to bend others—by some means—to their will?

Both his audience and the newspapers, for the lecture was widely reported, assumed that the 'people' to whom the Archduke referred meant the Inspector General of the army and his closest colleagues.

A few days later Johann Salvator held a Press conference during which he appeared to be perfectly at ease, and professed astonishment that tendencies should be attributed to him which he did not possess. He stressed that he had attempted to present only the technical and practical considerations relating to his subject intending no attack on anyone, certainly not on Archduke Albrecht who was not the creator of the present system but had merely inherited it. He refused to concede that his lecture constituted any breach of discipline, pointing out that if it was regarded as such it would be impossible to criticise any organisation and faults could never be remedied. Some journalists did not find his explanation convincing and Albrecht, as was to be expected reacted violently. Johann Salvator gave an account of what happened next to his mother:

> The lecture is over, and without boasting it does appear to me to have created a certain sensation. I asked the Minister (of War) if it could be printed; the Minister agreed but did not want to take the responsibility, saying he wished to await the return of the Emperor. Returned on the 6th from Hungary, His Majesty read the manuscript and, expressing himself very favourably on it, gave permission for its publication. In the meantime, however, Archduke Albrecht read the reviews in the papers and, apparently jealous and afraid that my lecture could be detrimental to his 'image', wrote and telegraphed to Beck and to the Emperor and to me. The Emperor suspended his permission but telegraphed to Albrecht that he still wished the lecture to be published, in order to correct various false versions which had appeared in the newspapers, and that he would only forbid publication if this displeased Archduke Albrecht. Albrecht naturally could do nothing else but agree. Then pressure was again put on the Emperor. There was a great struggle between Beck and the Minister of War, Beck wanting to stop the publication in order to curry favour with Albrecht. Finally the Minister won and the lecture was printed. The Emperor said 'it is very well written, I don't find the points too strongly put, and the end in particular is most patriotic and loyal'. Albrecht who asked me for an explanation which I have not given him is apparently very angry. [22]

Albrecht was very angry indeed. On returning to Vienna he went straight to the Emperor and protested that Johann Salvator's insubordination was such that were he an ordinary line officer he would be deprived of his rank and cashiered—the fate which had befallen Laaba. Franz Joseph found himself in a dilemma. The Archduke was not an ordinary line officer, and the printed version of his lecture, which he himself had authorised, had not only aroused so much interest at home that it was rapidly being sold out, but had attracted a great deal of attention abroad and was favourably commented on both in Prussia and in the French press. To take severe disciplinary action would create a bad impression in a number of foreign countries, and probably arouse dissatisfaction in the army where there were many officers who shared Johann Salvator's views. Some mark of displeasure must however be registered, and the only possible one was another posting to the provinces. On Christmas Eve 1883 the Archduke was transferred to command the 3rd Infantry Division in Linz and Rudolf, now also a Lieutenant-General, appointed to succeed him in command of the 25th Division in Vienna. The reshuffle appeared to please both young men. The Crown Prince had been pressing for a posting to the Vienna garrison. Johann Salvator professed himself delighted with his transfer to Linz saying that it would enable him to escape from the tedious social round in Vienna, to see more of his mother, and to supervise the alterations to Schloss Orth. Linz was within easy reach of the capital; it would be possible for him to remain in touch with events there, and with Rudolf of whom he was now seeing a good deal.

CHAPTER 9

An Uneasy Relationship

Rudolf and Johann Salvator were more alike than any other two members of the younger generation of the Imperial Family. Both of them had wide interests, active forward-thinking minds, were critical of the Catholic Church and inclined to religious free-thinking; disliked the aristocracy, and were convinced that the Emperor was in every way badly advised. They shared a love of the sea and the south, and felt a sense of claustrophobia within the Monarchy. Both of them had a compulsive urge to write, appreciated the importance of the Press, and used their journalistic contacts as a means of acquiring information and making their views known.

Because of their resemblance in intellectual ability and progressive ideas it has been suggested that the two young men acted together, and that Johann Salvator was Rudolf's only close friend in the family. Unfortunately, practically none of the correspondence between them has survived, but all available information indicates that their relationship was not consistently harmonious, certainly not intimate, and that the degree of collaboration generally assumed to have existed between them has been exaggerated. By no means all their tastes and views were identical. Johann Salvator unlike Rudolf was not a keen shot, and the latter, while enjoying gypsy orchestras and Viennese songs, had none of the former's real appreciation of music. Over foreign affairs they were both convinced of the necessity for the expansion of the Monarchy's influence in the Balkans, but differed over the question of Germany. The Crown Prince, whatever his dislike of the Prussian mentality, was until the last few months of his life a protagonist of the German alliance and feared Russia.

The Archduke was convinced that the Monarchy must come to terms with Russia and retained a lifelong hatred of Germany, writing caustically after his first visit to Berlin of 'the capital of the new Germany—built with Austrian and French money',[1] and of its monuments flanked by captured 'Austrian and French guns'.[2] At home, while agreed on the general necessity for social progress, there was a different emphasis in their objectives. Johann Salvator concentrated on the question of army reform, Rudolf once his early enthusiasm for the army had passed, became more concerned with the problems of reconciling the various nationalities in the Monarchy. Of the two the Archduke was the more forthright, speaking and writing what he felt without regard for the consequences to himself. If he was convinced that something should be done he went straight for it. Rudolf, pulled first one way and then the other by conflicting considerations, tended to vacillate. Highly strung and more timid than his cousin, he was more easily inclined to pessimism.

When Johann Salvator was first posted to a regiment in 1872 Rudolf was still a fourteen-year-old boy in the schoolroom. It seems unlikely that at this stage or for several years to come that the cousins knew each other well. The Archduke was away from Vienna a great deal, and the ideas of a boy in his teens are not of much interest to a young man in his early twenties. After the Crown Prince came of age the gap between them narrowed, but not at first happily. Johann Salvator was critical of Rudolf's visit to Egypt and the Holy Land before his marriage.

> It seems to me that this pilgrimage to Jerusalem is only a cloak for the real object of the journey, shooting and oriental parties in the Viceroy of Egypt's garden

and, he added censoriously,

> It is said that the Crown Prince has a mountain of debts.[3]

Writing a few days later on the subject of Rudolf's wedding he told his mother:

> If I were you I would not go to it because his Imperial and Royal Highness the most serene and august Crown Prince does

not merit this mark of respect for he has never paid proper attention to you either in Gmunden or in Vienna. Forgive me dear Mamma if I am so frank, but it is sad to see how this future sovereign treats his relatives, in spite of the fact that at his age he should show respect and attention to those who have seen a great deal before he was born. [4]

This is one of the more outspoken expressions of the jealousy which was endemic in Johann Salvator's attitude towards Rudolf. The Archduke was older than the Crown Prince, tougher physically and a strong character; he may have secretly considered himself the better man of the two of them. But there was no escaping the fact that he was a junior member of the Imperial Family of which—and Rudolf was very conscious of this and not backward in saying so—the Crown Prince would one day be head. In addition, as heir to the throne, Rudolf escaped some of the attacks suffered by Johann Salvator. The latter once said bitterly:

We agree about the Press, but my connections with it are much disapproved of and I have to put up with a great deal, while they do not dare to set about the Crown Prince. [5]

The Archduke felt that everything was easy for Rudolf, whereas he had to make his own way in the world, and because he resented this he was always liable to lash out with a sarcastic remark about his cousin.

However, for a time after Rudolf's marriage the two of them appeared to be getting on better. There is a story that when the Archduke visited Prague he and the Crown Prince filled a chamber pot with scent, suspended it out of a window of the Hradschin Palace and set fire to its contents. To their delight it exploded with a loud bang, much alarming the German Empress Augusta who was staying in the palace at the time. [6] 'Larks' such as apple-pie beds, soap in the cheese and booby traps were much in fashion amongst the younger members of the ruling houses and aristocracy of Europe. It is pleasant to think that Rudolf and Johann Salvator, both of whom were inclined to be serious and had not much sense of humour, may have been capable of behaving like their high-spirited contemporaries. After the Crown

Prince and Princess moved to Vienna in the spring of 1883 the Archduke saw more of them and found Rudolf agreeable and friendly, 'but I could wish he was more sincere'.[7] Towards the end of the year explaining that his lecture 'Drill or Education' had been partly directed at the Crown Prince, he was caustic about the latter's good reception of it. 'Because I highly praised the Prussians the lecture has made a good impression in Prussia, and because the Prussians are pleased Rudolf is pleased—a fine piece of logic!'[8]

Nevertheless, after Johann Salvator's transfer to Linz he continued to remain in touch with the Crown Prince, and before long public attention was focused on them both over an affair which had nothing to do with politics—the debunking of the famous medium Bastian. Spiritualism was one of the pastimes of the European aristocracy, producing startling experiences such as the occasion when, at a séance attended by a number of minor German royalties, a massive mahogany table bounced round the room and finally fell over, pinning to the ground the stout form of Princess Mary Adelaide of Teck. Rudolf loathed spiritualism and its adherents whom he described as the 'dark apostles of a still darker teaching',[9] and in this at least Johann Salvator agreed with him. For some time both of them collected accounts of Bastian's séances and the 'spirits' which he allegedly evoked, and in agreement with the Crown Prince, the Archduke invited the medium to Vienna with the intention of exposing him as a charlatan. The séances were held in Johann Salvator's house. Bastian was put in a room separated from the assembled company by a curtain and a pair of folding doors which were left open, but to which the Archduke had attached a device so that when a string was pulled they slammed. On the first two evenings he took no action, but at the third séance when after a 'twanging of instruments' a white shape appeared, pulled the string, the doors closed, and there were sounds of a most unethereal being desperately trying to retreat to the next room. This, grabbed by Rudolf and Johann Salvator, was revealed to be Bastian in his socks, some white muslin draped about him, conclusively exposed as a swindler. The Crown Prince wrote an account of the episode for the *Neues Wiener Tagblatt*. Johann Salvator held a Press conference and published a pamphlet on the whole affair which he privately asserted he had arranged because Rudolf, whatever he might say, was in danger of being impressed by Bastian.

The Archduke's inability to refrain from making derogatory remarks about his cousin did not augur well for their collaboration in a literary project on which they were at the time together engaged. This began at the end of 1883 when Johann Salvator completed and handed over to Rudolf the synopsis of a ten-volume study of the ethnography of the races within the Monarchy. Whether the Archduke prepared this at Rudolf's request, or whether it was his own idea is not clear. Certainly the Crown Prince was keenly interested in it, and in March 1884 made a formal application to the Emperor for permission to start work on the book. He suggested that it should be called '*Die Öster-reichische-Ungarische Monarchie im Wort und Bild*',[10] explaining to his father that it would give an unbiased picture of the varying national characteristics of his subjects which, demonstrating their interdependence on each other, would increase their sense of patriotism. He presented this as his own idea without any mention of the contribution made to it by Johann Salvator. Franz Joseph gave his approval. Rudolf appointed two sub-editors, Ritter von Weilen, a professor and President of the Journalists Club, and Maurius Jokai, a prominent Hungarian journalist, and formed a co-ordinating committee of which he himself took the chair, on which he invited Johann Salvator to serve. But the Archduke in the meantime had taken umbrage. He complained that he was too busy with his military duties to attend committee meetings in Vienna.

As I am paid to be a soldier I cannot adopt the profession of a scientist and be at the beck and call of the 'Neue Burg' (the Crown Prince) . . . I have extricated myself from the unpleasant and difficult situation in which I found myself with regard to the work inaugurated by Rudolf. I have told him that I cannot be either a member of the committee or his adviser. I am, however, ready to contribute to the enterprise, and as the Emperor knows I have offered to write about the architecture, peasant houses and monuments of Upper Austria, a subject which I believe can be free from any political angle.[11]

Evidently the Crown Prince attempted to make his cousin change his mind and for a time Johann Salvator wavered, but at the end of May, 'after long and careful thought', he withdrew from the committee 'without replying to Rudolf'.[12] Writing to Weilen in the following year he referred to 'an incident—which to my utmost regret—rendered my participation in the Crown Prince's great work impossible',[13] but gave no indication of what this incident was. Possibly he was jealous of Rudolf for taking the credit for an idea which he himself had originated, disagreed with certain alterations in his original synopsis, and resented working under his younger cousin. Whatever the reason the Archduke's withdrawal from the committee marked the end of his close collaboration with the Crown Prince. Both of them were impatient and touchy. Rudolf throughout his life chose as his friends older men and was only at ease with those of his contemporaries whom he could patronise. Johann Salvator resented being patronised. Each of them wished to dominate and both of them were Habsburgs, a family on which the capacity for sustained friendship was rarely bestowed. Although they thought along parallel lines, they were incapable of combining for joint action, and their mutual impatience with the older generation did not bridge the gap between them.

Amongst the older generation there was no one whom the Archduke and the Crown Prince disliked more than Field-Marshal Archduke Albrecht. Frederick the Great's rejoinder to the officer who relied on practical experience and neglected to keep abreast of modern tactics, 'I have in the army two mules which have been through forty campaigns, but they are still two mules',[14] summarised Johann Salvator's opinion of the Inspector General of the army. He privately referred to Albrecht as an old fool, and was sick and tired of hearing him still referred to as 'the Victor of Custozza', particularly since after a close study of the battle and the terrain over which it had been fought, he was convinced that the Field-Marshal's victory was only due to the incompetence of the Italian general opposing him. Rudolf shared this opinion, and in addition could not stand his elderly relative as a person.

He delights in nosing about, picking quarrels, in intriguing and doing harm for he is malicious. If he discovers a mistake or weakness in someone it gives him pleasure. . . . If one has the honour of being in his presence one must . . . sit there in admiration like the archangels around God. [15]

When Johann Salvator was in trouble with Albrecht and Beck after his lecture on 'Drill or Education', Rudolf wrote warning him:

They have again got you into a fine mess with Papa; you are undermining discipline. If a member of the most exalted ruling House, instructed in soldierly virtues, etc., sets an example of insubordination, the effect on young officers, etc., . . . you can imagine the rest. Papa was very irritated but controlled himself and said at the end of the recital: 'Gentlemen, you may be assured that I will not tolerate insubordination in my army. I await your further report on the case of His Imperial Highness.' There will not be much joy in a further report on you by Uncle Albrecht. You are no longer the good Johann who studies so industriously. [16]

The report was made and Rudolf wrote again:

Uncle Albrecht saw Papa and shouted at him. I tell you, Albrecht and Beck are agreed about you and they have Papa as always entirely on their side. If I say anything Papa will only be more annoyed. It is wisest for you to do penance and appease the injured hero of Custozza. [17]

The Crown Prince was not prepared to stand up for his cousin and a few months later when he clashed with Albrecht, Johann Salvator did not take his side. The clash occurred during the manœuvres at Bruck an der Leitha in August 1884. The manœuvres were an annual event and a penance for a number of

people, including it may be suspected Count Harrach on whose
estates they were held, and who was obliged to house the important personages attending them in his castle. They were presided
over by the Emperor, accompanied by Albrecht and Beck, before
whom the junior generals carried out exercises, set without
regard for the exhaustion of the troops, in the hottest and dustiest
month of the year. In 1884 Stephanie accompanied Rudolf and
both stayed with Count Harrach which meant, as Johann Salvator
said, that all the officers, on top of everything else had to put up
'with the boredom of the Court round', and in consequence a
series of long days.

> Morning manœuvres which finished at 2 p.m., lunch with
> Archduke Albrecht, military conferences, camp inspections,
> then the troops recreational amusements at which one had to
> be present, then tea with Albrecht or Rudolf and perhaps a
> serenade or torchlight procession.

He found that Archduke Albrecht

> got overtired, was really deplorably nervous and could leave
> nothing and nobody in peace for a moment.[18]

The Crown Prince described the Field-Marshal as being 'in a
frightful state of nerves, decrepitude, stupidity and irritability',[19]
and had a violent political argument with him. Albrecht then
proceeded to get his own back by ordering a general stand-to
when the Crown Prince had gone out shooting, pointing out
publicly that of all the officers only the heir to the throne was not
at his post. Rudolf found this 'infamous', stormed off to see the
Emperor at Laxenburg, announced that he wished to resign from
the army, and was with difficulty persuaded to return to Bruck.

In view of his own difficulties with Albrecht, Johann Salvator
might have been expected to sympathise with the Crown Prince,
but he did nothing of the sort.

> It was certainly not an opportune moment to order a stand-to;
> however, Rudolf is not interested in soldiering. . . . I only had
> command once, yesterday in the presence of the Emperor. . . .
> It was easy, went well, and the Emperor and even Albrecht

were pleased. His Majesty greatly praised me for pushing forward a detachment with decision and speed, while Rudolf executed a diversion some distance away which seemed ridiculous. [20]

The two young men were incapable of making a joint stand even against someone whom they both disliked.

The Field-Marshal now had no use for either of them, and particularly not for Johann Salvator, telling Beck:

The only one who I hoped might be my eventual successor— now that the heir to the throne appears to have lost interest in military affairs—Archduke Johann, has, alas, shown us that he lacks those essential qualities which distinguished Monte-cuccoli, Eugen, Archduke Karl. [21]

There is something pathetic about this admission, for it was part of Albrecht's creed that the head of the army should be a member of the Imperial Family. He could not realise that he was partly to blame for this disappointment, he was constantly on the defensive and, being of his generation, considered it improper to be candid either to the Crown Prince or the Archduke about misgivings such as at this time he confided to Beck.

When I look back on the dreadful shortcomings of the Generals which we have both seen in Vienna and Lemberg, and which I have also found in the IV, V and VIth Corps, I shudder to think what would occur in the event of war with these un-trained, mostly ignorant and often unpractical commanders. [22]

Incapable of explaining, he could only order, so failed to enlist the sympathy and support of his younger relatives, and they made no allowance for the difficulties with which he had to contend. Confident of the full support of the Emperor he remained however in a stronger position than either of them, with the power to block Johann Salvator's promotion and to turn down any ideas which he or the Crown Prince might put forward about army reform.

Much as he disliked Archduke Albrecht, Rudolf was less affected by him than Johann Salvator, for the army was neither his career nor his only sphere of activity. Although still allowed by the Emperor no voice in affairs of state, widening contacts and experience from 1884 onwards brought him a good deal of intellectual stimulus. He was engaged in writing the introduction to *Die Österreichische-Ungarische Monarchie im Wort und Bild*, personally directed the work on the book and enjoyed doing so, for his committee included a number of outstanding scholars, whom he liked and with whom he felt at ease. The recognition of his intellectual achievements by the award of an honorary doctorate by the University of Vienna delighted him. Foreign rather than home affairs were now his main preoccupation, a shift of interest which brought him within the aegis of Count Gustav Kalnoky von Korospatak who after a short interregnum had succeeded Andrassy as Foreign Minister of the Monarchy.

Of Franz Joseph's generation (he was born in 1832) Kalnoky began his career as a cavalry officer, but soon transferred to the Diplomatic Service. After twenty-seven years abroad he was recalled from St. Petersburg where he was Ambassador to become Minister of Foreign Affairs, a post for which it was said he had nearly been turned down because he wore a monocle which Franz Joseph considered 'too Prussian'. The Count was a dapper little man with a snub nose, a bachelor who according to a member of the German Embassy staff possessed one of the largest collections of pornographic literature in Europe. Chilly and reserved, he was unemotional, devoid of enthusiasms and had few friends. He boasted that he had never received a journalist. Self-confident, calm—whatever the crisis he always slept well—he lived for his job, worked very hard indeed, had a clear brain, a great deal of common sense, and detested any form of muddle or confusion. Bismarck remarked that it was possible to get through more business with Kalnoky in two hours than with Andrassy in two days.

The Count maintained that the Monarchy must act as a Great Power, for a strong foreign policy would make the various nationalities forget their internecine quarrels, but it was a theory which he was incapable of putting into practice. Unlike Andrassy he was not a statesman who, having decided on a plan, acted on it and then dealt with whatever unforeseen contingencies might arise, but a diplomat of the school which holds that diplomacy is the art of the possible. Franz Joseph, comparing the methods of the two Foreign Ministers said:

> Count Andrassy knew how to cut through a knot, Count Kalnoky had a talent for carefully unpicking it. [23]

Rudolf with his natural impatience was from time to time critical of what he considered to be the 'weakness' of Kalnoky's cautious policy. But he got on with the Count a great deal better than he did with Taaffe, and for this a great deal of credit must be given to the Imperial Foreign Minister. Kalnoky, realistic enough to appreciate that Rudolf's contact with Szeps could not be stopped, brought it to some degree under control by encouraging the Crown Prince to pass on anything useful which he learnt from the journalist, particularly about France, either to himself, or to one of his principal subordinates, Ladislaus von Szögyeny, of whom Rudolf had a very high opinion. Kalnoky also took the commonsense view that, as the Crown Prince was beginning to travel abroad on representational missions and met a number of foreign royalties, he must to some extent be briefed. By 1885 he managed to persuade Franz Joseph (who remained doubtful about Rudolf's discretion) to agree to the Crown Prince seeing carefully selected Foreign Office files. On the whole the differences of opinion between the Foreign Minister and Rudolf were not profound, and there were a number of subjects on which they thought alike. One of these was that, to promote the economic interests of the Monarchy, Baron Hirsch's project for a railway through the Balkans via Sofia to link up Vienna with Constantinople must be completed as soon as possible.

Rudolf had personal reasons for supporting this project; he owed Hirsch a great deal of money. There is no evidence to show that the Crown Prince gambled, but he had expensive tastes. Money had to be found from somewhere, and to obtain it he turned, as many a Prince and aristocrat had done before him, to the Jews, not however to the Rothschilds, the traditional financiers of the Habsburgs and the aristocracy, but to Baron Hirsch, a lone operator and a financier rather than a banker. The Baron, constantly on the move between Vienna, Paris, London and the Riviera, with powerful contacts in all the important financial centres of Europe, was a mysterious figure. Only three things could be said about him with certainty: he was a snob, he was immensely rich, his financial transactions were on a scale so vast as to be the subject of correspondence between governments, and more devious than those of many Orientals. His greatest coup was the extraction from the Porte in 1869 of the concession to build the Vienna–Constantinople railway, but work on this had proceeded slowly, and in 1884 the Turks were making difficulty about the stretch of the line which still remained to be laid. Few people knew more about the Balkans than Hirsch, and it is likely that Rudolf found him a useful source, not only of money but of information. The Baron was more than willing to help the Crown Prince; an occasional loan to him might bring in very big dividends in the future. Both of them found their relationship profitable, and when in the spring of 1884 Rudolf, who was about to visit Constantinople, was entrusted by Kalnoky with a mandate to press the Sultan to reach an agreement with Hirsch's company about the completion of the railway, he gladly undertook this task.

The journey to Turkey, on which Rudolf was accompanied by Stephanie, was part of a tour of the Balkans which included visits to Bulgaria, Roumania and Serbia. Before his departure the Crown Prince was carefully briefed by Kalnoky, who impressed on him that he must say or do nothing which infringed the Treaty of Berlin, and handed him prepared texts for all the speeches which he would be required to make. He kept to his brief admirably, achieved a considerable personal success, and the tour made a deep impression on him. In the report of it which he wrote after his return, he stressed his conviction that the time was favourable for the Monarchy to expand its influence in the Balkans, through trade, by the export of culture and intensive diplomatic activity, and that this must be done regardless of Russian opposition. It is possible that he did, as has been alleged, say in a moment of elation to Stephanie in Constantinople, 'one day you will be Empress here!'

The Balkan tour was followed by a number of other journeys abroad. Towards the end of the summer Rudolf went again to Roumania, and then to Berlin and Lithuania. In 1885 he visited Greece and Montenegro, going on from there to shoot in Syria and the Lebanon. He also accompanied the Emperor to Kremsier for a meeting with the Czar of Russia and Bismarck. Thanks to Kalnoky the Crown Prince had seen and learnt a great deal, but in the course of 1885 increased knowledge began to bring increased pessimism. Rudolf now feared that Bismarck was about to attack France. It seemed to him that the possibility of war with Russia in the Balkans was increasing—'The Russians are sending quantities of arms and ammunition to Serbia, and even to Bosnia to foment a revolt there'[24]—and he was now not so confident of its outcome. In this mood he seemed to be unable to concentrate on his intellectual activities. His Adjutant's diary shows that in the course of 1885 he spent over two hundred days shooting.

Rudolf, however powerless to influence events and however pessimistic about the future, was at least at the centre of affairs in the latter half of 1884 and 1885, while Johann Salvator was marooned in a backwater. A popular commander, he took the trouble to get to know the area in which his men were stationed, toured the outlying units and when visiting an officers' mess made a point of talking to the junior lieutenants. In his spare time he continued to make improvements to Schloss Orth, and in what he described as his 'sterile leisure' composed two waltzes 'one of which has had the unmerited luck to be orchestrated and performed by Johann Strauss'.[25] But he felt cut off from what was going on, it was a restricted existence and, as he complained, solitary.

At the end of 1884 the Archduke made an effort to put things right with Rudolf: 'Then I apologised and wrote very plainly to Franz Joseph's son; I hope he will not take my frankness badly.'[26] He renewed his offer, which the Crown Prince accepted, to contribute a chapter on Upper Austria to *Die Österreichische-Ungarische Monarchie im Wort und Bild*. In the spring of 1885 Rudolf helped him to arrange a journey to Montenegro. But contact between them remained tenuous, and Johann Salvator's jealousy of his cousin became more pronounced. He was sarcastic about the Crown Prince's journey to the Near East.

> As regards the political motives which are being attributed to Rudolf's journey, I can assure you that they do not exist: on the contrary it is a journey solely for the amusement of that Prince . . . I could wish that there were political motives and that one could see that the future Emperor of Austria thinks of serious matters and not only of entertainment. [27]

The publication of the first part of *Die Österreichische-Ungarische Monarchie im Wort und Bild* evoked a caustic comment.

> The Crown Prince's work which is so highly regarded by the Jewish press has started to appear. The South Slavs [28] are very much against it because of its stress on dualism . . . and the Croat papers are agitating against this work of the future ruler. All this is as many people have prophesied. [29]

The Archduke now considered that the Crown Prince (who by comparison with himself had every opportunity in the world) was wasting his time and could do nothing right. In this frame of mind he was exasperated, when the annual manœuvres were planned, to have to ensure that in whatever exercise Rudolf took part the force which he commanded won. Such an arrangement offended his military ethics, and for it he blamed Beck and Albrecht.

Johann Salvator's relations with Albrecht were now in a state of armed neutrality. At the end of the year the Field-Marshal agreed a recommendation that he should be promoted to command an Army Corps, but added a rider to the effect that however well the Archduke might sum up the character of individuals, the conclusions which he then drew were not always correct. 'He is too prejudiced.' This meant that Johann Salvator could expect no promotion in the near future. Frustrated and depressed, tired of peace-time soldiering, it seemed to him at the end of 1885 that only an international crisis, such as a flare-up in the Balkans, could provide him with scope for action.

CHAPTER 10

The Bulgarian Throne

The complications of the situation in the Balkans formed a knot
which defied Kalnoky's ingenuity to unravel, and which even
Szeps admitted made one's head reel. There was a power vacuum
in the peninsula in which the Monarchy and Russia each sought
to exert their influence at the expense of the other, and the
Russians were doing this most effectively. Czar Alexander II had
been assassinated in 1881, but hopes that his successor Alexander
III might be rather easier to deal with had not been fulfilled.
Queen Victoria remarked tartly of the new Czar that he was 'a
sovereign whom she does not look on as a gentleman',[1] an
apposite comment, for Alexander, a tall, broad-shouldered man
of great physical strength, dressed like a Russian peasant and in
many ways thought like one. Gruff, obstinate, narrow and
suspicious, he mistrusted England, disliked Germany—as Crown
Prince he refused to hear German spoken in his presence—and
still resented Franz Joseph's 'insults' to his grandfather Nicholas I.
He was determined that the interests of his country must be
defended and promoted whenever possible. Russian money and
arms continued to be poured into the Balkans. St. Petersburg was
inclined to say one thing and its agents and generals on the spot
did another. The Russians were impossible people to deal with
and Kalnoky, had he known of it, would have wholeheartedly
echoed the complaint of a British diplomat:

> What is rather unfair is that they have no hesitation in asking
> us for assurances and information, but when we ask for any-
> thing they either ignore the request, or are very rude or tell
> us a downright and obvious lie. It is not fair dos.[2]

No help was to be expected from Germany. Bismarck was nervy and irritable, beset by the fear that France might form an alliance with the Czar and launch a war of revenge. Kalnoky was certain that Germany would not support the Monarchy in a forward policy in the Balkans. Franz Joseph had not the slightest wish to adopt such a policy. He was not prepared to advance through those 'gates of the Orient' which Andrassy had declared were open to him, saw Bosnia Herzegovina as a rounding off of his possessions, not as a spring-board from which to extend them, and settled back into a determination to preserve the *status quo,* clinging to the German alliance, resolved at all costs to avoid provoking Russia and hoping for the best. There were however ominous signs that this hope might not be fulfilled, for developments in Bulgaria threatened to upset the whole situation in the Balkans.

The throne of Bulgaria was created in 1878 by the Treaty of Berlin, Article II of which stipulated that the Prince of Bulgaria should not be a member of any of the ruling dynasties of the Great Powers, and must be freely elected by the Bulgarian people. The appointment of a foreign Prince to rule over a newly independent state had already been successful in the case of Greece and Roumania, where Prince William of Denmark and Prince Karl of Hohenzollern-Sigmaringen, had managed to cling to their respective thrones. Alexander of Battenberg, a member of the German princely family of Hesse, accepted the Bulgarian National Assembly's invitation to become their ruler, but soon discovered that his position was very much more difficult than that of the sovereigns of either Greece or Roumania. The Czar was determined to bring Bulgaria within his orbit. A large Russian diplomatic mission, well supplied with money for bribes, was established in Sofia; Russians occupied all the key posts in the Bulgarian army and were entrenched in the Civil Service. Bulgaria was the main target of Russian activity in the Balkans, and Prince Alexander's subjects, sturdy peasants, ninety per cent of whom were illiterate, still regarded the Czar as their liberator from Turkish oppression.

Alexander was related to the Czar and a brother-in-law of Queen Victoria's daughter Princess Beatrice, a young man without money or political experience, but tall, handsome and like-able. He was considered not to be actively pro-Russian, but was nevertheless acceptable to the Czar who felt confident that Sandro, as he was generally known to his relatives, would do as St. Petersburg dictated. The Russians, however, overplayed their hand and the Bulgarians turned against them, rallying behind Alexander of Battenberg. In September 1885 when the inhabitants of East Rumelia revolted against the Turks and asked him to become their Prince, he accepted and informed the Powers that Bulgaria and East Rumelia were now united into one country under his sovereignty.

This establishment of a Greater Bulgaria contravened the Treaty of Berlin, and for the next two years the 'affair of Bulgaria' frequently occupied the first column of foreign news in *The Times*. The British Government was inclined to favour it, arguing that it made the country better able to resist foreign aggression. Czar Alexander III, now on extremely bad terms with his cousin Sandro, ordered the withdrawal of all Russian officers from Bulgaria, calculating that since they occupied every post in the Bulgarian army above the rank of company commander, that army would be rendered ineffective as a fighting force. In the Monarchy, as usual, reactions were mixed. A Press campaign was launched in favour of the annexation of Bosnia Herzegovina. The Hungarians were all for action in the Balkans and the Crown Prince saw 'a great opportunity' there. But the Emperor was still opposed to taking any action at all which might put the Monarchy in the wrong or offend Russia, and Kalnoky, to Rudolf's annoyance, sided with Franz Joseph.

Rivers of ink were expended in the Chanceries of Europe on the problem of how to restore the *status quo*, but before anything effective had been done Balkan internecine jealousy gave this another severe jolt, for in mid-November Serbia invaded Bulgaria. Alexander of Battenberg was under thirty and had no campaign experience. His Adjutant General was aged twenty-seven, and as a result of the withdrawal of the Russians there was no officer in the Bulgarian army with more than eight years service. Nevertheless the Prince placed himself at the head of his forces.

They proved to be some of the toughest troops in Europe. One regiment marched 60 miles in 32 hours and of a total of nearly 4,500 men only 62 fell out; another covered the same distance in 26 hours and went straight into action. On November 19th, five days after the start of the invasion, Alexander thrashed the Serbs at Slivnica; ten days later he was well inside the Serbian frontier, and nothing it seemed could stop him from entering Belgrade. This dazzling achievement horrified Vienna. King Milan of Serbia, of peasant origin with a veneer of Western civilisation, was unpopular with his subjects and Kalnoky privately described him as a catastrophe. But he had thrown in his lot with the Monarchy. If he lost the war and was toppled off his throne, the strong pro-Russian faction in Belgrade would gain the upper hand and this, as Serbia's northern frontier marched with Hungary, could not be allowed to happen. Under the threat of Austrian intervention the Bulgarians were forced to withdraw to their own side of the frontier and to cease hostilities. Even so, Alexander remained the hero of the hour and his achievement stirred the imagination of a great many people, including the Crown Prince of Austria and Archduke Johann Salvator.

Alexander of Battenberg had demonstrated that it was possible to stand up to the Russians. The Monarchy, Rudolf was convinced, must now display similar courage and initiative. It was useless talking to his father, but something might be achieved through Kalnoky. At the beginning of December 1885 the Crown Prince wrote to the Minister of Foreign Affairs urging that an active policy must now be pursued to ally Bulgaria, Serbia, Greece and Roumania with the Monarchy, so that if—or more likely when—war broke out, their combined armies would take the weight of the Russian attack in the Balkans, freeing the Imperial army to meet the other prong of that attack which would be launched in Galicia. Rudolf made no mention of a development of influence by the extension of Austrian culture and trade. He was now thinking in terms of straight power politics and ended with a plea to Kalnoky for immediate and decisive action, on which he stressed might hang the whole future of generations yet to come.[3]

Kalnoky's reply demolished the Crown Prince's thesis. He reasoned that whatever inducements were held out to them, the Balkan states could not be relied on in the event of a crisis, reiterated his perennial theme that Germany, the Monarchy's only firm ally, could not be counted on in the event of war with Russia in the Balkans, and concluded:

> I know that I am laying myself open to the reproach that my policy is not sufficiently clear cut and vigorous—but that is the lesser evil. The greater evil would be to involve the Monarchy in a war the outcome of which is uncertain. [4]

Rudolf did not attempt to argue further and his New Year letter to Szeps suggests that the fight was going out of him:

> We shall not have a peaceful year . . . the future may be dark, and there may be bloodshed.

He held firm to his conviction that the Monarchy had a mission to fulfil in the world, but saw himself playing little part in it:

> Don't overrate me because my speeches are not too bad and I can write fairly good books and articles . . . these are small things far removed from great achievements in world affairs. [5]

In the crisis which, as he correctly prophesied, arose in 1886 his role was passive compared to that of Archduke Johann Salvator.

Once again the crisis occurred in Bulgaria. The peace treaty which Alexander was forced to sign with Serbia seemed to his subjects to rob them of the fruits of their victory, and the wave of popular enthusiasm for the Prince evaporated. The Russians succeeded in suborning a number of officers who considered that after Slivnica they had not had the promotion which was due to them. Conspiracies multiplied—meetings at dead of night, oaths in front of Orthodox priests, secret comings and goings. Finally, late on the evening of August 21st, a group of Bulgarian officers forced their way into Alexander's palace and hustled him at revolver point to a Russian ship which was waiting on the Danube. For a few days there was no news and it was feared that he had been taken to Russia. Then on August 27th he turned up in Lemberg to hear that a government loyal to him had been formed forty-eight hours earlier, and to receive a telegram from it begging him to return to Bulgaria. Two days later he was back in Sofia, it seemed in triumph. But the Czar remained implacably hostile and Alexander's nerve broke. Within a fortnight of his return he abdicated, appointing a three-man Council of Regency to govern the country pending the election of his successor.

The kidnapping, triumphal return to Sofia and abdication of Alexander occurred within three weeks, and the whole episode was a severe shock to the fraternity of European rulers. Assassination they accepted as one of the hazards of their calling, but kidnapping with all the *lèse majesté* which it implied was another matter. No sovereign was more outraged than Queen Victoria, who lamented to the Prime Minister and the Foreign Secretary the 'cruel end' of the 'poor dear young Prince'. She fulminated against the 'Russian fiends' and demanded immediate action. Lord Salisbury, while denouncing the conduct of 'officers debauched with Russian gold', was, however, compelled to explain to Her Majesty that England was powerless to restore Prince Alexander to his throne. Bismarck was determined to do nothing except stop Austria and Russia from flying at each other's throats over Bulgaria. *The Times* came to the conclusion that:

> the fact must be faced that Austria is not prepared to burn a cartridge for the defence of Bulgaria. The discovery that the German alliance could not be depended upon has broken the nerve of the Empire's responsible rulers.[6]

Altogether the attitude to Bulgaria of the Powers resembled in the opinion of *The Times* that of

> five louts standing with their arms crossed while a girl is being maltreated before their eyes by a drunken Cossack,[7]

and nobody appeared to have any idea of how to prevent Bulgaria falling under Russian domination. Whether or not this would happen therefore depended on one man, the thirty-two-year-old leading member of the Regency Council in Sofia, Stefan Stambulov. While Bulgaria was ruled from Constantinople, Stambulov spent five years in Bucharest working for the revolutionary under-ground—five years of secret missions and hairbreadth escapes from the Turks. After his country was awarded her independence he became a deputy leader of the Liberal party, and eventually a firm supporter of Alexander of Battenberg under whom he fought as a private at Slivnica. When the Prince abdicated, the whole burden of preserving Bulgarian independence fell on his shoulders. Happily they were sturdy. Stambulov was an ardent patriot, a man of indomitable will and completely fearless who, from years of experience, knew how to match intrigue with intrigue. There was no tougher politician in the Balkans.

Stambulov attempted to persuade Alexander to return, but was unsuccessful. In November 1886 the Bulgarian National Assembly therefore elected Waldemar of Denmark, the brother-in-law of both the Prince of Wales and the Czar, as their Prince. It seemed a non-controversial choice, but the Czar refused to agree to it and put forward his own candidate in the person of one of his A.D.C.s, Prince Nicolas Dadian of Mingrelia. The name suggested the hero in the cast of an operetta. *The Times* informed its readers, most of whom had not the faintest idea of the whereabouts of Mingrelia, that the Prince came of an ancient family and was heavily in debt, observing no doubt accurately:

> It seems to be the opinion of the Czar that this 'Prince faineant' would make a very docile and submissive ruler of Bulgaria.[8]

Kalnoky described him as a 'Parisian boulevadier'. Queen Victoria sent a sharp telegram to Lord Salisbury:

> We must not and cannot agree to a Russian of very bad character being proposed for Bulgaria.[9]

Stambulov and his fellow Regents at once declared that under no circumstances would they accept Mingrelia as their Prince.

What *The Times* described as an 'interminable' string of possible alternatives for the Bulgarian throne (eventually totting up to a baker's three dozen) was then mentioned in the European Press and languidly discussed by the Powers. It included an assortment of German princelings, the Kings of Roumania, Serbia and

Montenegro, the Dukes of Edinburgh and Cumberland, a Turk, two of Louis Philippe's grandsons, the American General Sherman, the Belgian General Brialmont, several Russians, Prince Oskar of Sweden, and a Croatian Count who claimed descent from the original Kings of Bulgaria. Hungary was said to be teeming with noblemen who would be delighted to rule in Sofia. But amongst these candidates there was nobody both willing to accept the throne and acceptable to all the Powers and the Bulgarians and, apart from Russia, who continued to push the Prince of Mingrelia, no Power was prepared to come out in support of any of them. A total impasse seemed to have been reached. In an endeavour to break it, Stambulov and his fellow regents decided to send a three-man delegation abroad to hawk their throne round Europe. The delegation arrived in Vienna on the evening of December 7th. A few days later a strange combination of people—Princess Clementine of Sachsen-Coburg-Kohary, her son Ferdinand and Archduke Johann Salvator—became actively involved in the affairs of Bulgaria.

Princess Clementine, a daughter of the ex-King of France Louis Philippe, and the widow of a nephew of King Leopold I of Belgium was an immensely rich and formidable old lady nicknamed in Vienna 'Clementine de Medici'. Although she was so deaf that she was compelled to use a silver ear trumpet, little escaped her and she was regarded as having all the political ability and ambition of the House of Orléans. Of her three sons Philip, the eldest, was married to Crown Princess Stephanie's sister Louise, and August to a member of the reigning house of Brazil. Both these marriages were gratifying to the Princess's sense of rank, but she had even higher ambitions for her third son Ferdinand. To Clementine kingship was the most exalted profession in the world and therefore the only one which Ferdinand, on whom she doted, could contemplate. She was prepared to devote a great deal of effort and money to secure him a throne.

The object of these aspirations was not an attractive young man. Tall and plump with a slight stoop, he had a pale face, a nervous tic, furtive blue eyes and a very large nose. He spoke in a high pitched drawl, and it was difficult to discover what he really thought about anything. At the age of twenty he entered the cavalry, an unfortunate choice since he had a deplorable seat on a horse, and an almost hysterical fear of those animals. Before long he transferred to the infantry, but did not advance beyond the rank of lieutenant. However, if quite devoid of military ability, Ferdinand was no fool and could, if he chose to exert himself, flatter, cajole, get the best of any argument or tear a reputation to rags. Generally he did not so choose, and spent his time sauntering round Vienna, collecting stuffed birds and taking a dilettante interest in science. This Coburg Prince was not a popular member of the *jeunesse dorée* of the capital. They mocked his equestrian incompetence, could not understand his lack of interest in shooting, and gossiped about his curious habits, his love of wearing rich furs and his passion for jewellery. It was rumoured that he slept in pink nightgowns trimmed with lace, and his sister-in-law Louise alleged that he dabbled in black magic. Altogether there was much to suggest that he would be well cast as the Oscar Wilde of Central Europe.

The Prince however had no imperfections in the eyes of his mother, who when Alexander of Battenberg abdicated, evidently let it be known that her son was prepared to be considered as his successor. In November 1886 Kalnoky mentioned him as such to the British Chargé d'Affaires in Vienna, but added that while Ferdinand 'was undoubtedly very clever and intelligent . . . he had very delicate health and would never seriously think of accepting the post, though he might like to see his name brought forward'.[10] Kalnoky himself was certainly not going to do this, on the contrary he was bending over backwards to assure everyone that the Monarchy had no interest in any candidate whatsoever. It was soon apparent to the Princess that no official support for Ferdinand would be forthcoming, and that another means of drawing the Bulgarians' attention to him must be found. Towing her son in her wake who, while fancying the idea of himself in princely robes, was uncertain about exchanging the comforts of the Coburg Palace in Vienna for the rigours of Sofia, Clementine joined forces with Johann Salvator.

The Archduke possessed the means of putting Ferdinand in

touch with the Bulgarians, and for his own reasons was prepared to do so. Alexander of Battenberg's victory at Slivnica had impressed him with the fighting quality of that nation, and he was convinced that if trained in modern methods of warfare, they would provide an important bulwark against Russian expansion in the Balkans. Johann Salvator had a vision of himself as Commander-in-Chief of the Bulgarian army, a position which would give him the scope which, towards the end of 1886, he had abandoned all hope of achieving in the Monarchy. When Clementine's ambitions became known to him he saw his chance. The Archduke had the lowest opinion of Ferdinand as an officer, reporting when the Coburg Prince had served under him in Linz that he was totally unfit for promotion. But because Ferinand was flabby and quite uninterested in military affairs he would, Johann Salvator calculated, welcome a strong man at his side to deal with them. He therefore struck a bargain with Clementine. He would provide the introduction to the Bulgarians which she needed, and in return for this her son, if elected to the throne, would summon him to Sofia to take up the post of Commander-in-Chief there. It appeared that the Archduke's interests and those of the Princess coincided to their mutual benefit.

Some devious manœuvres now took place. Shortly after the Bulgarian delegation arrived in Vienna Ferdinand came secretly to Linz to see Johann Salvator, and over lunch discussed the question of his candidature for the Bulgarian throne. He appeared still 'to be divided between desire for a throne and fear of the dangers which always accompany such a position',[11] but presumably allowed himself to be overruled by his mother, for a few days later the Archduke acted. On the evening before the Bulgarian delegates were due to leave Vienna they went to Ronacher's, the Viennese music hall. There, in Box 27, they met a fellow countryman who introduced them to a retired Austrian officer, 'a certain Major Laaba', Johann Salvator's protégé whose reinstatement in rank the Archduke had finally wrenched out of Albrecht a few months earlier. Laaba after some general conversation remarked casually that he understood the delegates were looking for a Prince, and said that he could introduce them to Prince Ferdinand of Coburg. The Bulgarians, although many people in Vienna had been astonished to find 'three polished gentlemen speaking several languages', instead of 'three uncouth creatures wearing some national peasant costume and led about by an interpreter',[12] had been rebuffed by Kalnoky and the Russian Ambassador, both of whom said that they had no official status, and had made no progress with their mission. They therefore accepted Laaba's suggestion with alacrity, and postponed their departure. On the following day they were taken to a side door of the Palais Coburg and ushered into Ferdinand's presence. Although he was wearing full uniform they were not impressed by his appearance, but found that he knew a good deal about conditions in Bulgaria. It was agreed that his name should go forward for the throne, provided he could get the Emperor and the Czar of Russia to agree to his candidature.

So far Johann Salvator had used Laaba as his intermediary and remained in Linz away from the scene of action. He now decided that, agreement in principle having been reached between Ferdinand and the Bulgarians, he must take steps to further it. A few days later he came incognito to Vienna to meet his journalist confidant Heinrich Pollak in a private room in an unfashionable hotel, in order to discuss Ferdinand's candidature and the attitude of the Press towards it. At this meeting, according to Pollak, the Archduke gave two reasons for his support of the Coburg Prince. The first was his conviction that it was vital for the Monarchy to have a commanding position in the Balkans. The time had now come to seize it, and since Kalnoky would take no action, it was necessary to go over his head, say nothing to the Emperor, and produce a *fait accompli*. The second reason was that Ferdinand was a good choice for Bulgaria. He was rich, with powerful family connections and had behind him a mother of exceptional shrewdness and determination. The Bulgarian National Assembly could certainly be 'fixed' so that he would be elected, and once he was on the throne all the Powers would accept him. When the journalist queried Ferdinand's military ability Johann Salvator replied:

I shall be there. . . . I will simply get myself summoned by the Prince to Sofia where I will be nominated Commander-in-Chief and place myself at the head of the army. You can imagine how the future pattern will then develop.[13]

When Pollak asked the Archduke if the Crown Prince had been consulted about Ferdinand's candidature he received an evasive reply. In fact Johann Salvator had not taken Rudolf into his confidence because little if any confidence now existed between them. Therefore, although the news of the arrival in the field of this dark horse for the Bulgarian throne had appeared in the Press the day after the delegation had visited the Coburg Palace, for a few days the Crown Prince had no more idea than anybody else as to how, or by whom, the contact between Ferdinand and the Bulgarians had been effected. He then received a note from Kalnoky informing him that there was reason to suspect that the intermediary in the affair was Archduke Johann Salvator. Within a few hours the following tirade was on its way to the Foreign Minister:

Vienna, December 22nd
1886.

My dear Count,

As instructed by you Bombelles has just given me the very peculiar communication about Archduke Johann's role as an intermediary. I have already experienced a great deal of incorrect behaviour on the part of this gentleman, but to carry out a negotiation with a foreign deputation without permission of the Emperor, and behind his back and that of the Minister of Foreign Affairs in this critical time, is an action on the part of someone who is an Archduke and a General which must be most severely punished. What are we coming to when such things are possible within the Imperial Family and the army, when the Emperor can no longer rely on those who should be guided by no other principles than unquestioning obedience and absolute loyalty? If I may be permitted to offer you advice it is that after you have fully established the facts you should go to the Emperor, tell him what has occurred, and request him to put an absolute ban on such activities, for how can anyone carry on as Foreign Minister when behind his back Archdukes pursue their own foreign policy. . . .

Yours, Rudolf.[14]

In view of the Crown Prince's connection with Szeps he could hardly complain about anyone going behind the back of his father's Ministers. Johann Salvator was attempting to do what he himself had failed to achieve in his approach to Kalnoky a year earlier, to force some action to improve the position of the Monarchy in the Balkans. It might have been expected that, if Rudolf considered it impolitic to be enthusiastic about this initiative in public, privately he would have applauded it and if possible given it his support. The violent terms of his letter to Kalnoky suggest it seems that on the contrary, all he wished to do was to get the Archduke into trouble, and evidently this was not a passing mood. After seeing Johann Salvator in early January 1887, he told the Foreign Minister that he considered it desirable that a watch should be kept on his cousin whom he described as 'very agitated'.[15] It was the nadir of their relationship.

The Emperor's attitude remains an enigma. In view of his conviction that nobody, and particularly not a member of the Imperial Family, should presume to take action or even express an opinion about matters which did not concern them, it was to be expected that some form of punishment, or at least a severe reprimand, would be meted out to Johann Salvator. Nothing apparently happened. Possibly Franz Joseph was told nothing, possibly Kalnoky played the whole matter down. Certainly when, towards the end of January, the Archduke applied for permission to go abroad on leave, the Emperor raised no objection.

Johann Salvator travelled first to Trieste and from there went to Venice to keep a strange appointment for a Habsburg Archduke:

On the piazza I found the person who was waiting for me. After taking over the document which he had brought and discussing it with him, we lunched together and went to the Lido where we continued our conversation. The person left by the night express. I remained in Venice.[16]

The 'person' whom he met was Kaltchev of the Bulgarian delegation. He described to the Archduke the appalling position of Bulgaria and the poor impression which Ferdinand of Coburg had made on himself and his colleagues, and then came to the point. If Alexander of Battenberg persisted in his refusal to return to Sofia, would Johann Salvator himself be prepared to accept the Bulgarian throne? It was a flattering offer, but the Archduke firmly turned it down replying that he did not feel capable of succeeding Alexander and all he wished was 'to place his sword at the service of Bulgaria' should she have to fight to preserve her independence.[17] There the matter rested, and when his leave was up Johann Salvator returned to Linz.

By now Ferdinand's name was no longer discussed in connection with Bulgaria. The Czar dismissed the idea of his candidature as 'ridiculous', and Queen Victoria for once agreed with him. When she first heard of what had occurred Lord Salisbury received two telegrams in rapid succession:

16.12.86. Hope there is no truth in respect of Prince Ferdinand of Coburg as a candidate. He is totally unfit—delicate, eccentric and effeminate. Only seen it in *The Times*. Should be stopped at once.

17.12.86. It is important that it should be known that *I* and my family have nothing to do with the absurd pretensions of this foolish young cousin of mine.[18]

A few days later Princess Clementine, who in an endeavour to conjure up support for her son had appealed to Queen Victoria's Coburg family feeling, received the following snub from Windsor Castle:

Windsor, 21st December
1886.

My dear Clem,
I received your letter ... I must confess with some astonish-

ment. . . . Knowing how much you love your son I am astonished that you have even considered this proposal; in your
place I would be thankful if it were dropped.

I am as always your devoted cousin and faithful friend,

V.R.I.[19]

Bismarck continued to assert that what happened in Bulgaria was
a matter of perfect indifference to Germany, and Kalnoky maintained an attitude of silent detachment. It seemed that Prince
Ferdinand's candidature had disappeared below the political
horizon. Other names were discussed from time to time in the
Press or in diplomatic despatches, but without any great interest.
The throne of Bulgaria had been a problem for so long that
everyone had grown accustomed to living with it, and as no
disaster had yet occurred it was generally assumed that the
Regency could carry on.

In Linz, judging from his letters to his mother, Johann
Salvator was in an unsettled frame of mind. There was considerable international tension, and preparations were being made for
a possible war with Russia—somewhat belatedly for Albrecht,
still the Commander-in-Chief designate in the event of the outbreak of hostilities, was obliged for health reasons to spend the
winter at Arco in the Trentino, from where he conducted the
affairs of the army by post. Like other generals Johann Salvator
was occupied with preparations for mobilization, but he appeared
to have lost interest in his military career, writing in February:

> If there is no war I intend to take a year's leave if not more, in
> order to rest and enjoy the only diversion which really appeals
> to me, which is sailing.[20]

In April after an audience with the Emperor he told his mother:

> His Majesty explicitly declared that he would make me Com-
> mander of an Army Corps when the first vacancy occurred,
> and that he would 'order' me to accept this, for he could not
> approve of my doubts as to my ability. . . . This declaration
> may soon be implemented. . . . There is nothing which I can

do but to resign either before or after the appointment is made.[21]

He rearranged his financial affairs.

Tomorrow the 1st March 400,000 florins will be paid to me from the Family Fund . . . in return for the cessation of my allowance. It is not profitable for me, but circumstances could arise in which it would be to my advantage to have nearly half a million in hand. . . . All my patrimony which consists of Austrian and Italian bonds is deposited in Switzerland. . . . In this way I think I can deal with any eventuality.[22]

In this mood of uncertainty about the future Johann Salvator became increasingly reckless of what he said or did. He delivered a lecture to the Officers' Club in Linz on the theatre of war against Russia, and followed this up by calling in Vienna on the Russian General Kaulbars. The former was embarrassing to Kalnoky who was struggling to preserve peace; the latter could be construed as having contact with a hostile foreign national. Kaulbars had been forced by the Czar for a time on to Alexander of Battenberg as Minister of War in Bulgaria, and while there he had made himself notorious by his efforts to align the Bulgarians on the side of Russia. He was not regarded as a friend of the Monarchy, and was evidently under surveillance while on leave in Austria. The Archduke's call on him was immediately reported to the Emperor, and Johann Salvator received a curt note asking him to explain to His Imperial Majesty why he had made it, what had been discussed at it and the reason for his 'long-standing' contact with Kaulbars. In his reply the Archduke made out the best case he could. When Kaulbars had first written to him from Sofia[23] he had passed the letter on to Kalnoky. Since then the General, when on leave in Austria, had sought him out, and had offered to arrange a visit to Russia for him (of which Kalnoky had been informed and which had come to nothing), but their meetings had been purely social. The recent call was a matter of courtesy, although in the course of it the General's time in Bulgaria had been discussed. At a subsequent audience with the Emperor Johann Salvator succeeded in reassuring Franz Joseph both about his lecture at Linz and about his contact with Kaulbars. Astonishingly, the question of his activities in connection with Ferdinand of Coburg's candidature for the Bulgarian throne was not raised by the Emperor. He may still have been ignorant of them, or he may have been advised by Kalnoky that, while no official support could be given to Ferdinand, he would serve the interests of the Monarchy better than any other candidate. If therefore he managed to get himself elected Prince of Bulgaria so much the better, and in the meantime the best thing to do was to turn a blind eye to the whole affair. Whatever the explanation, the fact that at this audience Franz Joseph reiterated his decision to appoint Johann Salvator to command an Army Corps suggests that he entertained no doubts of the latter's personal loyalty.

The Archduke had developed a talent for sailing very close to the wind of Imperial displeasure without disaster, and continued to do so. Within a few days of seeing the Emperor he was in touch with Stoilov, another member of the Bulgarian delegation. Whatever attitude the Powers might adopt, Stambulov was insistent that Bulgaria must have a Prince, and as soon as possible. Stoilov had been sent back to Vienna with a mandate to persuade Ferdinand to go to Roumania to await his election by the Bulgarian National Assembly, and from there to make his formal entry into Sofia. The Prince procrastinated. 'It appears,' Johann Salvator wrote to his mother, 'that he has not got the courage to do this.' His own attitude he assured her remained unchanged. 'I have *explicitly declined* the renewed request. I do not want a throne, only peace.'[24] He returned to his post, leaving Laaba to keep in touch with the situation.

Some weeks later Stoilov came to see the Archduke in Linz. He told him that he could make no progress with Ferdinand who imposed impossible conditions and seemed to be incapable of making up his mind. Once again in the name of the Regency he offered Johann Salvator the Bulgarian throne. Once again, and this time finally, the Archduke refused, explaining that since his election would contravene the Treaty of Berlin it would not be in

Bulgaria's interests, but reiterating that in the event of war he would gladly fight to defend that country. Shortly after this he went abroad on leave. When, on July 7th, the Bulgarian National Assembly formally elected Ferdinand as their Prince, Johann Salvator was sailing off the coast of Belgium.

PART THREE

Rien ne va plus

CHAPTER 11

The Beginning of the End

During his leave in the summer of 1887, Johann Salvator based himself on an hotel in Ostend, did not go to the Kursaal, avoided meeting people, and although he assured his mother that he was taking no unnecessary risks while sailing, had a foreboding of some unspecified disaster. 'I am certain I shall not have seventy years of activity, even if the Lord spares me for so long.'[1] He returned to his post, however, on August 5th for the summer manœuvres, and appeared to have no immediate plans for a change in his career. But on September 14th he suddenly left for England and ten days later it was announced in the *Military Gazette* that at his own request he had been relieved from the command of the 3rd Infantry Division. Within six weeks something unexpected had happened to justify his foreboding.

Three days after the Archduke's return to the Monarchy, Ferdinand of Coburg, accompanied by a small suite, departed to Sofia. The coincidence of dates has led to the assumption that the Emperor, enraged by Johann Salvator's excursion into politics when promoting Ferdinand's candidature for the Bulgarian throne, either sacked the Archduke or forced him to resign from his command. There are, however, a number of grounds for querying this. When Ferdinand finally agreed to go to Bulgaria, Johann Salvator was a thousand miles away in Belgium, and so could not have influenced this decision. Moreover, neither the Emperor nor the Crown Prince were now wholly averse to it, for as Rudolf told Kalnoky, they had come round to the point of view that once Ferdinand was established in Sofia he might be of some use to the Monarchy. Admittedly Laaba, known to be Johann Salvator's intermediary in the whole affair, said that he was going on a visit to Roumania and Serbia, and then accompanied Ferdinand to Sofia as the latter's 'invited guest', a deception which gave grounds for suspecting that the Archduke might be planning some further intrigue in Bulgaria. But the Emperor knew about this on August 10th. Why then did he wait until mid-September to take action against Johann Salvator? Alternatively, why, if he considered that the Archduke should be punished for promoting Ferdinand's candidature had he not done so before? A possible explanation may be that Johann Salvator had very nearly made himself liable for punishment, but not quite. He had not attempted to emulate the example of Ferdinand Max and establish himself on the throne of a separate kingdom; nor could he be accused of acting unpatriotically, for the result of his initiative was to provide a Prince for Bulgaria more acceptable to the Monarchy than any of the other candidates who had been suggested. Therefore, from Franz Joseph's point of view, while his interest in politics was undesirable and he must certainly be watched, his behaviour had not yet been such as to call for his summary dismissal from the army.

A clue as to what may have precipitated the premature end of the Archduke's military career is to be found in a letter which Ferdinand, his elder brother, later wrote to their mother, Grand Duchess Maria Antonia.[2] In this Ferdinand gave a long list of Johann Salvator's mistakes and failings but made no mention of the Bulgarian affair. He did, however, refer to an incident which evidently occurred during the summer manœuvres of 1887.

> I can understand that having ability and talent and having made a real success in Bosnia, it upset him to be condemned to appear to be beaten in an exercise, which perhaps was strategically not very well conducted, by his nominal opponent Archduke Rudolf.

But, the Grand Duke of Tuscany went on to indicate, Johann Salvator instead of accepting that this was necessary because Rudolf was heir to the throne 'behaved and acted in a manner which made bad blood. Then came the distressing flight to London. . . .' The credibility of this account is enhanced by the fact that the Archduke had already complained about being ordered to 'fix' exercises so that Rudolf appeared in them to the best advantage. He could well have lost his temper, told Albrecht exactly what he thought about this, and a great deal else besides, and when ordered to apologise refused to do so.

Certainly shortly after he returned from leave Johann Salvator was convinced that he was under surveillance, his letters were being opened, and that his enemies were insinuating to the Emperor that his ultimate aim was to seize the Bulgarian throne for himself. He now bitterly regretted that he had not gone to Sofia under some assumed name in order to hold Ferdinand, from whom there was no word, to his promise. It seemed probable that the army appointment for which he had hoped in Bulgaria would not now materialise, and if he had lost Franz Joseph's confidence there was no future worth naming for him in the Monarchy. When the Archduke received from Rudolf the 'shattering news' that the Emperor no longer trusted him, it was the last straw. He could no longer combat his persecutors; all he could do was to place himself beyond their reach. He wrote to Franz Joseph, resigned his command, asked for permission to go abroad, and left for England to seek the only means of escape now open to him—the sea.

From England Johann Salvator sent a farewell message to all ranks who had served under him. He also wrote to the Mayor of Linz, thanking him for his unfailing help and co-operation and saying that he would always remember the city and its inhabitants with the utmost affection. During the time the Archduke was stationed there he had taken care to promote good relations between troops and civilians, and supported and encouraged a number of cultural and charitable activities. As a result he had become exceptionally popular, and after his departure the city council unanimously voted that he be awarded the freedom of Linz, a mark of appreciation never before conferred by any place in the Monarchy on any Archduke. When the news of this honour, the highest which the citizens of Linz could bestow, reached Johann Salvator he telegraphed accepting it with enthusiasm and gratitude. So far as the Emperor was concerned this hammered another nail into the Archduke's coffin.

Franz Joseph first learnt of the award from the newspapers, and at once wrote in a state of extreme irritation to Count Taaffe.

I see from the newspapers that the Linz city council has awarded Archduke Johann the freedom of the city. As far as I know nothing like this has ever occurred. Such an award seems to be hardly compatible with the status of a member of the Imperial Family and creates a precedent for the future. I request you to let me know whether you consider it would be possible to annul the city council's resolution. The papers also contain a letter from Archduke Johann thanking the Mayor of Linz which is tendentious and full of misstatements; it therefore appears to be all the more necessary to take firm action in this affair.[3]

Taaffe replied that unfortunately no legal means existed for annulling the resolution, but agreed that it was most undesirable that anything of the sort should occur again, for it could involve members of the Imperial Family in undesirable local affiliations and political entanglements. He suggested that the Emperor should address a letter to all Archdukes, informing them of Johann Salvator's misdemeanour and ordering them to refuse any similar award which might be offered to them. Franz Joseph did this and also sent a sharp note to Johann Salvator:

The announcement in the Press of your thanks for the freedom of the city awarded to you by Linz, compels me to draw your attention to the fact that the acceptance of such a distinction by any member of my armed forces is dependent on my permission. In this case I am not prepared to give it, because the acceptance of the freedom of a city is not compatible with the position of a member of the Imperial Family. I leave it to you to refuse the offer made to you by the city of Linz.

Franz Joseph.[4]

To insubordination and meddling in politics Johann Salvator had added the cardinal sin of becoming too popular. And, although no longer actively employed in the army, he had only achieved a partial freedom. Whether in the Monarchy or abroad, as an officer and an Archduke he was still subject to Imperial discipline; this, as he learnt from an order which reached him at the beginning of October, meant that he must inform the Emperor of his plans and whereabouts. Meanwhile Franz Joseph had received a report from his Military Attaché in London, according to which the Archduke's behaviour gave no grounds for complaint. He was staying incognito at the Hotel Victoria, Charing Cross, accompanied by Baron Mensshengen and an Austrian naval officer, Count Messey, had contacted the Embassy, giving instructions about the forwarding of letters, and was engaged in the innocuous occupation of buying a yacht, in which he proposed to sail as soon as possible to Nice and the Riviera.

The report said nothing of the Archduke's frame of mind. Of this his mother was better informed. Johann Salvator wrote to her on September 23rd shortly after reaching England, describing his search for the yacht, 'which will be my home for some time'. He was waiting anxiously for the Emperor's reply to his letter.

> His Majesty can always either graciously give me the only possible satisfaction, or permit my 'effacement'. . . . If neither one or the other are explicitly conceded and they thus expect to get hold of me, I assure you dearest Mamma that I shall await the necessary guarantee *outside the Monarchy*.[5]

A week later defiance was turning into bitterness and depression.

> I see from the Gazette of the 24th of September that His Majesty the Emperor has deigned to permit my retirement from active service. No other notification has reached me, and I sense from this the manner in which my action has been judged. Ferdinand too, to whom I sent the draft of my letter to the Head of the Family, has up to the present shown no sign of life. I am well aware that something like this cannot be done without causing trouble but—I am honest enough to admit it—I assumed that the rights and undeserved sorrow of a loyal individual, perhaps too loyal, and possibly also able,

would be appreciated. However, there it is, and I do not assume that they are saying I am a loss to the State. In addition my plans to sail to the Mediterranean have met with no comment.

'Silence gives consent' says the proverb. . . . The yacht which I have bought cost £1,500 . . . which does not seem to be excessive given that I have a small palace transportable to wherever I like in the world—or to put it better—wherever I dislike least. Afloat and sailing at least I cannot be accused of political intrigues.[6]

At Cherbourg two days out from England Johann Salvator was still thoroughly dispirited.

I have only received a notification from the Emperor repeating what is already in the Gazette, and informing me that His Majesty wishes to be informed from time to time of my plans and whereabouts. . . . Otherwise nobody has written to me . . . which shows the general feeling. If they knew how much I have suffered to see myself so misjudged after a voluntary sacrifice . . . they would be less indignant.[7]

When he reached Lisbon in early December he embarked on a passenger steamer for Madeira and the Canary Islands, planning to rejoin his yacht in the Mediterranean, and telling his mother:

Knowing my sorrows as you do only too well, you can equally well understand that I must seek for new impressions to distract and comfort me. . . . It is certain that I shall be pardoned if it is known that I am still voyaging in search of far off lands.[8]

But by the beginning of 1888 when Johann Salvator rejoined his yacht no pardon was forthcoming. Mensshengen had been relieved from his post at his own request. The Archduke (for he still considered himself as such and therefore entitled to a gentleman-in-waiting) telegraphed the head of the Emperor's Military Chancery for a replacement, and eventually Baron de Fin arrived, a dull old gentleman who frankly admitted to Johann

Salvator that he had been instructed to observe and report on the latter's mental state. For a while anger replaced depression. The Archduke was 'furious with those who have made the Emperor believe that I am insane', furious with the rumours that were circulating about him—that he had gone to Russia, would marry the Queen of Spain, had married secretly in Linz; furious because 'they' wanted to stop him from entering the Monarchy to visit his mother at Arco on Lake Garda, 'saying that it would be better for me to make further journeys and what do you think they have suggested . . . that I should go to Massawa where the poor Italians are being exterminated by cholera!'9

At the end of 1887 the British Military Attaché in Vienna informed London:

> It is reported that the Archduke Johann is returning to Austria and will take up his residence at Gmunden under an assumed title. It is to be hoped that in the event of war his services may be utilised.10

Johann Salvator, however, saw no prospect of re-employment in the army when early in the following year he obtained permission to visit his mother at Arco. Two other questions therefore preoccupied him. Would it be possible to effect some sort of reconciliation with the Crown Prince? Was there any chance of a post in Bulgaria? He wrote to Weilen who was in close contact with Rudolf about the former problem:

> I would gladly have written long ago to the Crown Prince . . . but I feared and still fear to be met with an unfavourable reception . . . I believe that I can only hope for a return of his good will through a wholehearted apology for a decision which I took, not without reason, but which was incorrect and which I deeply regret.11

Weilen was reassuring, and in a further letter the Archduke told him:

> I wrote to the Crown Prince and told him what I feel and hold to be true. Believe me I know I have been at fault, but I have been through an inquest on myself which I would not have

wished on my worst enemy and which—I confess to you
frankly—has for the time being broken my spirit and clouded
my soul.[12]

The result of Johann Salvator's efforts to ascertain whether there
was any future for him in Bulgaria were not so happy, and finally
in despair he sent a letter by special messenger to Laaba.

At the New Year I telegraphed to you both in Sofia and in
Vienna, but you have made no sign of life. As I know you too
well to assume that you have forgotten me, I must conclude
that you have some reason for being annoyed with me. . . .
I should be grateful if you would tell me how I can write to
Prince Ferdinand, for I cannot send letters from or transitting
Austria: some of them are opened, some confiscated. I long to
tell my cousin how much I admire his noble and courageous
bearing, and also to clarify things between us in a friendly
manner.

Since I—overwhelmed by my Emperor's mistrust of my
not dishonourable part in the Bulgarian affair—have been
wandering the world seeking forgetfulness, I have had to suffer
the meanest intrigues and suspicions, and have been the object
of the most fantastic newspaper reports . . . I cannot wait for
war to break out.[13]

Two days later the Archduke left Arco to resume his aimless
sailing round the Mediterranean. At the beginning of May he
put into Venice where he offended von Warsberg, the Imperial
Consul-General, by failing to report his arrival, and outraged de
Fin, still reluctantly in attendance on him, because he made no
attempt to conceal the presence of 'a lady' on board his yacht.
de Fin removed himself in dudgeon to an hotel on the mainland
and wrote to the Emperor about the Archduke's scandalous
behaviour. Johann Salvator also wrote complaining about the
Baron. Franz Joseph ordered the Archduke to return at once to
Schloss Orth. After his departure de Fin and von Warsberg
discussed His Imperial Highness's misdemeanours at length.
The latter reported to Kalnoky that de Fin had no words bad
enough for this delinquent Habsburg and considered that his

Crown Prince Rudolf

Crown Princess Stephanie

undisciplined and immoral character could only be cured by
expelling him from the Imperial Family and giving him what
he apparently wished, the chance under another name of enjoying the freedom which he apparently prized more than anything else. . . . He was so arrogant that when he discovered
what it was like to be treated as an ordinary citizen he would
beg to have his title restored. I myself, [the Consul General
concluded], have observed this gentleman's arrogance in spite
of his radical talk.[14]

Franz Joseph did not compel the Archduke to remain at
Schloss Orth, and in the course of the summer allowed him to
make another cruise in the Adriatic. But now even sailing failed
to raise Johann Salvator's spirits. By the end of the year when,
having laid up his yacht for the winter, he once again returned to
his house, he felt himself to be looking down a long dark tunnel
at the end of which there was no light.

Here in Orth it is very lonely . . . my life—it is no life—my
existence is like the misty, gloomy, blank empty autumn days
in the mountains.[15]

Rudolf too was looking down a long dark tunnel. In his case
however the trouble was not lack of occupation, but a sense of
futility combined with apprehension for the future. He did not
conceal this from Szeps when the latter congratulated him on his
thirtieth birthday in 1888.

'The age of thirty marks a dividing point in life and one that
is not too pleasant either. Much time has passed, spent more or
less usefully but empty so far as real acts and successes are
concerned. We are living in a time of slow, drawn-out rotten-
ness, no one knows for how long we are to continue in this
way, and each year makes me older, less fresh and less efficient.
The necessary daily routine is, in the long run, very tiring and
this eternal preparing of oneself, this constant waiting for times
of great reform, wears out one's creative power. . . . A time
of war must come soon, a great time in which we will be
happy, since after its glorious end we can build the foundations

of a great and peaceful Austria. A lifetime that is spent in cease-
less movement often, in fact usually, exhausted and strained
by manifold activities, is short when one measures it in terms
of real spiritual activity.[16]

Unable to see any means of reconciling the conflicting claims of
the various nationalities in the Monarchy Rudolf, although it
outraged his liberal ideals, now reluctantly subscribed to the
Emperor's belief in the necessity of a strong centralised government supported by the army. He still dreamt of reigning over a
Danubian Empire, but had no idea of how that dream could be
fulfilled except by a war and this, whatever he might write to
Szeps, he was torn between longing for and dreading. And he
now had serious misgivings about the value of the keystone of
his father's foreign policy, the German alliance. There had been
changes in Berlin which, from the Crown Prince's point of view,
were not for the better.

In the spring of 1888 'Old Wilhelm' died at the age of ninety.
His successor Friedrich, fatally ill with cancer of the throat, only
reigned for a hundred days, and his son then ascended the
throne as Emperor Wilhelm II. The new German Emperor was
self-willed, tactless and impulsive, a militarist with inflated dreams
of glory and a tendency to strike attitudes. When made an
Admiral of the Fleet by his grandmother Queen Victoria, he
wrote to the British Ambassador in Berlin:

Fancy wearing the same uniform as St. Vincent and Nelson;
it is enough to make one quite giddy. I feel something like
Macbeth must have felt when he was suddenly received by the
witches with the cry of 'All hail who art Thane of Glamis and
of Cawdor too.'[17]

He was capable of extreme rudeness, and before his succession
had grossly insulted Rudolf in public. The Crown Prince did not
conceal the fact that the two of them had absolutely nothing in
common, and that he both disliked and mistrusted Wilhelm. The
latter's accession to the throne increased the doubts which he
already entertained about the value of the German alliance. In
despair he began to toy with the idea of seeking a rapprochement

with Russia, a change of stance which did not escape notice in Berlin. Bismarck evidently was not greatly perturbed. He agreed with Prince Reuss, the German Ambassador in Vienna, that Rudolf's moods fluctuated, and was confident that his views constituted no serious danger to the alliance, for he was still allowed by his father no share in the framing of policy.

Although Franz Joseph had no opinion of his son's political theories, he required him to undertake an increasing number of representational duties. In the spring and early summer of 1887 the Crown Prince was sent to Hungary, to Berlin for the celebration of the German Emperor's ninetieth birthday, and then to England for Queen Victoria's Jubilee celebrations. While Rudolf was in London the Prince of Wales, who was fond of him, entertained him at several parties which were 'very animated' and lasted into the small hours of the morning. Queen Victoria invested him with the Order of the Garter, and he sat next to her at one of the State lunches, in the course of which she found that he 'spoke most warmly and kindly of how anxious he was for a friendly alliance'.[18] Count Karl Kinsky, who was attached to the Austro-Hungarian Embassy in London, confirmed to Kalnoky that the Crown Prince had made an excellent impression on everyone with whom he came in contact. Kinsky, a prominent member of the Marlborough House set and regarded, as the Duke of Portland said, by London society as 'one of us' after he had won the Grand National, added that he found His Imperial Highness, whom he had not seen for some time, greatly altered for the better.

I noticed two things which particularly pleased me. First he has—I was previously not quite sure of this—what I call the 'Austrian grace of manner', and secondly I noted how much he looks up to the Emperor and regards him as an example. This too I had not expected, assuming rather . . . that his motto was opposition for the sake of opposition . . . I was delighted.[19]

The Crown Prince left England and the Count retreated thankfully to Newmarket to recover from the rigours of the visit, each day of which he complained had lasted from dawn until dawn.

Rudolf however two days after returning to Vienna set out on an extensive tour of Galicia. It was a success, but he returned from it exhausted and, determined to get away for a few days before the Bruck manœuvres began, requested that the newspapers should make no mention of his whereabouts.

> For otherwise I will not be left in peace by the Ballplatz, by officials, by Weilen, by relations and friends. From my return I have done nothing but see people, and now I must have a few days complete rest.[20]

The rest, such as it was, evidently did not help a great deal. The manœuvres began a fortnight later and the Crown Prince was soon complaining of the heat:

> I am dripping with sweat all day and all night. Of course that makes me fearfully thirsty, so I am constantly drinking champagne which makes me sweat still more.[21]

of inability to sleep, 'something which I have practically given up', and that he was dead tired.

In 1888 the pressure on Rudolf increased. The Emperor appointed him Inspector General of the Infantry, announcing that this was a mark of Imperial regard for the main branch of the army. In this newly-created post it was incumbent on the Crown Prince to visit units in the outlying provinces of the Monarchy. Once again as soon as spring began he was constantly on the move. By the end of August he had been twice to Galicia and once to Hungary to inspect troops, toured Bosnia and Herzegovina, and represented the Emperor in Berlin both at Wilhelm I's funeral and at the celebration of the accession of his shortlived successor Friedrich III. There was no prospect of a let up in the autumn. The Prince of Wales, who had been appointed Honorary Colonel of the Austrian 12th Hussars, was due to arrive in early September to attend the manœuvres in which his regiment was taking part, after which he proposed to spend several weeks in the Monarchy shooting. At the beginning of October the Prince's nephew, the new German Emperor Wilhelm II, was coming to Vienna for his first State Visit since his accession.

The juxtaposition of visits proved to be unfortunate. Wilhelm II, on extremely bad terms with his uncle, announced that he did not wish the latter to be present during his State Visit. The two of them in Kalnoky's view could quarrel as much as they liked, but not in Vienna. The Prince of Wales must therefore be persuaded to absent himself while the German Emperor was there. The news of this unhappy situation was broken to the Prince by Rudolf and Kalnoky when he arrived. Predictably very annoyed indeed by his nephew's attitude, he nevertheless agreed, out of consideration for Franz Joseph, to go to Bucharest at the beginning of October to stay with the King of Roumania while Wilhelm II was in the Imperial capital. In the meantime he must be entertained, and entertaining the heir to the English throne was, as many European royalties had discovered, a test of endurance. The Prince had unending vitality, disliked going to bed before the early hours of the morning, was a charming guest when amused, but if bored made no attempt to conceal the fact. State dinners at the Hofburg were no solution to the problem, for they were over by ten and the rest of the evening had still to be filled in. Shooting must be arranged. Much of this devolved on Rudolf. 'Wales . . . is in excellent spirits, and wants to see and do everything; as ever he is quite untiring.' The Crown Prince could not say the same of himself, 'I am tired and long for a rest'. Nevertheless he gladly invited 'Wales' to a bear shoot at Görgeny on his return from Roumania.

I am happy to invite Wales. Wilhelm I would only want to invite in order to arrange a neat hunting accident which would remove him from the world.[22]

After some late evenings in Vienna and Budapest followed by shooting in Hungary, the Prince of Wales left for Roumania. Rudolf returned to Vienna to endure the German Emperor's visit during which, at a State banquet, he was obliged to listen to his father proposing a toast to the Germany army, 'that perfect model of all military virtues',[23] and to put up with insinuations by Wilhelm that he was an incompetent Inspector General of the

Infantry. Eventually the German Emperor, showering the Order of the Black Eagle studded with diamonds about him, departed and Rudolf left at once for Görgeny to continue the entertainment of the Prince of Wales. Unfortunately the shoot was not a success for no bears appeared. 'The Crown Prince,' Wales wrote to the future King George V, 'was dreadfully put out . . . but we were a very cheery party—capital cook, Hungarian band and splendid weather.'[24] The party then moved on to Neuburg in Styria where a chamois shoot provided better sport, and which the Prince found 'the prettiest spot I have seen for a long time'.[25] He left for Paris in a very good humour having, thanks to Rudolf, thoroughly enjoyed his stay in the Monarchy.

Although the Crown Prince was capable of rising to an occasion, it became apparent during the second half of 1888 that he could not always be relied upon to do so. He was noticed to be distrait at public ceremonies, late for parades and inclined when he eventually arrived to gaze vacantly into space, or to be more interested in the removal of mud from his riding boots than the troops whom he was reviewing. Many people remarked that he looked grey and unwell. In fact Rudolf had not been fit for three years. Early in 1886 he was laid up with an illness which a recent study of the medicines, prepared for him on his doctor's orders by the Court Dispensary, indicates was gonorrhoea.[26] A year later he had a severe attack of bronchitis and violent attacks of coughing which, while on an official visit to Berlin, he could only control by taking morphine, as he acknowledged 'an injurious drug'.[27] In the following spring inflammation of the eyes for a time prevented him shooting, and towards the end of the summer of 1888 after a riding accident he began to suffer from bad headaches.

The treatment for gonorrhoea was painful, and in those days it was seldom completely cured. The knowledge that he had contracted this disease with its possible effect on his virility must have been devastating to Rudolf whose attitude to women resembled that of a huntsman out for a series of kills. Moreover, it seems probable that he infected Stephanie. She herself in her reminiscences alleged that this was so and, bitter and biassed though she then was about everything to do with the Crown Prince, the fact that she became ill shortly after he did and was attended by a gynaecologist, suggests that on this point she may have been truthful. It is likely therefore that, in addition to the shock of the discovery that he had damaged his own health, Rudolf was burdened with the knowledge that he himself had probably destroyed his chance of having a son.

The Crown Prince and Princess continued to make some public appearances together and to exchange letters (which in his case although they ended with some expression of affection now opened coldly 'Dear Stephanie' and became shorter and shorter), but behind this façade their marriage had collapsed. That Rudolf should be unfaithful to her from time to time, as he had been for several years, can hardly have surprised Stephanie. She must have known of her father's behaviour, and learnt that there was nothing extraordinary in married Princes indulging in an occasional extramatrimonial adventure. But, unlike Princess Alexandra, who managed to regard the Prince of Wales's affairs as a necessary diversion for him, and who continued to dote on him, providing a base to which he could and did return, Stephanie was incapable of handling the situation and regarded it as an insult to herself and her position. According to one story she discovered that Rudolf and some brother officers were entertaining an opera singer, drove in her State carriage to the house in question, found the Crown Prince's private fiaker standing outside, ordered it to take her home, and left Rudolf—his incognito destroyed—to return in her carriage with a liveried coachman on the box.[28] This incident may well have occurred. Concerned above all with the dignities and representational aspects of her position, opening exhibitions and patronising balls as if the future of the Monarchy depended on it, the Crown Princess made no effort to understand her husband, preaching and nagging at him when he came home late, in a voice which was said to resemble a foghorn. Homecoming became less and less attractive, and Rudolf absented himself more and more. Stephanie by this time bored him. She shared none of his intellectual interests, their values were different and no form of mutual respect existed between them. Each became towards the other calculating, ungenerous and egotistical.

Frustration and depression about the future, a wrecked marriage and frequent ill-health were enough to impose a strain on any man, however equable his temperament, who was obliged to make continual public appearances. Rudolf did not possess an equable temperament. Kinsky noticed his lack of nervous stamina when he was in London.

> Only one thing distresses me; he is nervy. It is a fact. I knew this from before and noticed it here. It is his misfortune. He fights against it, but it persists. . . . He can do nothing about this.[29]

The Count was right. Rudolf tried to get his nerves under control, to beat them down, by fast reckless driving, by taking risks out shooting. He endeavoured to steel himself against the fear of death by a constant contemplation of it—in the autumn of 1887 he obtained a skull which thereafter stood on his writing table. It was a lonely struggle, and one in which there was little to help him. A prayer which he wrote and which was found amongst his papers after his death, shows that he was not an atheist, but he was an agnostic and the comfort of orthodox religious belief was therefore denied to him. He had no intimate friends and was becoming estranged from his family. Elisabeth, the one person capable of understanding him, was preoccupied by her own ailments, by her new interest in classical Greece, and she was spending more and more time abroad. When Rudolf saw his mother he could not bring himself to confide in her. At a Court banquet in 1888, alarmed by his paleness and the black lines under his eyes she asked him if he was ill. He fobbed her off by saying that he was merely tired.

The Empress noticed that her son did not look well; his relatives found the Crown Prince cold and sarcastic, and some of them observed that he appeared to be on bad terms with Stephanie. The Crown Princess knew that her husband was drinking. Otto, one of the wilder of the young Archdukes, knew that Rudolf, in order to have money available to meet expenses which he did not wish to come to the knowledge of his secretariat, had borrowed heavily from Baron Hirsch. Count Orsini Rosenberg the A.D.C., one of whose duties was to keep His Imperial Highness's engagement diary, must have noticed the change in the names which appeared in it. Intellectuals were now replaced by aristocrats interested mainly in shooting such as Count Josef Hoyos and Prince Philip of Coburg, interspersed with Hungarian magnates such as Count Pista Karolyi who were identified with the movement to obtain still more privileges for the Magyars. Rosenberg also knew, for from time to time he had to make discreet arrangements for her to accompany the Crown Prince when he went on tours of inspection, that a certain Mitzi Caspar played an important part in Rudolf's life.

Mitzi Caspar has been variously described as a soubrette, a dancer or a photographer's model. In fact she had no profession other than that of a '*süsses Mädel*—sweet girl'—and like most of her kind in Vienna was sentimental but endowed with a great deal of cheerful common sense, soothing and holding love lightly. She probably came to Vienna from Graz in 1882, and if Rudolf's sister-in-law, Louise of Coburg, is to be believed, shortly after that became the Crown Prince's mistress; certainly by 1887 she was in a position to buy an expensive house. She appears to have played something of the same role in Rudolf's life as Milli Stubel did in Johann Salvator's—someone from whom he might stray and absent himself for a time, but to whom he returned, someone with whom he could spend a few hours in a world of Viennese *gemütlichkeit*. In 1887, as his struggle to control his nerves failed, and as, through lack of concentration he was unable to write, Rudolf began to escape more and more into this world, slipping out of the Hofburg by a back entrance to be taken by Bratfisch, his private fiaker driver, to some rendezvous, or to a tavern where he remained until the early hours of the morning, drinking and singing Viennese songs with his father's humbler subjects, returning as dawn was breaking to be helped to bed by his valet Loschek.

Rudolf was careful to conceal his nocturnal adventures, and probably only Bratfisch and Loschek were fully aware of them.

But whereas a number of people had noticed a change, or at least a physical deterioration, in the Crown Prince, the Emperor apparently had noticed nothing. Communication between father and son was down to a minimum, and it is likely that when they had a discussion alone together Franz Joseph treated his heir as he did his ministers, confining the interview to whatever point he wished to raise and then terminating it. Although quick to notice a button out of place on a uniform or a mistake in ceremonial, where people were concerned the Emperor had no insight and was not an observant man. When they were out shooting together he had one personal experience of his son's tendency to lose control of himself and act wildly. Rudolf disobeyed one of the cardinal rules, left his stand, swung round and fired, narrowly missing his father and wounding his loader. He was sent off the beat for the rest of the day, but apart from that Franz Joseph took no further action.

The Emperor was also astonishingly inactive about another and very much more reprehensible episode. Three of the younger members of the Imperial Family when out riding encountered a peasant funeral procession, set their horses at the waggon carrying the coffin, and jumped over it. The story leaked out and a German nationalist deputy Pernerstorfer quoted it in Parliament. There was an uproar and what the British Ambassador described to Lord Salisbury as:

> Disorderly conduct for which it would hardly be possible to find a parallel in Continental Europe. . . . Certain members of the Extreme Left party indulged in the most disgraceful language, making hardly concealed references of the most insulting character to members of the Imperial family, and personal allusions such as have never been employed in any parliament. [30]

A few days later Pernerstorfer was beaten up by two unknown assailants. Stephanie many years later alleged that the members of the Imperial Family involved in the incident were Rudolf and the Archdukes Otto and Franz Ferdinand. Otto certainly was and so, according to several Italian newspapers, was the Crown

Prince. By his own admission Rudolf organised the beating up of Pernerstorfer, about which he wrote with some satisfaction to Stephanie:

> The police have given me some anxious hours; they have been on the trail, and have discovered the regiment from which the riding whips came. They could not get hold of the men concerned for we spirited them off in good time, one of them to southern Hungary, and the other to Herzegovina. Still it took all my brazenness to save myself and Bolla[31] from trouble.[32]

The Emperor did very little about the whole affair. After Pernerstorfer's disclosures he interviewed some unidentified younger members of his family, but was not in the least severe with them. After the deputy had been beaten up he ordered a full enquiry, but did not pursue it with any vigour. The same principles appeared to pertain in the Pernerstorfer case as in the Laaba case many years earlier: anyone who impugned a member of the Imperial Family, even if what they said was true, was in the wrong. It is perhaps not altogether surprising that nobody dared to tell Franz Joseph about the deterioration in Rudolf.

1888 was a year of wonderful weather. During the summer and autumn Vienna was bathed in golden sunshine and its inhabitants, carefree and gay, danced to the *Kaiserwaltz* which Johann Strauss composed to celebrate the fortieth anniversary of the Emperor's accession to the throne. It marked the end of a hard time for Franz Joseph, during which he had been haunted by the fear of war and lonely and unhappy for Elisabeth was often unwell and away a great deal. By 1888, however, much had improved. Russia had suddenly lost interest in Bulgaria, international tension had relaxed, and the Emperor told the British Ambassador that he 'scarcely remembered a time when the general aspect of affairs in Europe was so peaceful as at the present moment'.[33]

Above all Franz Joseph at last had someone during the Empress's absences to whom he could talk. Elisabeth, who loved him in her own way and understood him very well, realised his loneliness. Since she personally could not alleviate this, for she now found it psychologically impossible to remain for long in the Monarchy, she determined to find someone who could and, having noticed that the Emperor admired Frau Schratt, an actress at the Burgtheater, encouraged him to strike up a friendship with her. It was an inspired choice. Katherina Schratt, the daughter of a shopkeeper and twenty-three years younger than Franz Joseph was, as everyone agreed, an exceptionally nice woman, incapable of malice or intrigue, amiable, cheerful and natural. The Emperor's letters to her, warm, easy, full of Viennese expressions, show that he found in her someone with whom he could forget his position and behave like a human being; to whom he could confide fears such as his horror of making speeches, and small domestic details such as the state of his corns. Frau Schratt was an excellent listener, uninhibited in her comments, discreet, and invariably welcoming even when Franz Joseph arrived for breakfast with her at 7 a.m. after she had been up late at the Burgtheater. She arranged informal supper parties to amuse him, and thought of small additions to his comfort. Although the Emperor became utterly devoted to her, it is most unlikely that they were lovers. He told her: 'I love my wife and I will not abuse her trust and her friendship for you',[34] and some months later wrote to Elisabeth: 'I have with heartfelt gratitude the wonderful feeling that your love increases as the years go by . . . and this makes me infinitely happy.'[35] Both women were essential to him; Elisabeth as the never quite attainable object of his adoration, Katherina Schratt as a beloved friend who gave him the companionship which his wife could not provide.

Inevitably there was gossip. That it never became damaging was due to the Empress who made a point of inviting Frau Schratt to come and see her, and lost no opportunity of indicating that what was going on had her complete approval. Always at ease with simple people, she liked the actress. They compared notes of their cures and slimming diets. When she was abroad the Emperor relayed news of the one to the other. It was a remarkable triangular relationship from which all three emerged very well and, thanks to Elisabeth's unfailing protection of it, Franz Joseph was able from time to time to enjoy with Frau Schratt something which he had never known before—a few hours of domestic happiness.

By 1888 the Emperor complained that he was beginning to feel like an old man, but he was still at his desk at five in the morning, and when on manœuvres was far less tired after a long day on horseback than Rudolf. Archduke Albrecht too was remarkably active. In a laudatory letter addressed to him on his seventieth birthday which was read out to all units of the army, Franz Joseph spoke of the Archduke as being 'in full manly vigour, with unimpaired energy and strength'.[36] This was not quite true, for Albrecht's sight was now very bad indeed. But apart from this his health had not deteriorated, and he had no intention of resigning from his post as Inspector General. At the end of 1888 both he and Franz Joseph were in far better shape and far happier than Archduke Johann Salvator and the Crown Prince, each of whom was engulfed in his own world of private misery. Had either of them known that Johann Salvator had written to Weilen: 'Why can't the human soul be tuned up for five gulden like a piano?'[37] and Rudolf to Szeps: 'I find I cannot get worked up any more about anything, and least of all about things which concern me personally',[38] they would have been astonished and, totally unaware of the despair of having no *raison d'être*, quite uncomprehending.

CHAPTER 12

Mayerling I

At the end of 1888 the Crown Prince told Szeps that, although international tension had diminished, he had a feeling of 'almost unnatural calm' like 'the thickening of the atmosphere before a storm'. He added 'Things cannot go on like this, that is my only consolation'.[1] However, in the opening weeks of the New Year although not looking well, he appeared to be in relatively good spirits, visited the theatre, went on several shooting expeditions and carried out a number of official engagements. At a dinner party Lady Paget, the British Ambassadress, had a long conversation with him, and found him 'somehow, different, less sarcastic and, for the first time he looked me in the eyes when speaking'.[2]

Lady Paget did not speculate on the reason for the change she noticed in Rudolf; she may have heard that he was involved with an eighteen-year-old girl, Mary Vetsera, but if so probably attached no great importance to this. Nor, at this stage, did anyone else in Vienna. The Crown Prince now seemed to conduct his amorous adventures on the principle of the newer the better; this particular girl it was generally thought was not, and not likely to be, his only iron in the fire. Nevertheless the affair aroused interest; for although not yet out of her teens, Mary Vetsera had already attracted a great deal of attention. Contemporary descriptions of her vary. Some people found her 'exceptionally beautiful' or 'bewilderingly lovely' and walking 'with a seductive swaying grace that was irresistible'.[3] Lady Paget was more restrained:

> She was short and rather stumpy, with one shoulder higher than the other, but otherwise well developed. She had very

large blue eyes, with black hair, well marked brows and long dark lashes, a thick red mouth and a complexion of lilies and roses. [4]

But, although opinions about her beauty differed, there was general agreement that there was an aura of 'oriental' sensuality about her which men found wildly attractive.

Mary inherited this 'oriental' allure from her mother Hélène whose father Thermistokles Baltazzi, a Levantine banker, after having amassed an immense fortune in Constantinople settled in Vienna. The Baltazzis were devoid of quarterings and so could never hope to be received at Court, but they had no difficulty in carving out a position for themselves in Viennese society, for they possessed the two essential qualifications for success in that milieu, a great deal of money and a keen interest in horses and racing. Mary's aunts married into the lesser aristocracy; of her uncles Aristide owned a large stud and was a prominent member of the Jockey Club, Hektor became an outstanding gentleman rider and Alexander, a leading member of the international racing set patronised by the Prince of Wales, won the Derby with his horse Kisbar in 1876. The brothers attracted the attention of the Empress, who, provided people were good horsemen, was not discriminating about their origins. Two of them hunted with her on one of her visits to Leicestershire, to the great disapproval of Countess Festetics her lady-in-waiting, who conceded that they were clever, rode splendidly and had 'beautiful interesting eyes', but noted 'no one knows exactly where these people come from with all their money, but they make me feel uncomfortable . . . they push themselves in everywhere'. [5]

Mary's mother, a small, dark temperamental woman always beautifully dressed, pushed herself in everywhere with even more determination than the rest of her family. She did not accompany her husband, Baron Albin Vetsera, a minor diplomat, when he was posted abroad, and they were seen so rarely together that some people wondered if he really existed. Through her brothers she managed to hook herself on to those members of the aristocracy who hunted with the Emperor and Empress at

Gödöllö, and there her attempts to make up to Rudolf were so blatant that they were noticed even by Franz Joseph who was much annoyed. In Vienna, where society gossiped more than in any other capital in Europe, few people were more gossiped about than Hélène Vetsera but, whatever they might say about her behind her back, stigmatising her as an adventuress and a social climber, some of the aristocracy of the First Society came to her parties, for the food was excellent and the company entertaining. The Baroness was impervious to snubs, adept at manufacturing connections, and not in the least fastidious about the way in which she did so. Her admirers were said to include Archduke Wilhelm, and there were people in Vienna who nicknamed her daughter Mary '*le picque nicque*', alleging that any one of half a dozen men might be her father. Hélène Vetsera was in the terminology of the day 'fast', but she was also successful. In 1886 having apparently finally discarded her husband (who died unmourned in Cairo in the following year) she settled down to achieve her next ambition, a brilliant marriage for Mary.

Mary was virtually uneducated, interested only in clothes and racing, spoilt, impulsive, inclined to fly into tantrums if she did not get her own way, and brought up to think only of pleasure. At home she could be silly and tiresome, but at the social functions to which her mother started to take her when she was sixteen she had an immediate success. The Prince of Wales, to whom she was introduced at a race meeting in Germany, found her pretty and charming as did a great many other men. By 1888 the Duke of Braganza was amongst her most ardent admirers, and it seemed as though he might propose to her. The Duke was a widower and twice Mary's age, but his family had been kings of Portugal and he was a Royal Highness. It was exactly the sort of marriage which the Baroness aimed at for her daughter. Moreover, it would settle Mary's infatuation with the Crown Prince which was becoming embarrassing, for whenever she saw Rudolf at the races, at the theatre, or out riding in the Prater she never took her eyes off him.

At the opening of the new Burgtheater in October 1888 the Prince of Wales drew Rudolf's attention to Mary Vetsera, but

Milli Stubel

Mary Vetsera

found he appeared to take no interest in her. It seems doubtful whether this lack of interest was genuine. A few weeks later the Crown Prince arranged for Mary to be smuggled by the back way used by Szeps (and no doubt a number of other people) into his apartment in the Hofburg, employing as an intermediary for this purpose Countess Marie Larisch-Wallersee, his cousin and a friend of Baroness Vetsera's. Marie Larisch, the daughter of the Empress's brother by his morganatic marriage to a Jewish actress, was the same age as Rudolf. She was an excellent horsewoman which endeared her to Elisabeth, and so, when a girl, was frequently invited to stay by the Empress. Although she was attractive and had a lovely figure she was not liked. There was something devious about her which made Countess Festetics feel 'uncomfortable'; in Latour's opinion she had set her heart on marrying Rudolf and, frustrated in this ambition was only too delighted to do anything which would upset Stephanie. Marie Larisch's own marriage was not a success. Her husband's estate was in Bohemia where she was bored, and she was also constantly short of money. By the age of thirty she had become a hard, discontented, amoral woman, prepared to intrigue for the sake of amusement; prepared to volunteer to chaperone Mary on shopping expeditions when in fact she was taking her to Rudolf; perfectly willing to act as a *procureuse,* particularly if the reward for her services was adequate.

Rudolf's first meeting with Mary was followed by others. Countess Larisch was not always there to facilitate them, for her husband only allowed her to make short visits to Vienna. When she was away Mary manufactured excuses to slip out of the house and disappear round the corner, where Bratfisch was waiting to drive her to the Hofburg. Her care to conceal what was going on suggests that she knew her mother would not approve of it, and this was probably correct. Baroness Vetsera was ambitious for a brilliant marriage for her daughter, not only for Mary's sake but because it would improve her own position in society. An affair with the Crown Prince could not lead to marriage, was unlikely to last, and might cause a scandal which would wreck her calculations. Social climber though she was, and close to the wind though she herself had sailed in the past, it seems likely that the Baroness would have been horrified had she known that at some time between November 1888 and mid-January 1889 Mary became Rudolf's mistress.

On the evening of Sunday, January 27th, 1889, Prince Reuss the German Ambassador gave a reception in honour of Wilhelm II's birthday. All Vienna was there—ministers, officials, leading scholars such as von Arneth, and that very large section of society which was on the Embassy calling list, including Baroness Vetsera and Mary. The Emperor himself came, so did a number of members of the Imperial Family. Rudolf, wearing the uniform of the German Uhlan regiment of which he was honorary colonel, arrived with Stephanie shortly before his father. When Franz Joseph entered the room the Crown Prince broke off the conversation he was having with Kalnoky, took the hand which the Emperor extended to him and bowed very low in an attitude of the utmost respect. He then moved round the room talking to Archduke Albrecht and other members of the Imperial Family, to Reuss and Lady Paget, and to Count Hoyos about arrangements for a shoot. One or two people, Lady Paget and the historian von Arneth among them, noticed that he seemed depressed. One or two people also noticed that Mary Vetsera never took her eyes off him and Monts, a member of the Embassy staff, found the keen interest which she displayed in every detail of Rudolf's German uniform a little surprising. But, contrary to what Marie Larisch (who was not at the reception) later asserted, she apparently made no scene, neither did Monts, who escorted the Crown Prince and Princess to their carriage and talked to the former while the servants searched for Stephanie's ermine cloak, notice anything unusual.

The shoot which Rudolf discussed with Count Hoyos during the reception was, he told the Count, to take place on January 29th and 30th in the Imperial game preserve near Mayerling, a house which together with some land the Crown Prince had acquired from the neighbouring monastery of Heiligenkreuz in 1886. Mayerling was built round a courtyard one side of which Rudolf converted into accommodation for himself, Stephanie and their guests, making a large combined bedroom and study for his own use on the ground floor, with a bathroom leading off it and a room beside it opening, like his bedroom on to an entrance hall, for his valet. Immediately above this was Stephanie's bedroom, bathroom and sitting room, and a room for her maid. The Crown Prince and Princess's private apartments therefore consisted of a compact block separated from the reception and guest rooms by the main entrance hall and staircase. As the servants' quarters, kitchen, storerooms and a suite of rooms for Rudolf's small daughter Elisabeth took up the remainding buildings round two sides of the courtyard, the fourth of which was occupied by a church, the Crown Prince bought a villa about five hundred yards away from the main house in order to be able to put up additional guests when he had a large shooting party.

Apart from the island of Lacroma in the Adriatic, Mayerling was the only property which Rudolf personally owned. The view from the shooting lodge over meadows and wooded hills, if not spectacular was peaceful, and it was within easy reach of Vienna, either through the Wienerwald or, if this was not feasible in winter because of ice on the steep hills, by train to Baden followed by a fifteen kilometres drive up a good road. The whole journey could be done in two and a half hours. Stephanie played little if any part in the planning of Mayerling and after the house-warming party in the autumn of 1887, seldom went there. It was Rudolf's creation, not elaborately but comfortably furnished, ornamented with his shooting trophies, lit by oil lamps. It provided him with a retreat and a respite from the pressure which during 1888 he found more and more acute.

At the German Embassy reception the Crown Prince asked Hoyos to arrange with Prince Philip of Coburg, who had also been invited to the shoot, to catch an early train to Baden on the morning of Tuesday, January 29th in order that they might reach Mayerling in time for breakfast. When they arrived Rudolf told them that during his drive out from Vienna on the previous day the carriage had stuck on an icy hill and he had caught a cold trying to help push it. He thought it wiser therefore to remain indoors, and after a cheerful breakfast wished his guests good sport and left them to their own devices.

A family dinner party was due to take place in the Hofburg at 6 p.m. that evening. Philip of Coburg left for Vienna to attend it, and arranged to spend the night in the capital, returning to Mayerling early on the following morning for the next day's shoot. About an hour before the dinner party was due to begin Rudolf sent a telegram to Stephanie asking her to explain to his father that he could not come because he had a severe cold. Details of all banquets and dinners given by the Emperor were minutely recorded in the Court archives. The entry in the *Zeremoniell-Protokoll* for January 29th notes that the table plan approved by His Imperial Majesty had to be altered at the last moment because the Crown Prince had sent word from Mayerling that he could not be there. Last minute changes of this sort irritated Franz Joseph. The table plan shows that Stephanie sat between him and Archduke Albrecht, not the sort of person likely to help out in a difficult situation. She must have had a ghastly evening, and in her memoirs recalls that she was anxious in case Rudolf was seriously ill but dared not say so. By the time the family dinner party began there was in any case no means of finding out how he was. The telephone had yet to be invented. Rudolf had given orders that the Court telegraph office installed in Mayerling should not be manned. The nearest public telegraph office closed at 6 p.m. and was at Alland, a village two and a half miles away. Over the night of January 29th–30th Mayerling was cut off from all rapid communication with the outside world. What was occurring there was not known in Vienna until shortly before 11.30 a.m. on the morning of the 30th, when Hoyos burst into Bombelles' room on the second floor of the Hofburg and told him that Rudolf and Mary Vetsera had been found together in bed, dead from cyanide poisoning.

The news of the tragedy must be broken to the Emperor. This was a task which no Court official had the courage to face, and they agreed that it could only be done by the Empress. Baron Nopsca the head of her household told Elisabeth what had happened. She wept for a few minutes, then pulled herself together and, head held high, went to Franz Joseph. The British Ambassador reported to Lord Salisbury:

I hear on the best authority that the manner in which the Empress comforted herself, though completely stunned by the blow, and the fortitude and courage with which she prepared the Emperor and finally broke to him this overwhelming misfortune surpasses the power of words to describe.[6]

By 1 p.m. no further news from Mayerling had reached the Hofburg. None was to be expected for a while, for although Widerhofer, the Emperor's physician, had been telegraphed for by Hoyos to go there at once, he was unlikely to arrive before midday at the earliest, and then had to examine the bodies. Rumours were, however, already circulating that Rudolf had been seriously wounded in a shooting accident and might not live. It was imperative to issue some official statement.

Talleyrand is said to have observed: '*Il n'y a rien qui s'arrange aussi facilement que les faits*'—'Nothing is easier to fix than facts'. The facts accompanying the Crown Prince's death were, for those who had to deal with them, extremely intractable. The Imperial Court, rooted in tradition, functioned on precedent, following with slight variations the same procedure and observing the same ceremonial for each Habsburg birth, marriage and death. But for the events of Wednesday, January 30th, 1889—the heir to the throne dead in bed with his mistress, a commoner, and both of them having apparently died from unnatural causes—there was no precedent at all. It was a problem with which the hierarchy of Court officialdom was quite unequipped to deal. To make matters worse, Prince Hohenlohe the Lord Chamberlain of the Emperor's household, was away in the country; Count Tisza the Minister President of Hungary was in Budapest; the Emperor had retreated to his study and was in no state to think fast. A good deal therefore devolved on Count Taaffe, the Minister President of the Austrian half of the Monarchy.

The problem was how to conceal the circumstances of the Crown Prince's death, which if revealed would gravely damage the prestige of the Imperial House. If scandal was to be avoided

Rudolf must be laid to rest in the Habsburg family vault in Vienna with the full blessing of the Catholic Church, and all traces of Mary Vetsera's presence and death in Mayerling must be obliterated. As the first step to achieving this, the official announcement of the Crown Prince's death must give no hint to the world in general of the circumstances under which it had occurred. At this stage, on the early afternoon of Wednesday, January 30th, no information had been received to contradict or throw further light on Hoyos's statement that Rudolf and Mary Vetsera had 'poisoned themselves with cyanide'. This could mean, as the Emperor and Empress were convinced it did, that Mary had poisoned first the Crown Prince and then herself. In this case neither the chaplain to the Hofburg, who was directly answerable to the Vatican, nor the Papal Nuncio could object to Rudolf's funeral taking place with full religious rites. But this version of what had occurred could not be publicly announced for to do so would reveal the scandal of Mary's liaison with the Crown Prince. It was impossible to say that Rudolf had poisoned himself, for under canon law a suicide could not be given a Christian burial. To confirm the general rumour that the heir to the throne had been killed in an accident while out shooting was not feasible. Imperial Highnesses did not go out shooting by themselves. Some account of the circumstances of the accident would have to be given and witnesses named. There seemed to be only one way out of the predicament. A special edition of the official *Wiener Zeitung* appeared early in the afternoon carrying the announcement that the Crown Prince had died at Mayerling that morning of apoplexy. A diary of events was kept at Court. The official whose duty it was to write this up, noted on January 30th that the announcement in the *Wiener Zeitung* had been drafted by Count Taaffe in conjunction with Count Kalnoky and made no mention of it having been approved by the Emperor. Possibly at that time Franz Joseph, overwhelmed by grief, was unapproachable.

An announcement successfully concealing (it was to be hoped) the circumstances of the Crown Prince's death had been issued. His body must now be brought to Vienna for a State funeral and, since Mayerling was an Imperial property over which neither the civil authorities nor the police had any jurisdiction or right of entry, arrangements for this must be made by the Court. In addition a Court Commission must be sent to Mayerling to search for a will, take any inventory which they considered necessary, and incorporate the doctor's report of the cause of death in their statement for the Emperor. This was the traditional procedure when a member of the Imperial Family died, and there was no question of departing from it. From midday until midnight on the day of the Crown Prince's death the situation at Mayerling was therefore in the hands of people who belonged to the Court hierarchy—Widerhofer Franz Joseph's physician, Bombelles the head of Rudolf's household who reached the shooting lodge shortly after him, and the Court Commission, a miscellaneous collection of officials which did not arrive until darkness had fallen. Amongst them there was nobody with any police training, that is to say nobody capable of noting and assessing details which might throw a light on what had occurred.

By eight o'clock on the following day a number of people knew that the coffin containing Rudolf's body had reached the Hofburg in the early hours of the morning. By this time the *Wiener Zeitung* and the equivalent official newspaper in Hungary were on sale, repeating the original announcement of the Crown Prince's death, but now giving the cause of it as a heart attack. And by this time the Emperor who saw Widerhofer at 6 a.m., had learnt from him what nobody at Court on the previous evening had the courage to reveal. This was that when the doctor arrived at Mayerling he found Rudolf slumped over the edge of the bed, a wound in the top of his skull from which blood and brains were oozing, a mirror and a revolver near his right hand, Mary Vetsera lying beside him shot through the head, and that everything in this horrifying scene pointed to one horrifying conclusion: the Crown Prince had killed his mistress and then shot himself.

On the previous day when he first heard of Rudolf's death Franz Joseph was stunned by shock. Now, informed by Widerhofer of an even more bitter reality he collected himself and, wearing full uniform complete with sword and gloves, went to see his son's body. Then he summoned his ministers, Hohenlohe and other Court officials. His habit of command reasserted itself and he took the decisions as to what must now be done. The Emperor was an honest man, practical and, although in no way bigoted, obedient to the laws of the Church. There was a degree beyond which he was not prepared to deceive his people nor, he realised, could success in doing so be guaranteed. Widerhofer's discretion was absolute but, a man of the utmost professional integrity, he could not be expected to certify that the Crown Prince had died from apoplexy or heart failure. The members of the Court Commission could be sworn to silence, but what about the servants who would have to clear up the bloodstained mess at Mayerling? To ask for religious rites at Rudolf's funeral would be tricking the Church authorities into breaking canon law. The majority of the inhabitants of the Monarchy were Catholics and the consequences of such a deception, if discovered, could be disastrous. Franz Joseph's first decision was therefore that the public must be told part of the truth (not all of it for no mention must be made of Mary Vetsera) and it must be announced that the heir to the throne had committed suicide. His second decision was that, since canon law provided that if medical evidence showed that suicide had been committed while of an unsound mind, the blessing of the Church would not be withheld, an autopsy must be performed on his son.

The autopsy began at nine o'clock that evening and lasted until midnight. A report of the findings was handed to the Emperor by Hohenlohe on the following morning, February 1st. Kalnoky communicated the gist of it to Galimberti the Papal Nuncio. The public were informed in the *Wiener Zeitung* that the first reports of the cause of the Crown Prince's death had been mistaken, that Widerhofer when he arrived at Mayerling on January 30th had found that Rudolf had died instantaneously from a bullet wound which had shattered the top of his skull, and that the position of a revolver by his right hand established unquestionably that the wound was self-inflicted. A number of people, the statement said, had noted that during the last few weeks of his life His Imperial Highness appeared to be suffering from some form of nervous disturbance, and it must be assumed that he had taken his life in a moment of insanity. It was also known that the Crown Prince after a riding accident in the autumn, which he had ordered should be kept secret, had frequently complained of headaches.

Next day the arrangements for the funeral were announced, and a summary of the results of the autopsy published. This reiterated that Rudolf had died from a self-inflicted revolver wound, adding that the examination had revealed certain malformations in the structure of the skull which it was known could cause an abnormal mental state. No further official statement on the circumstances of the Crown Prince's death was ever made.

The funeral took place on February 5th. On a cold grey winter afternoon as dusk was falling the coffin was borne in solemn procession from the chapel of the Hofburg where the Crown Prince had been lying in state, through the narrow streets of the old city of Vienna to the church of the Capuchins. When the religious ceremony was over it was carried down to the vault and Rudolf was laid to rest amidst one hundred and twelve ancestors. By the Emperor's request, apart from the King and Queen of Belgium, no crowned heads were there. Stephanie's parents were of little comfort to anyone. (The King's first act on arriving in Vienna was to make an appointment to see a financier about his Congo venture.) Elisabeth, by now prostrate with grief, did not go to the funeral. Franz Joseph managed to retain his self-control until he followed the coffin into the vault, when he broke down and wept bitterly.

Another funeral had already taken place. Mary Vetsera had been buried at Heiligenkreuz a few miles away from Mayerling, after a complicated series of manœuvres devised by Taaffe which involved the Court, the police, the local civil authorities and the Abbot of Heiligenkreuz, and in which the law was, to put it mildly, very severely bent. Several people were required to do things which they greatly disliked and which went against their conscience. Auchenthaler, Rudolf's doctor was ordered on January 31st to go to Mayerling accompanied by Slatin, a junior Court official, examine Mary's body, and produce a statement describing it as 'having been found in the parish of Mayerling' giving the cause of death as suicide by shooting. Count Stockau, Baroness Vetsera's brother-in-law, together with Alexander Baltazzi were ordered to meet Auchenthaler and Slatin at the shooting lodge, provide formal identification of their niece, dress the corpse, seat it in Stockau's fiaker and drive it to Heiligenkreuz. Pressure was brought to bear on the Abbot of Heiligenkreuz to agree to the burial of Mary Vetsera in the graveyard under his jurisdiction, although she was formally certified as having committed suicide. The police were instructed to ensure that the body was driven from Mayerling to Heiligenkreuz without attracting attention, and then buried under conditions of the utmost secrecy. To maintain an appearance of complying with the law, the head of the civil administration of the district was told to make the necessary entries in the official records required by the ponderous bureaucratic procedure of the day, and to ensure that they tallied with Auchenthaler's statement.

The burial took place as planned, and was a macabre affair. Although Mary had been dead for a day and a half, her body had neither been washed nor laid out, and was with difficulty propped up in Stockau's fiaker. The drive through the dark to Heiligenkreuz over icy roads was a nightmare. A gale and pouring rain next morning delayed the digging of the grave. Eventually the operation was completed and—the police reported—without attracting undue attention. This was hardly true. Admittedly no journalist had been present, but the unusual amount of coming and going had attracted notice in the village. And, since the police, local officials and inmates of the monastery had all been involved, the number of people who knew that something very curious connected with the Crown Prince's death had occurred at Mayerling was considerably increased. None of this however appeared to worry Count Taaffe, who was to be seen in Vienna, his hat on the back of his head as usual, smoking a cigar, walking with a jaunty air as though he had nothing more serious on his mind than the arrangements for a Hofball.

On the day of Rudolf's funeral the British Ambassador reported to Lord Salisbury:

There is I hear considerable indignation amongst the Public at the way in which they have been hoodwinked and deceived by the varying official accounts which have been published.[7]

This was an understatement. The first announcement that Rudolf had died of apoplexy had been greeted with amazed incredulity; he was only thirty and generally held to be as *The Times* put it 'in the flower of manly strength'.[8] Twenty-four hours later *The Times* commented:

Everyone will have his own version of how the Crown Prince died, and the official statement of the facts is the only one which finds no general acceptance.[9]

The next announcement that Rudolf had shot himself was therefore too much, even for a public conditioned for years into a docile acceptance of the idea that the Emperor and his Ministers knew best about everything. If the Crown Prince had shot himself this must have been apparent when his death was first discovered. Why then had an announcement to this effect not been made at once? There seemed to be only one possible explanation—officialdom had something to hide about the manner of his death, or the reason for it, or both. Speculation now ran riot. Rudolf had died after a duel, or shot himself after a drunken orgy. Or he had been killed by a jealous forester whose daughter he had seduced, or assassinated for some unknown reason, or hit over the head with a bottle in a brawl. These allegations that he had been murdered persisted for years and the wildest theories were evolved as to the identity of his killer. When the statement of the results of the autopsy appeared, every point in it was queried. The statement described the wound and said it could have been made by a shot from a revolver of medium calibre. Could such a weapon have made such a wound? The wording of the sentence giving the cause of death as a head wound was equivocal. Were there other injuries which had not been mentioned? Was there really a malformation of the skull which had caused insanity, or was this announcement simply made (as it had been done before in the case of suicides) to ensure the Crown Prince a

Catholic funeral? Rumours were also circulating that Mary
Vetsera too, had died at Mayerling. Had she been shot by Rudolf
who had then committed suicide? Had she killed him first and
then herself? And to all the speculation as to how the Crown
Prince had died were added queries as to the reason for his death.
Despair at a collapsed marriage from which there was no escape
by divorce? Because he was engaged in some form of political
intrigue? Because he had quarrelled with his father? Or was he
really insane?

A week after the discovery of the tragedy it was clear that
official attempts to avoid scandal by concealing the circumstances
of Rudolf's death were a dismal failure. Too many people knew at
least something of what had occurred at Mayerling, and far too
many of them had talked. By February 5th Sir Augustus Paget,
obliged to his embarrassment by Royal command to inform
Queen Victoria of everything which he could discover, had learnt
'from an unimpeachable source' of the early history of Mary
Vetsera's affair with the Crown Prince, that Countess Larisch
had both promoted this and been involved in the girl's dis-
appearance from Vienna, and a great deal which, he informed
his sovereign, only 'the sternest sense of duty' compelled him to
write, about the scene when the two bodies were discovered at
Mayerling.[10] Other members of the Diplomatic Corps too had
no difficulty in obtaining information from 'well informed
sources'. Galimberti the Papal Nuncio, an experienced smooth
diplomat, told the German Ambassador that although his official
conscience was clear, for he only had to believe the version of
Rudolf's death which had been officially communicated to him
by Kalnoky, nevertheless it was the first time in history that the
Papal Nuncio in full vestments had attended 'the funeral of a
murderer and suicide'.[11]

A number of people had some idea of what had happened, but
nobody made any headway in discovering why it had happened.
It was known that the Crown Prince had appointed Szögyeny of
the Ministry of Foreign Affairs as his literary executor with
responsibility for dealing with all his papers, and that before his
death he had written a number of farewell letters—accounts

varied as to whom they were addressed but according to most of them there was none for the Emperor. This suggested that father and son had quarrelled and the Russian Chargé d'Affaires reported that this was confirmed by Szögyeny. To other people, however, Szögyeny asserted that he could find no explanation of why the Crown Prince had killed himself. The consensus of opinion was that he had not shot himself because of a hopeless love affair with Mary Vetsera. As the British Ambassador observed to Lord Salisbury, it was not the first time a young lady had been 'lured from the path of virtue, and there was no earthly reason why, as in other instances things should not have been quietly arranged in this case'.[12] He doubted if the full truth would ever be known 'it is all mystery, mystery, mystery',[13] and fell back on the explanation that Rudolf had gone to his death because through his mother he had inherited the Wittelsbach insanity, and Mary Vetsera to hers because she was 'a silly vain exaltée young person, quite without religion or principle'.[14]

Mayerling became a European sensation. In the Monarchy official policy remained unaltered for nearly three decades. No further information was released to the public, and anything in print on the subject of the Crown Prince's death was banned. It was a policy which could not however be enforced. Under the Press law in the Austrian part of the Monarchy newspapers could be muzzled, but the equivalent law in Hungary was less strict. Nothing could suppress rumours, censorship was inadequate to prevent the transmission of information abroad, no control could be exercised over what was published in other countries, and the police were unable to confiscate all the innumerable copies of newspapers and books containing speculation about what had occurred at Mayerling which for years flooded into the Monarchy. When in the summer of 1889 Baroness Vetsera's apologia protesting that she had no idea of the extent of her daughter's involvement with Rudolf, reproducing Mary's farewell letters and giving a detailed account of the macabre circumstances of the disposal of her body, appeared as a privately printed brochure, several copies of it escaped confiscation and found their way abroad. Extracts from it appeared in the French press, and the entire brochure was reprinted in Germany where it ran through a number of editions.[15] In the summer of 1897 when it became known that Countess Larisch intended to publish her memoirs the Emperor himself intervened, bought the copyright of the book, suppressed it, and personally burnt the original manuscript. In 1913, however, the memoirs were published in London adding to the very large volume of sensational literature which had been produced on the subject of Mayerling.

The reactions provoked by Rudolf's death are revealing. The extent to which he was mourned throughout Hungary is illustrated by a moving telegram of condolence to the Emperor:

> The humble inhabitants of a small faraway village add their tears to the sea of sorrow.
>
> The Parish of Bögöz.[16]

In the Austrian half of the Monarchy his death was a great blow to many people of progressive ideas who had seen in him their hope for the future, and there too he was mourned by those who had known and appreciated his intellectual qualities. On the other hand, those whom he had attacked while he was alive became his detractors after his death. Archbishop Schönborn and other leading members of the ecclesiastical hierarchy made it clear that they were sceptical of the official finding of suicide while of an unsound mind, and there were instances in all parts of the Monarchy of priests omitting to toll the bell for the dead, and of their reluctance to say Mass for the repose of the Crown Prince's soul. Many courtiers, officials and members of the aristocracy, shocked though they were by the death of the heir to the throne, were unanimous in condemning his behaviour towards the end of his life and talked of little else.

Official pedantry and red tape, adherence to the tradition that the death of a member of the Imperial Family must be dealt with by Court officials, and the Emperor's instinctive clinging to the idea that it was only incumbent on the House of Habsburg to tell its subjects as much as it considered desirable for them to know all contributed to the inept handling of the aftermath of the Crown Prince's death, the fatal delay in announcing his suicide and the failure to conceal the part which Mary Vetsera had played in it. Neither the ineptitude nor the failure however in any way impaired the prestige of the Emperor whose courage, self-control and dignity commanded universal admiration. They did, however, have two consequences. One was to damage the memory of Rudolf by concentrating attention on the discreditable period of his life to the exclusion of any appreciation of his better qualities. The other was to convey the impression that although some of the truth had leaked out, much was still concealed. When Franz Joseph died in 1916 an aura of mystery still hung about Mayerling.

CHAPTER 13

Mayerling II

The First World War brought about the fall of the House of Habsburg and the final collapse of the Monarchy. The government of the Austrian Republic saw no reason for protecting either the honour or the secrets of the deposed dynasty. Censorship was lifted and archives gradually became available for research. The publication of reminiscences, letters and historical studies incorporating hitherto unknown material, began and has continued until the present day. Between 1928 and 1932 the statements of two key witnesses to the discovery of Rudolf's death—Count Josef Hoyos and the Crown Prince's valet Loschek—and the recollections of Slatin, the junior member of the Court Commission sent to investigate it, appeared. Considered in conjunction they throw some light on what occurred at Mayerling on the morning of January 30th, 1889.

Count Hoyos wrote his statement within weeks of Rudolf's death and deposited it for safe custody in a sealed envlope in the State Archives. Its existence was known only to a very few people until, in 1928, it was reproduced by Oskar von Mitis in his important study of the Crown Prince.[1] This statement, generally referred to as the Hoyos *Denkschrift,* consists of three documents. One is a copy of a letter to Hohenlohe in which the Count asserts that, in spite of an equivocal message sent to him by Mary Vetsera in a farewell note found at Mayerling from Rudolf to Loschek, he had never exchanged more than a few words with the young Baroness, and was quite ignorant of her liaison with the Crown Prince. One consists of a series of notes, dated February 1889, in which Hoyos summarises information he has picked up about the development of Rudolf's affair with Mary, his suicidal tendencies, his relationship with Mitzi Caspar, his debts, his farewell letters, Mary's farewell letters, her determination to die and her burial at Heiligenkreuz. In this Hoyos cites the names of his informants, among them members of the Crown Prince's household, Archduke Otto, Philip and Louise Coburg, Szögyeny, Kubasek one of the senior officials on the Court Commission. It reads like an attempt at amateur detection, and gives the impression that a number of people on whose silence the Emperor might have been expected to rely had been far too talkative. In the third and longest document the Count gives a detailed account of his experiences at Mayerling during the twenty-four hours which he spent there between the mornings of January 29th and January 30th, 1889.

Hoyos recorded only two things on the 29th which struck him as being in any way unusual. One was that when he and Prince Philip of Coburg arrived at the shooting lodge at 8.10 a.m., having caught the early train from Vienna to Baden and driven up from there, the shutters of all the windows facing on to the road (these included three windows of Rudolf's bedroom on the ground floor) were closed as if the place was uninhabited. The other was the Crown Prince's account of his journey to Mayerling on the previous day, when instead of coming by train to Baden, he had driven from Vienna over the icy roads of the Wienerwald and taken an incredibly long time to do so. The Count found this 'somewhat mysterious' but made no comment. He appears to have considered it no way odd that, although there were three spare rooms in the shooting lodge, and he was the only overnight guest (as Philip of Coburg had to return to Vienna for the Family Dinner), he should be put up in the villa which was about five hundred yards from the main building. Nor did he notice anything amiss with Rudolf when they dined alone together that night. On the contrary the Crown Prince was apparently relaxed, at his most charming, drank very little and ate well in spite of his cold. Shooting was the main topic of conversation. Rudolf made only one reference to politics when he produced three telegrams from Count Pista Karolyi, a vehement opponent of the new army law which the Emperor and his

Ministers were endeavouring to push through the Hungarian Parliament, and commented that embarrassing articles implying he supported Karolyi had appeared in Hungarian opposition newspapers. But he appeared to be quite philosophic about this. Coburg was due to return from Vienna shortly after 8 a.m. on the following morning for the second day's shooting, and the Crown Prince said that as soon as he arrived they would all three breakfast together. At nine o'clock he announced that he must go to bed to tend his cold, refused the offer of some more handkerchiefs, wished his guest goodnight and withdrew. According to Hoyos's statement nothing had occurred during the day which gave the slightest hint of what was to come. Nor, as he dressed on the following morning was he aware that anything was wrong until, 'some minutes' before eight, his valet announced that Zwerger the caretaker at the shooting lodge wished to see him.

Hoyos records the events of the next hour and a half in minute detail. Zwerger was brought in and said that he had been sent by Loschek to report that the Crown Prince could not be wakened. The Count's reaction to this was that Rudolf should not be disturbed. Zwerger then explained that His Imperial Highness had appeared at 6.30 a.m., fully dressed, in the antechamber off which both his and Loschek's bedrooms opened and gave orders that his breakfast was to be ready and Bratfisch's fiaker harnessed at 7.30, at which time he was to be called. He then returned, whistling, to his room. Since 7.30 Loschek had knocked in vain at the Crown Prince's door. Both doors to Rudolf's bedroom were locked from the inside. This convinced the Count that there was every reason to fear 'a disaster' and he hurried to the shooting lodge. Loschek repeated what Zwerger had already said. Hoyos, having knocked and shouted to Rudolf in vain, and ascertained that the room was not heated by coal so that there could be no question of carbon monoxide poisoning, ordered Loschek to break down one of the doors. Loschek then revealed that Mary Vetsera was with the Crown Prince, a fact of which the Count states emphatically he was totally unaware and which 'utterly dismayed' him. 'Now the worst was to be feared . . . and my responsibility was crushing.' He looked at his watch, it was 8.9, which meant that Prince Philip of Coburg should be arriving, and seconds later the Prince drove into the courtyard.

Hoyos then relates that he took Coburg into the billiard room, told him of the situation and, after a 'brief consultation' they decided to take the responsibility of breaking down a door. But, 'in view of the extremely delicate circumstances' they also decided that only Loschek would enter the room to see what had happened, and that the designation of any other witnesses, 'unless there was danger in delay', was to be left to His Imperial Majesty.

Loschek in the presence of Hoyos and Coburg first tried to spring the lock with an axe, and then having failed to do this, smashed through a panel of the door. Peering through the hole he reported that both Rudolf and Mary Vetsera lay on the bed, 'apparently dead'. Hoyos continues his account:

> Our dismay and sorrow were indescribable. The question of whether a doctor should be called was debated. In view of the circumstances this was not desirable if there was no sign of life. The most important thing to determine was whether help was useless, and this Loschek must do.

Loschek put his hand through the smashed panel, turned the key on the inside of the door and went into the room. 'A few moments later' he announced that:

> there was no sign of life in the bodies, the Crown Prince was slumped over the edge of the bed with a great pool of blood in front of him, and that death was presumably due to poisoning by potassium cyanide for this caused such haemorrhages.

'Death by shooting,' Hoyos adds, 'was only established later.'

The Emperor must be informed at once. Coburg overwhelmed by sorrow was 'barely capable of action'. After a brief discussion it was agreed that Hoyos should undertake this task while the Prince remained on guard at Mayerling to bar entry to everyone except an emissary from His Majesty and Dr. Widerhofer. The Count drafted a telegram to Widerhofer asking him, without giving the reason why, to come out to Mayerling urgently and gave it to Loschek to send off, sent a servant to get his fur coat from the villa, and at 'about 8.37' as he carefully notes, started for Baden in Bratfisch's fiaker.

Bratfisch, urged on by the Count, drove fast although the road was icy and slippery. During the journey he tried to find out what had occurred and asked what he should say if questioned. Hoyos refused to give him any information, ordered him to say nothing and, overriding his contention that he should at once return to Mayerling because he had an errand to perform there, told him to wait at Baden station to meet Widerhofer.

> When we arrived at the station, [Hoyos continues], the 9.18 express from Trieste which took on no passengers at Baden was awaited. I sent a further telegram, to the Lord Chamberlain Prince Constantin Hohenlohe asking him to go to the Hofburg at once and, indicating that I was travelling in the service of His Majesty, succeeded in boarding the train. I was concerned until further orders were given by the Emperor to keep everything as secret as possible, and that nobody should learn anything either in Mayerling or during my short journey.

There are several puzzling features in Hoyos's statement. Why did he and Coburg not go into the bedroom to see what had happened and personally make sure that Rudolf was beyond all human aid? Coburg was the Crown Prince's brother-in-law, Hoyos had been made a Privy Councillor by Franz Joseph. That they should consider that the Emperor would prefer them to rely on information from a servant instead of ascertaining the facts for themselves seems extraordinary.

Loschek must have made some examination of the bodies in order to be able to say that there was no sign of life in them and, however cursory this was, he can hardly have failed to notice the wounds in the heads of both Rudolf and Mary. He had started his career as a gamekeeper and loader and therefore had the experience to recognise a bullet wound when he saw one. Why then did he announce that the pool of blood in front of the Crown Prince was the result of a violent haemorrhage presumably caused by potassium cyanide poisoning (which in fact causes no such thing)? Why did Hoyos and Coburg accept this verdict without question?

How did Hoyos, according to the timings which he gives, manage to catch the 9.18 express from Baden? The station at Baden is fifteen kilometres from Mayerling and on the far side of the town. While one or two exceptional instances are on record of a fiaker driver covering a kilometre in 2–2·3 minutes, the average speed was 5 minutes a kilometre. [2] Bratfisch was driving slightly downhill all the way from Mayerling to Baden, but on a slippery road at the end of which he had to cross the town. It seems unlikely that he could at most have achieved a speed of more than 3 minutes a kilometre, and therefore would have taken at least 45 minutes to reach the station, the entrance to which is up a flight of steps. Having got out of the fiaker Hoyos had to hurry up these steps, send his telegram to Prince Hohenlohe, and argue the station master or some other railway official into waiving the rules and allowing him to board the train, all of which must have taken a minimum of 5 minutes. It would seem therefore that less than 50 minutes cannot have elapsed from the time the Count left Mayerling until the time he got on to the express. He says, however, that he started from the shooting lodge at 'about 8.37'. If in fact he started at 8.37 or later he would have had at the most 41 minutes and possibly less in which to catch the train. It is difficult to see how he could possibly have done so unless it was late. But it was due to reach Vienna at 9.50, and Hoyos says he reached the Hofburg, several kilometres drive from the station, at 10.11. It could only therefore at the most have been a very few minutes behind schedule. Did Hoyos's 'about 8.37' in fact mean that he started at least 10 minutes earlier? To assume that he did so solves the problem of how he managed to catch the train but raises another, for it reduces the time which he had with Coburg after the latter's return to Mayerling to approximately 17 minutes. Neither the Prince nor the Count had held any important public office; neither therefore was accustomed to dealing with crises which demanded rapid thinking. On a cold winter morning before breakfast they were confronted at Mayerling with a situation which appalled both of them, and aspects of which were enough to make anyone feel physically sick. That they should have accomplished all Hoyos says they did in barely half an hour is almost incredible; that they should have managed to do so in just over a quarter of an hour would seem to be miraculous. This difficulty which the timings given by the Count presents, together with the other puzzling features of his statement, makes the recollections of the other key witness, Loschek, of particular interest.

Loschek dictated his recollections to his son on January 19th, 1928, thirty-nine years after Mayerling. A fair copy was made and certified by the local mayor as being an exact reproduction of what the son had taken down, and this was published in Germany and in the *Neues Wiener Tagblatt*[3] a few weeks after the valet's death in 1932. Loschek says he was compelled to record what he knew because 'as the only remaining living witness of the drama of Mayerling (in any case there were only two—valet Johann Loschek and Count Hoyos),' he did not want to take his knowledge with him to the grave, and so dictated 'the simple truth'. He confirms Hoyos's statement that on the evening of January 29th the latter and the Crown Prince dined alone together, but gives a different version of what occurred on the following morning.

At 6.10 Rudolf fully dressed came to me in the room I was in and ordered me to arrange for the fiaker to be harnessed. Before I had reached the courtyard I heard two shots. I ran back at once and was met by the smell of gunpowder. I rushed to the bedroom, but contrary to Rudolf's usual practice the door was locked. What was to be done? I at once fetched Count Hoyos and with a hammer smashed in a panel of the door so that I could put my hand through and open it from the inside. It was a dreadful sight. Rudolf, fully dressed, lay dead on his bed, Mary Vetsera, also fully dressed, lay dead on her bed. Rudolf's army revolver was beside him. Neither of them had gone to bed at all. The heads of both were hanging down. At the first glance one could see that Rudolf had first shot Mary Vetsera and then killed himself. Only two well aimed shots had been fired. The presence of a third person, or that splinters of glass were lodged in Rudolf's head is, like so much which has been said about Rudolf's death, pure invention.

Loschek goes on to say that he telegraphed for Widerhofer who arrived at 8.30, locked up everything and laid out Rudolf and Mary on their beds which 'were not like the beds of a married couple side by side, but along the two walls'. He then found on the Crown Prince's bedside table a note from Rudolf addressed to him which read:

Dear Loschek. Fetch a priest and arrange for us to be buried together in one grave at Heiligenkreuz. Deliver my dear Mary's valuables and her letter to her mother. Thank you for your invariably loyal and devoted service during the many years which you have been with me. Get the letter to my wife to her as soon as possible. Rudolf.

'And then,' Loschek says, 'I broke down. I knelt and laid my head against Rudolf's arm and wept bitterly.'

It is unlikely that by January 19th, 1928, when Loschek dictated this statement, Mitis's study of the Crown Prince, reproducing the Hoyos *Denkschrift,* although published in the same year, was already on sale. Therefore, unless Mitis had consulted Loschek while he was writing the book, and neither of them make any mention of this, it seems improbable that the latter knew what Hoyos (who had died in 1899) had said.

Loschek's account differs from the Hoyos *Denkschrift* on three important points. He states that he last saw the Crown Prince alive at 6.10 a.m., and minutes later heard two shots; that as soon as he went into the bedroom he saw that Rudolf had shot first Mary and then himself; that he and the Count were the only witnesses of what occurred—he makes absolutely no mention of Philip of Coburg. Hoyos wrote his statement only a few weeks after the events he describes. Loschek dictated his version many years later at the age of eighty-three. He was inaccurate about many details, and his memory could have failed him about the exact time when he last saw the Crown Prince alive. It seems however unlikely that he would have been inaccurate about the shots he heard or the state of the bodies when he first saw them—these are the sort of stark events which remain imprinted on the mind. The versions of the two key witnesses as to what happened at Mayerling therefore conflict. Where does the balance of credibility lie?

No evidence has yet appeared to show that anyone besides Loschek heard any shots, and his statement about this therefore remains uncorroborated. There is, however, one indication that the time when he says he heard them may be fairly accurate. It appears, surprisingly, in the summary compiled by Hoyos of information derived from various sources. According to this summary, Bratfisch told Wodiczka the Mayerling gamekeeper when the latter was preparing to leave at 7 a.m. on the morning of January 30th to prepare for the day's shoot, that it was pointless for him to do so: there would be no shoot because the Crown Prince was dead. Hoyos cites as witnesses for this two members of Rudolf's household one of whom heard of it direct from Wodiczka. He adds that the gamekeeper did not set out as he had planned.

As regards Loschek's version of the cause of death, two responsible people, as soon as they walked into the Crown Prince's bedroom and saw the bodies, also came to the conclusion that Rudolf had shot Mary Vetsera and then himself. One was Dr. Widerhofer, the other Slatin of the Court Commission. Widerhofer himself never wrote about this, but that he was in no doubt as to what had occurred is confirmed not only by the summary of his findings in the official announcement of suicide, but also by an entry in Archduchess Valerie's diary recording what he told the Emperor.[4] Slatin, who wrote the first draft of the report of the first Court Commission sent to Mayerling on the day of the Crown Prince's death, and a few days later was ordered to draw up an inventory of the contents of the shooting lodge, made a number of shorthand notes of his experiences. In 1924, by then a retired senior civil servant, he wrote these up into a memorandum which he checked very carefully indeed five years later. Extracts from this were published in the *Neues Wiener*

Tagblatt after his death,[5] and in addition a number of quotations from the original copy of it appear in a recent work on Mayerling.[6]

In 1929 when Slatin rechecked his memorandum it is likely that he had read the Hoyos *Denkschrift* published by Mitis in the previous year, but improbable that he knew of Loschek's recollections, for these were not published until 1932. He describes the scene in the Crown Prince's bedroom as he noted it at the time.

In the bedroom we found two corpses: that of the late Crown Prince, his face hardly disfigured at all, but the top of his skull burst open and from this blood and brains oozed, it seemed to me as the result of a shot fired at very close range—and the corpse of a beautiful girl, Mary Vetsera.[7]

Later he added some more details.

Although I did not note this I remember absolutely clearly that the Crown Prince lay on the left of the bed and the young Baroness on the right, and I am almost equally certain that to the left of the Crown Prince's bed on a chair or a low table or something of the sort there was a hand mirror and a revolver, the presence of both of which Hofrat Kubasek confirmed to me after the Commission's visit of February 4th, 1889.[8]

His conclusion is quite unequivocal. 'The Crown Prince in agreement with Mary Vetsera shot first her and then himself.'[9]

Widerhofer's and Slatin's immediate reactions and conclusions as to the way in which Rudolf and Mary Vetsera died were the same as Loschek's. About this it would seem that Loschek was speaking the truth. But then how is Hoyos's cyanide story to be explained? Slatin provides a possible clue when he quotes as one of the proofs of the cause of death:

An ashtray surrounded by tiger's teeth with the inscription 'A revolver would be better—deadlier', which we found on the morning of January 31st on the writing desk in Vienna.[10]

According to Polzer-Hoditz who became *chef de cabinet* to Karl Franz Joseph's successor and the last Habsburg Emperor, a leather brief case containing a few of Rudolf's possessions from

Mayerling which had been kept in the Emperor's Chancery was found to contain a flat onyx ashtray, ornamented with gilded eagle's claws, on the inside of which Mary Vetsera had written in violet ink: 'Rather revolver than poison. Revolver is more certain.'[11] It may have been that from Loschek's recollection of these ashtrays, or some similar indication that Rudolf and Mary had considered ways of killing themselves other than by shooting, that the cyanide story was originated.

If shooting was admitted as the cause of death the conclusion that Rudolf had killed Mary and then himself was inescapable—nobody would believe that she was capable of handling a revolver. But if it was reported that death had occurred from poisoning—a possible means for an eighteen-year-old girl to kill her lover—then the blame could be shifted on to her and Rudolf made to appear as her victim. Possibly this idea occurred to Loschek as soon as he saw what had happened and he lied to Hoyos. Or he may have told the Count the truth, or the latter went into the room and saw it for himself. According to Monts of the German Embassy in Vienna, the station master at Baden telegraphed the head of the Vienna branch of the Rothschilds (who had a controlling interest in the railway) to report that when Hoyos was arguing his way on to the express he shouted: 'The Crown Prince has shot himself. I must go to His Majesty at once.'[12]

Hoyos would, however, certainly have clutched at the idea that the cause of the Crown Prince's death could be said to be poisoning by Mary Vetsera. It made it possible to represent Rudolf in a somewhat better light which would make the tragedy easier for his parents to bear, and it averted the ultimate disgrace of the heir to the throne, whose ancestors had held the august title of Holy Roman Emperor in almost unbroken succession for four hundred years, being denied a Christian burial. A rumour later circulated in Vienna that Hoyos had offered to Franz Joseph to spread the story that while out shooting he had accidentally killed Rudolf, and then leave the Monarchy for good. This suggests that the Count had the reputation of a man who was utterly loyal to the Emperor, placed the interests of the dynasty above all other considerations, and was willing to sacrifice himself to defend them. It would therefore be in character for him to be willing to say because it protected the House of Habsburg that Rudolf had been poisoned even if he knew that this was not true.

What part did Coburg play in all this? Hoyos writes that he was there when the door was broken down. Loschek however makes no mention of him at all. The Prince himself beyond saying that he was at Mayerling, 'saw everything' and that the details were too frightful to relate,[13] apparently remained silent. Possibly the door was broken down before he arrived; in which case Hoyos could have informed him in a few minutes of several *faits accompli* and left for Baden in reasonable time to catch the train. But Loschek's statement containing as it does many lapses of memory, cannot be taken as conclusive proof of this. All that can be said with any certainty is that Hoyos did by some means catch the train, and that if he deliberately misrepresented the cause of Rudolf's death to the Emperor, he did so from honourable motives in an attempt to salve something from the wreckage of an appalling situation. That this attempt would make the position worse rather than better; causing the fatal delay in the announcement of the Crown Prince's suicide which gave Mayerling what today would be described as sensational news value, and which led to damaging theorising and fantasy as to the truth, was something which he could scarcely be expected to foresee.

The findings of the Court Commission probably contain information which would clear up a number of obscure points as to what happened at Mayerling on the morning of Rudolf's death, but they, together with the full report of the autopsy on the Crown Prince, have disappeared. Franz Joseph, presumably determined that they should not be deposited in archives to which future generations of officials would have access, handing them over to Count Taaffe, who removed them to Schloss Ellischau, his castle in Bohemia. What happened to them after that remains a mystery. Both Taaffe's son and grandson hinted that some documents relating to Rudolf's death, the absolute secrecy of which they considered it a sacred duty to preserve, were in their possession. It is possible that the grandson, Count Eduard Taaffe, removed them to Ireland with his family archives when in 1937 he sold the Ellischau estate and returned to the country from which his ancestors emigrated to the Monarchy at the beginning of the eighteenth century. The relative who inherited those archives when Eduard Taaffe died in 1967, has, however, found no trace of them. Should they eventually be discovered, the seeming discrepancies between Hoyos and Loschek's statements might be resolved, but it is unlikely that they would contradict Loschek's, Widerhofer's and Slatin's findings as to the manner of Rudolf's death. Slatin states he distinctly remembers that one of the reports of the Court Commission contained the sentence: 'It is evident that the Crown Prince used the mirror in the last moment of his life.' It sounded better, he adds, 'than the crude words: "The Crown Prince shot himself with the help of the mirror".'[14]

The Court Commission reports and other documents entrusted by Franz Joseph to Count Taaffe may one day reappear. The file on Mayerling kept by Baron Krauss the Police President turned up after a gap of sixty-six years, when it was discovered in a house in Berlin amongst the papers left by an impoverished actor. Presumably it had been removed from the Vienna Police Archives, where it had been buried since 1889, by some Nazi after the Anschluss. This file throws no additional light on the actual circumstances and discovery of the Crown Prince's death, for the only time when a police officer was allowed into the shooting lodge was when Mary Vetsera's body was removed to Heiligen-kreuz. But it does contain a note, made by Krauss, of information obtained by one of his agents from Mitzi Caspar, which puts into perspective the part played by Mary Vetsera in Rudolf's decision to end his life. According to Mitzi Rudolf had talked about killing himself since the summer of 1883, and at some point proposed a suicide pact to her, a suggestion which she refused to take seriously. She said that he spent the greater part of the night with her before he went to Mayerling.[15] In other words, Rudolf, obsessed from time to time with the idea of suicide, had become afraid to die alone. Mary was not the love of his life, but she was unique in that she was the only person prepared to accompany

him in death. He did not kill himself because of her, but she made
it possible for him to do so.

The Crown Prince wrote farewell letters to several people,
amongst them Stephanie and Szögyeny. A facsimile of his letter
to Stephanie is reproduced in her memoirs.

Dear Stephanie,
    You are rid of my presence and tiresomeness; be happy in
your own way. Be good to the poor little one, all that remains
of me. Give my last greetings to all friends, particularly
Bombelles, Spindler, Latour, Wowo, Gisela, Leopold etc. etc.
I am going tranquilly to death, which alone can save my good
name.

I embrace you most warmly,
Your loving Rudolf.[16]

Expert opinion considers both the letter from which this
facsimile was derived and the letter to Szögyeny, photographic
plates of which were discovered in the State Archives in 1958, to
be authentic.[17] In the latter Rudolf wrote in Hungarian:

Dear Szögyeny,
    I must die, it is the only way in which to leave this world
at least like a gentleman.
    Be so good as to open my writing desk here in Vienna in
the Turkish room where in better times we so often sat
together, and to deal with the papers in it as laid down in my
final wishes—enclosed herewith.
    With the warmest greetings to you and to our adored Hun-
garian fatherland, and all good wishes to you,
I am,
your faithful Rudolf.

The wishes, which were drafted in German, contained the
following instructions:

Sektions-Chef von Szögyeny-Marich is to be so good as to open
alone and *immediately* my writing desk in the Turkish room in
Vienna.

Rien ne va plus

The following letters are to be delivered:

1. To Valerie.
2. To my wife.
3. To Baron Hirsch.
4. To Mitzi Caspar.

All the money which is there is to be given to Mitzi Caspar. My valet Loschek knows her exact address.

All letters to me from Countess Marie Larisch-Wallersee and the little Vetsera are to be destroyed at once.

Szögyeny can dispose as he thinks best of other papers, consulting Colonel Mayer about anything of a military nature.

Rudolf.[18]

These are the only farewell letters from the Crown Prince of which the full authentic text is known. What Rudolf said to Hirsch has never been revealed. According to Hoyos Szögyeny hinted that the letter to Mitizi Caspar was 'overflowing with love'.[19] Count Corti, who had access to excellent sources of information, relates that Rudolf also wrote to Elisabeth and, referring to the Emperor, said: 'I know quite well that I am not worthy to be his son'. He told his sister Valerie: 'I do not die willingly'.[20] It seems that in each letter he reiterated the same theme, that he must die. He did not reveal why, except for undefined references to his honour.

It has been suggested that Rudolf shot himself in despair after having learnt that there was no possibility of getting a divorce from Stephanie, but there is no evidence to show that he ever attempted to obtain one.

The greeting to Hungary in the Crown Prince's letter to Szögyeny and the fact that the situation there was the only political subject which he mentioned during his final evening with Hoyos, indicate that Hungary was much in his thoughts at the end of his life. Opposition politicians in Budapest such as Pista Karolyi were agitating for more independence for Hungary than the Compromise permitted. Had Rudolf entered into some commitment to declare himself on their side and then realised that to do so would be aligning himself with his father's opponents? Did he then, lacking the courage to resolve this dilemma, shoot himself? Rudolf may, in one of his wilder moments, have told Count Karolyi and his colleagues that they could count on his support, but whether he was involved in any major conspiracy with them is debatable. If he was why has no account of it emerged from any source, Hungarian or otherwise? The Emperor's undoubted sorrow at the time of Rudolf's death, his letters to Elisabeth every year at the end of January recalling sadly 'our dear Rudolf', 'our dear one whom we shall never forget', do not convey the impression that he considered his heir guilty of treason. That the Crown Prince was in close touch with Hungarians of whom Franz Joseph did not approve, and that at the end of his life he felt guilty about this is likely. But that these contacts were the only reason for his suicide seems improbable and remains non-proven.

A few weeks after Mayerling Franz Joseph wrote to Frau Schratt that he and Widerhofer had spent over an hour together, during which 'we once again went over the whole tragic affair, tried to find some coherence in it, searched for causes. It was all no good.'[21] In view of this letter, the persistent rumours that Rudolf shot himself after a violent quarrel with his father would seem to be exaggerated. But it is possible that some interview took place at which the Emperor, quite unaware of the effect which it would have on his son, brusquely criticised or reproved him for some aspect of his behaviour. 'You are drinking too much. I do not like the company you keep. Your marriage is going to pieces, your affair with the Vetsera girl is becoming notorious and must stop.' Or, 'I know of your futile intrigues with the Hungarians.' Or, 'As you know I have never approved of your political ideas, which I can assure you are quite impracticable.' Or 'You seem to be forgetting the responsibilities of your position. Now go away and pull yourself together.' Although he considered that the Emperor was badly advised, Rudolf retained a deep respect for his father. These or similar criticisms, made at a time when his physical and nervous stamina were both at a low ebb, could have had a devastating effect.

The absence of any farewell letter to Franz Joseph and

Rudolf's statement to his mother that he was unworthy to be his father's son, make it likely that the Emperor, perhaps unknowingly, had a part in the final breaking down of the Crown Prince's fragile self-confidence. Once that collapsed all that remained to him was the knowledge that he was a failure, coupled with a good deal of self disgust. He had neither the robust temperament nor the necessary strength to pull himself together, and in any case saw no point in doing so. He was tied to Stephanie for life. There was no prospect of succeeding to the throne in the near future. He might spend years as an impotent spectator before he got the chance of playing a decisive part in affairs of state. Like his mother Rudolf was incapable of sustaining a long haul: like her too when the situation became intolerable his instinct was to get away from it. He was feeling ill and all sense of proportion had deserted him. Mary Vetsera was intent, as her farewell letters published by her mother show, on one thing only, that if there was no future in her affair with Rudolf she would die with him so that nobody else could have him. She was not the person to restore his equilibrium. The Crown Prince had no conventional religious belief to which to cling, and nobody to whom he felt he could turn who might have suggested to him that his sense of guilt and failure was exaggerated. There was nothing to stop him from deciding, in loneliness and perhaps reluctantly, for he delayed shooting himself until the last possible moment at Mayerling, to take the action traditionally expected of an officer in the Imperial Army who had failed to preserve his honour—suicide.

Baron Gorup who, as a young police officer was sent to Mayerling to assist in the removal of Mary Vetsera's body, alleged many years later that while there he found in a drawer and copied the following note by Rudolf:

Mayerling, 30th January 1889.

Farewell!

Time is short. I sum up:

The Emperor will not abdicate in the foreseeable future. He is heading for decline. Eternal waiting with unending painful set-backs and repeated grievous struggles unbearable.

Aspirations with regard to Hungary magnificent, but dangerous. B. be on guard!

No understanding anywhere for rotting marriage. Baroness has chosen the same way because of the hopelessness of her true love for me. Expiation!

Rudolf. [22]

This note may not be authentic, but if a fabrication it is brilliant, for it could well have been written in the early hours of the morning by a young man, a glass of brandy by his side, who was very near the outside edge of sanity, his mind blanketed in despair and about to seek the only means of escape which he believed remained to him.

Even that escape was not quite complete. In his farewell letter to Loschek and, according to Count Corti, to Elisabeth, Rudolf asked to be buried at Heiligenkreuz in the midst of the Wiener-wald where he had so often found peace. By the Emperor's orders he was brought back to Vienna to the dark enclosed vault under the Church of the Capuchins filled with the marble tombs of his ancestors. Death brought no release from being a Habsburg.

CHAPTER 14

Cape Horn

According to one of the many rumours which circulated in Vienna after the Crown Prince's death, Johann Salvator went to Mayerling, quarrelled with Rudolf, and killed him by hitting him over the head with a bottle. That this was quite unfounded is conclusively proved by a telegram from the Archduke to the Emperor expressing his deep sorrow at 'the loss we have all suffered', which was despatched from Fiume several hundred miles from Vienna at 7.40 p.m. on the day of the Crown Prince's death.[1]

There was also a rumour, which has never been entirely dispelled, that Johann Salvator and Rudolf were conspiring together, and one version of this alleges that they planned to dethrone the Emperor and divide the Monarchy between them. Countess Larisch says in her memoirs that the Crown Prince entrusted her with a steel box, instructing her only to hand it over to a person who would give the password R.I.O.U. On the day of Rudolf's funeral she received a message quoting this password and summoning her to a rendezvous at half-past ten that evening. When, heavily veiled, she reached the appointed place, she was met by a mysterious stranger whom she eventually recognised to be Johann Salvator, and who told her as he took the box from her that it contained papers so damning to Rudolf and himself that had they fallen into the Emperor's hands they would both have been court martialled and shot.[2] Ten years later Milli Stubel's sister wrote her reminiscences of Johann Salvator, which were published by a Viennese newspaper. Marie Stubel asserted that the steel box described by the Countess had been handed by the Archduke to Milli for safe keeping, and that it contained a number of letters in cipher.[3] Neither she nor Countess Larisch can, however, be considered as accurate sources of information, and both published their recollections of the steel box after a considerable lapse of time.

There are indications that there had been a rapprochement between the Archduke and the Crown Prince—it may have dated from a meeting they had in Pola in July 1888. Heinrich Pollak the journalist who saw the Archduke in Vienna on the day before Rudolf's funeral, found him barely able to control his grief. According to Pollak Johann Salvator spoke in the warmest terms of his cousin's charm, many talents and 'good heart' making (in contrast to many people at that time) only one adverse comment, that Rudolf was hot tempered, and that anyone who wished to remain on good terms with him had to be extremely careful. 4 But a rapprochement does not necessarily mean a conspiracy, and if the two young men were plotting together it is unlikely that they had made a great deal of progress before the Crown Prince's death. Both of them suspected that their letters were liable to be opened. To conspire it was necessary to meet, but Rudolf during the last year of his life was much occupied with representational duties, while Johann Salvator spent the greater part of it cruising in the Mediterranean and the Adriatic, or at Fiume where by early 1889 he was working to acquire, astonishingly for a Habsburg Archduke, a master's certificate in merchant seamanship.

Johann Salvator's nephew visited him in Fiume in the winter of 1889. Milli Stubel was there and they all sat and drank tea together by the light of an oil lamp in the unpretentious lodgings where the Archduke was studying for his exams. In April he reported to his mother:

> I am continuing my lessons in navigation, and devoting more time to them as the professor has more to spare. I hope to be able to master all the material in the course of the two months which I propose to spend by the sea. 5

A few weeks later in order to put into practice what he had learnt he cruised down the Dalmatian coast. In the second half of June he told her that, in addition to mathematics, he was learning a little about how to run a ship and engineering, 'thus I think before long I shall be ready for the examination which will qualify me to command all kinds of vessels'.[6] When at the end of the month he was compelled to interrupt his studies to go and see the Grand Duchess and attend to affairs at Schloss Orth, he asked his professor to come there in August, for he was determined to pass the examination by the end of September.[7]

Having managed by some means to do this, the Archduke then took a step which he had planned for some time. On October 7th he left secretly for Zürich. From there, on the following day, he returned the insignia of his Order of the Golden Fleece to the Emperor together with a startling letter.

Zürich, 8.10.89.

Your Majesty,

My behaviour for nearly two years, during which time I have obediently refrained from anything to do with matters which did not concern me, will have convinced your Majesty that I have endeavoured to regain your Majesty's favour.

Too young to sit still for ever, too proud to be paid for doing nothing, my existence has become unbearable. My sense of honour, which is certainly justified, prevents me from requesting re-employment in the army: I have the alternative either of continuing the unworthy existence of an idle prince, or of becoming an ordinary citizen and seeking a new profession. I have finally been forced to decide for the latter, because I do not fit into my present circumstances, and to be personally independent offers a compensation for what I have lost.

I therefore voluntarily renounce my rank and position, and respectfully return my title and rights as an Archduke and my military rank to Your Majesty, humbly requesting that Your Majesty will confer on me a bourgeois status.

I shall seek an existence, a means of earning my living, probably at sea far from the Fatherland, and endeavour to create for myself a position which although modest will be worthy of respect. Should, however, Your Majesty one day call your subjects to the colours, I trust I may be permitted to return home and—if only as an ordinary soldier—to offer up my life in Your Majesty's service.

I entreat Your Majesty to believe that this step has been made harder for me by the knowledge that it will be disagreeable to Your Majesty, to whom I am eternally grateful and who commands my entire devotion. As, however, I am paying dearly for it—with my entire social standing—with everything which stands for hope and a career—I hope Your Majesty will find it possible to forgive me.

Your Majesty's loyal and most
obedient subject
Archduke Johann FML.[8]

The Emperor received this letter two days later. During the eight months since Rudolf's death in addition to his personal grief he had endured a great deal. Elisabeth was in a state of semi-collapse and it seemed doubtful if she would ever appear in public again. There had been trouble with the Hungarians, trouble with the Czechs, Taaffe's position as Minister President of Austria was shaky, Milan of Serbia had abdicated and the international situation gave cause for anxiety. Now, at the time when it was necessary for the House of Habsburg to close their ranks and stand together, Johann Salvator opted out. His references to princes who were paid for doing nothing was insulting, for it applied to a number of his relations, and his action, for which there was no parallel in the history of the dynasty, registered a mark of no confidence in it for all the world to see. To Franz Joseph it was the equivalent of desertion in the face of the enemy, for which there could be neither understanding nor forgiveness. He summoned Johann Salvator's eldest brother Ferdinand of Tuscany to Vienna, and they conferred together on the behaviour of this Habsburg who had 'renounced his family, his position and his duties and fled from them like a thief'.[9] The Emperor, while appreciating Johann Salvator's declaration of loyalty to himself, was no longer prepared to put up with his behaviour. Major Csanady was sent to Zürich with a curt letter in which Franz Joseph granted the Archduke's request to resign his army rank

233

and relinquish 'the right to be publicly recognised and treated as a Prince of the Imperial House', and demanded to know what name he now proposed to adopt. The Emperor went on to say that he was terminating Johann Salvator's appointment as Colonel Proprietor of the 2nd Artillery Regiment, striking his name off the list of knights of the Order of the Golden Fleece, and giving orders that his appanage and other allowances were no longer to be paid. He forbade the Archduke to re-enter the Monarchy without his express permission, and ordered him to sign an acknowledgement of his letter. Johann Salvator signed.[10] Csanady took the document back to Vienna and handed it over to the Emperor. Franz Joseph received it without comment. Two days later Johann Salvator wrote again to the Emperor. He said that he had decided to adopt the name of Johann Orth and, since he was no longer a Prince of the Imperial House with extra-territorial rights, requested that he be granted Austrian or Hungarian citizenship or, if this were not permitted, that he should receive orders as to what foreign nationality he should acquire. Franz Joseph instructed Kalnoky to reply that it was his express wish that the former Archduke should take the necessary steps to become a Swiss citizen. This was the final mark of Imperial displeasure. It caused a great deal of confusion, and led to graver consequences for Johann Salvator than perhaps the Emperor realised.

Johann Salvator's departure from the Monarchy has been cited as further proof that he was involved in some conspiracy with Rudolf. But in that event he would not have delayed his departure abroad for eight months after Mayerling, and it seems likely that the date of this was determined by the necessity of first acquiring a master's certificate in seamanship in order to ensure a means of earning his living. When writing to his eldest brother he stressed that the step which he had taken was not the result of a sudden impulse. He asked his mother's forgiveness for leaving without saying goodbye to her.

It was not from lack of devotion but from lack of courage, because I knew that I would not be able to withstand the pleadings of your maternal heart. . . . It is true that for a time you will not see me so much; but please believe me that this thought has also cost me a great deal. . . . Being sure of your forgiveness I implore your blessing from the depths of my deeply disturbed soul at this grave moment of my life.[11]

It had not been an easy decision to take.

Grand Duchess Maria Antonia was seventy-six, and the renunciation of his rank by her adored youngest son shocked her profoundly. But she wrote giving him her blessing and, if she could neither understand nor approve what he had done, her affection for him was unaltered. Johann Salvator's sister Luisa Princess Isenburg at once invited him to spend Christmas at Birstein. Others, as he told his mother, adopted a different attitude.

The promptness with which my renunciation was sanctioned is the best proof of how little importance has been and is attributed to it, and most of the relations, while deploring the step think it a good thing that the family should be rid for ever of that member of it who according to their ideas has never done it credit.

He then endeavoured to reassure her:

To be successful I must no longer look behind me but must look ahead. Do not be afraid dear Mamma, that I will speculate with disastrous consequences for my finances. I am well aware that the little which I now have is *everything* and I will not buy a ship before having made long and searching investigations. I am now going to travel to make the necessary inquiries and to gain experience in the service.[12]

At the beginning of November Johann Salvator, then in London, received an Austrian passport (there was no common citizenship of both parts of the Monarchy) valid for six months. The issue of this had been authorised by Taaffe. It was accompanied by a letter from Kalnoky informing him of Franz Joseph's order that he should apply for Swiss nationality. He replied that he would obey the Emperor's command 'although it pains me inexpressibly not to be allowed to remain an Austrian and a subject of our most gracious Monarch'.[13] Shortly after this he embarked for Hamburg, travelling via Stockholm as a volunteer ship's officer. The voyage was rough and, as Johann Salvator admitted, not an agreeable experience.

> This trial was full of disillusionments, both as regards the interests of this profession for an educated person, as regards the contact which it afforded with the captain and the officers, and finally because it is an existence full of privations and dangers, and with little about it of glory or merit.

However, he was determined to continue with his plan.

> The information which I have been able to acquire . . . has convinced me that capital invested in a ship can give a satisfactory return provided the owner captains the vessel. For this reason I am dropping the idea of acquiring a ship now and concentrating on the practical study of the art of seamanship, in order not to take up this profession until I am sure that I am capable of practising it.[14]

Then he discovered that if he became a Swiss citizen, the master's certificate which he had acquired in the Monarchy would no longer be valid. This was a very serious blow. He wrote to Kalnoky imploring the Foreign Minister to persuade the Emperor to rescind his decision or, if this was not possible to induce the Minister of Trade to agree that, even if he became Swiss, his master's certificate would still entitle him to command his own ship sailing under the Austrian flag.[15] Kalnoky did not receive this letter with enthusiasm: it added another complication to a thoroughly tiresome problem.

No official statement about Johann Salvator's renunciation of his title had been issued; the Emperor, understandably, was anxious to keep the whole affair out of the newspapers. But formalities which nobody contemplated waiving had to be complied with and therefore, as in the case of Rudolf's death, altogether too many people had to be told what had happened. The Emperor might order secrecy; Kalnoky could not ensure it.

It was, for example, useless to mark all official communications with regard to the former Archduke as 'strictly confidential' and to restrict their circulation. As the Austro-Hungarian Embassy in London pointed out, if Johann Salvator was going to lead a seafaring existence he might put in at a port anywhere in the world, and therefore all Consuls must be informed of this possibility and instructed as to the attitude which they should adopt. [16] In a matter of weeks the Press got hold of the story, and it was featured in newspapers throughout Europe. In England and France in particular Johann Salvator was described as highly gifted, the hope of the Imperial army and one of its most popular and distinguished generals. The *Daily News* prophesied that he would follow the example of Peter the Great and enter a shipbuilding yard,

> Johann will of course soon become 'Jack' in the yard; and as Jack Orth we may expect to find the new mate hail fellow well met with half the hammer men of Deptford. [17]

The Times, summing him up as 'a Prince of remarkable ability and character', announced that he had laid down his rank because:

> The most recent military appointments . . . have convinced him that no real change has come over the spirit in which the organisation of the army is worked—a spirit which the Archduke believes to be injurious to the efficiency of the service. [18]

Such comments were calculated to displease the Emperor. They did not ease the task of Kalnoky and his colleagues on whom, since Johann Salvator was now a private citizen and therefore no concern of the Court, the burden of dealing with his affairs fell, and who were confronted, like the Court hierarchy over Mayerling, with a situation for which there was no precedent.

Johann Salvator's plea that the question of his change of nationality be reconsidered was therefore altogether most unwelcome. Kalnoky consulted Taaffe. Taaffe consulted the Minister of Trade who was responsible for the Merchant Marine. The latter wrote a very long memorandum, saying that if the former Archduke became a foreign national his master's certificate was no longer valid. Nobody apparently dared to submit the problem to the Emperor. Meanwhile Johann Salvator, anxiously awaiting the reply on which his future depended, left Hamburg for England. From the North Western Hotel, Liverpool, an address evocative of black horsehair sofas, a swirl of fog round the windows, the dank greyness of Merseyside in winter—a world removed from the colour and elegance of the Court of Vienna—he wrote to Heinrich Pollak. Should he be compelled to change his nationality, he wanted to ensure that Pollak would publish a statement that he had only done this in obedience to the Emperor's command.

> It matters very much to me that I should not be regarded as a disloyal son of the Fatherland, as many people who have attacked me anonymously assume.[19]

To add to his depression he heard that Laaba had died, and was anxious in case the Major had failed to destroy a number of compromising letters. Altogether Johann Salvator's nerves were on edge when shortly before Christmas a letter, addressed to 'Herr Johann Orth', arrived from Kalnoky informing him that he must acquire Swiss nationality, and that nothing could be done to solve the consequent problem of his master's certificate.[20]

Johann Salvator spent Christmas with his sister and her family at Birstein, and came to the conclusion that there was only one course of action open to him. His Austrian passport did not expire until the end of April, and he could not be expected to complete the formalities for changing his nationality before then. He must acquire a ship, sail while his passport was still valid and present everyone with a *fait accompli*. Shortly before the end of January he called on the Austro-Hungarian Consul General in London to say that he had bought a ship, completed the negotiations for a cargo, and proposed in the near future to set off for South America. He requested that the vessel be registered at a port in the Monarchy in order that he might sail under the Austrian flag. Reporting this interview to his Ambassador the Consul-General observed:

Since Herr Johann Orth, as he called himself when talking to me, has not yet acquired foreign nationality and so de facto is still an Austrian citizen, his request conforms with the law and the necessary action can be taken. [21]

Ten days later he forwarded to the maritime authorities at Fiume an application from Johann Salvator for the registration there of the *Saint Margaret*, an iron three master of 1,368 tons.

Unlike his Consul-General the Ambassador still had doubts about the former Archduke's nationality, and wrote to Vienna asking for a definite ruling as to whether 'Herr Orth is or is not still an Austrian citizen'. [22] Kalnoky passed the query on to Taaffe. The latter replied that in his opinion Herr Orth, until such time as he acquired other nationality, was still a citizen of the Monarchy and therefore his master's certificate entitled him to command a ship sailing under the Austro-Hungarian flag. [23] The Foreign Minister marked Taaffe's letter for file and took no further action. Then, in rapid succession, Kalnoky received two further communications. The first was a despatch from the Embassy in London reporting that Johann Salvator had requested papers to enable him to make the voyage across the Atlantic. But according to regulations these could only be issued to the owner of a ship if he was a citizen of the Monarchy. What, the Embassy asked once again, was the position with regard to this applicant's nationality? The second was a letter from the maritime authorities in Fiume pointing out that, according to the law, a ship could only be registered there if the owner was a Hungarian national, which Herr Johann Orth was not, since he had been born in Florence and was domiciled in Gmunden. Should an exception be made because of his former rank? Kalnoky now felt compelled to submit the problem to the Emperor. Franz Joseph was emphatic that under no circumstances would he permit Johann Salvator to become a Hungarian citizen. Taaffe, once again consulted, advised that the former Archduke should be directed to withdraw his application for the registration in Fiume of the *Saint Margaret,* and apply for her to be registered in Trieste, the port in the Austrian half of the Monarchy. [24] It was by now very nearly the end of February. Since the beginning of the year a great deal of red tape had been deployed round Johann Salvator's affairs.

To buy and equip the *Saint Margaret* Johann Salvator had realised all his available capital, and raised a loan on the security of Schloss Orth. He had contracted to carry a cargo to South America, and was in process of engaging a crew. His financial future now depended on this venture, and he must be on the high seas before his passport expired at the end of April. But he could not sail until the question of the *Saint Margaret*'s registration had been settled. Time was running out. The former Archduke, never a patient man, was temperamentally inclined to oscillate between optimism and depression. He had renounced his title and a large income in order to be free to do as he wished and to earn a living in a way to which nobody could object. But it seemed that he could not escape from the fact that he had been born an Archduke, and this meant that the liberty he sought was illusory, for restrictions could still be imposed on him which he was powerless to combat. Attributing deliberate malevolence to what was probably no more than bureaucratic dithering; disillusioned and convinced that he would never be permitted to follow the profession which he had chosen, he made a desperate bid for an alternative. On March 2nd, travelling under the name of Moritz Schenk, he arrived in Sofia and late that evening was received in audience by Prince Ferdinand of Bulgaria.

Von Burian, the Imperial Ambassador in Sofia, telegraphed and later wrote to Kalnoky a summary of Ferdinand's report of this interview which ended at one in the morning. According to the Prince, Johann Salvator in a state of nervous collapse, said that his plan for earning his living at sea had been frustrated and that he was penniless. Swearing that he would expect no promotion for ten years, he begged for an appointment as lieutenant in the Bulgarian army, adding that if this was refused he would seek a similar appointment in Turkey. Ferdinand rejected his request and ordered him to leave Sofia at once.[25]

When the first news of Johann Salvator's visit to Sofia reached Vienna Kalnoky went straight to the Emperor. No doubt with

Franz Joseph's full approval, he then telegraphed Calice the Imperial Ambassador in Constantinople informing him that any application which the former Archduke might make to join the Turkish army was in direct contravention of His Imperial Majesty's wishes. [26] Later he wrote to von Burian telling him that Prince Ferdinand had acted admirably in putting a rapid end to the adventure of the 'intriguer' Herr Orth who, painful though it was to have to say this about a member of the Imperial Family, had certainly misrepresented the truth about his personal position. [27]

By March 8th Johann Salvator was back in Birstein having achieved nothing. He then drafted a final petition to the Emperor which, with a covering letter to Kalnoky, he sent to Vienna by the hand of his brother-in-law Prince Isenburg. His enquiries, he told Franz Joseph, had revealed that whereas it would take him two years to acquire Swiss nationality, he could become a German citizen in a very much shorter time, and this he proposed to do if the Emperor agreed. As a special act of grace he begged that His Imperial Majesty would permit him to command a ship flying the Austro-Hungarian flag even when he was no longer a citizen of the Monarchy. [28] Franz Joseph did not reply to this petition, but he discussed it with Kalnoky. When the Ambassador in London reported that, if Herr Johann Orth did not sail within a few days, he would incur a serious financial loss, and again asked for permission to issue him with temporary papers for the voyage, Kalnoky telegraphed authorising this. Possibly the Emperor and he had come to the conclusion that the farther away the former Archduke was the better.

On March 26th, 1890, Johann Salvator sailed in the *Saint Margaret* for South America. A quarter of a century earlier another Habsburg had also left for the New World, but under very different circumstances. Archduke Ferdinand Max, accompanied by an embryo court, set out as Emperor of Mexico. Johann Salvator, with no companions except his crew, was bound for Port la Plata with a cargo of cement.

Before leaving Chatham he made a new will, signing it 'Johann Orth formerly Archduke Johann', in which he left Schloss Orth to his mother, and his house in Vienna and 100,000 gulden absolutely to 'my dear companion in life Ludmilla Stubel'. For over ten years in many ways Milli Stubel had occupied the same position in his life as that of Mitiz Caspar in Rudolf's—someone to whom it was always possible to return, who did not argue. She stood by him in adversity, joined him in his wanderings round the Mediterranean after he gave up the Linz command, and did not abandon him when he ceased to be an Archduke. Her relations later alleged that he then married her, but could produce no documentary proof of this; had he done so, it seems likely that he would have described her as his wife in his final will. Possibly they exchanged some vow which both considered binding; certainly she was the sole remnant of the past which he carried forward with him into his new existence as Johann Orth. He asked her, and she agreed, to follow him to South America.

In view of his lack of experience in handling a ship of any size Johann Salvator designated himself second-in-command of the *Saint Margaret*, engaging an experienced seaman, Captain Sodich, to take her across the Atlantic. He proposed to assume command himself for the next stage of the voyage to Valparaiso, where he had contracted to load a cargo of saltpetre and transport it back to Europe. It was a prospect which he viewed without enthusiasm, describing himself in a farewell letter to a friend as 'joyless and lonely' with only one objective left, to complete this venture successfully as a self-justification for his new existence. [29] The order for his change of nationality still rankled and writing to his mother to ask for her prayers he allowed himself one bitter comment, 'I venture to say that as I was legally born an Archduke I should not be compelled to become the subject of another Sovereign'. [30]

In spite of contrary winds, a severe storm and an outbreak of fire, the *Saint Margaret* reached the roadstead off la Plata on May 30th. Johann Salvator then however was left without officers. According to him, Captain Sodich was insulting and handed in his resignation, the Second Officer had to be dismissed for dishonesty, and the Third Officer had lost his nerve for seafaring. Sucich the Second Officer on the other hand later implied that 'Johann Orth' retained the mentality of an Archduke and a General, insisted that his orders be obeyed even though he was nominally second-in-command; that he refused to listen to the advice of those more experienced than himself, and was altogether so impossible that none of his officers were prepared to continue to serve with him.

Whether or not Sucich exaggerated, Johann Salvator's first experience of working as an ordinary citizen with no privileges of birth or rank had not been happy. He admitted to having derived 'little satisfaction' from the voyage, and on landing in South America was depressed to find that no letters from anyone in the Monarchy awaited him. There were rumours about his motive for renouncing his title in various newspapers on which he commented irritably, '"*cherchez la femme*" is often correct, but not everything in life is to be ascribed to this'.[31] When Milli Stubel who, accompanied by a maid, had travelled second class on a passenger ship to Buenos Aires, joined him on July 4th, he blamed her for indiscretion about their relationship. She wrote to her mother complaining that this was unfair: 'But I don't need to tell you what he is like, you know him well enough.' Altogether it was not a wholly joyful reunion, and Milli did not look forward to the immediate future, a further two months at sea. 'God knows if I will survive it. . . . Think of your poor unhappy Milli.'[32]

Johann Salvator interpreted Kalnoky's silence as implying that the order that he must change his nationality was tacitly dropped. But this did not mean that there was any employment offering him if he returned to Europe, and he could only carry on as planned. He assumed personal command of the *Saint Margaret*, engaged two new officers and replaced some of the crew. By the time Milli arrived all his ambition had hardened into one fierce resolve. He must go on to Valparaiso. Regardless of the fact that it was the worst season of the year, regardless too of his own inexperience of seamanship outside the Mediterranean, he must accomplish what he had set out to do, and this meant that he must surmount the dangers of one of the most hazardous voyages in the world—round Cape Horn. On July 12th with Milli on board he set sail from la Plata. On October 9th Kalnoky received a telegram from the Consul in Valparaiso reporting that the *Saint Margaret* was overdue. Lloyds were informed on November 5th that she was presumed lost, but declined to post her as missing because there was no conclusive evidence that she had sunk. On December 9th they were notified from Hamburg that the *Saint Margaret* had been sighted off Cape Horn on July 31st, when there was a raging hurricane and five degrees of frost. After that there was silence. Franz Joseph ordered that a search be made, but no trace of the *Saint Margaret* was discovered.

It is difficult to accept that a man who has vanished in the prime of life is dead, particularly a man as vital and unusual as Johann Salvator. Rumours that he was alive circulated for years. It was said that he had retreated to live in solitude in a remote part of South America, or journeyed on to Japan and finally died on an island in the Indian Ocean. There were reports that he had been seen in the province of Concordia in the Argentine, at the Paris Opera, at Cannes. A Miss Percy Fergusson from Biloxi in South Carolina, wrote a very long letter on bright pink paper in which she described meeting him when he had assumed the guise of a Russian sailor educated at a Russian university. Many of his family refused to believe that he would not return; his mother never wore mourning for him and made him her sole heir. There was a story that when she died a mysterious stranger arrived, prayed by her coffin and then disappeared.

Twenty-one years passed. Every rumour proved false. The *Saint Margaret* had disappeared, and nobody who sailed in her was ever seen again. In 1911 Johann Salvator was presumed dead and his estate finally wound up. In the petition for this submitted by his nephew's lawyer to the Obersthofmarschallamt he was described as:

> An Archduke without external privileges. . . . Archduke Johann who called himself Johann Orth, but nevertheless an Archduke and a member of the Imperial Family. The privileges were done away with, the Archduke remained.[33]

The legal definition was psychologically true. Johann Salvator had achieved the physical liberty for which he craved: his body lay, not in the vault under the Church of the Capuchins, but far away beneath the waves of the South Atlantic. But mentally he remained to the end of his life an Archduke and a Hapsburg, never quite able to divest himself of the conviction that he was therefore different from other people, unable to fit into the ordinary world, and driven by his endeavour to do so to self-destruction.

Epilogue

Rudolf was dead. Johann Salvator was dead. The Emperor and Archduke Albrecht, sustained by the power to make decisions which the young men had craved and been denied, toiled on. Franz Joseph never mentioned Johann Salvator and, except to Elisabeth, rarely spoke of his son. As in the dark days after Königgrätz he continued to work punctiliously as if nothing had happened. But then there had been a vestige of hope, and now there was none. At Mayerling he had lost the future. It was noticed that the heart seemed to have gone out of him.

Archduke Albrecht was appalled by the damage to the Hapsburg mystique inflicted by 'Rudolf's horrifying suicide . . . Johann's flight or desertion . . . two unparalleled stains in one year on the untarnished honour of our House',[1] a disgrace from which he declared he personally would never recover. Although almost completely blind he remained Inspector General until his death in 1895 at the age of seventy-eight. Over a thousand officers attended his State funeral, and the Emperor issued an Order of the Day describing him as the 'ornament and pride' of the army.

Franz Joseph lived for another twenty-one years, and during this time nothing was spared him. Elisabeth was assassinated by an anarchist in 1898; Franz Ferdinand his Heir Apparent was murdered at Sarajevo in 1914; the Great War broke out mortally threatening the Monarchy to the preservation of which he had dedicated his life. Some three and a half centuries earlier his great ancestor Karl V, the Habsburg who ruled over an Empire on which the sun never set, abdicated and retired to end his days in a monastery in Spain. He told the assembled Knights of the Order of the Golden Fleece that he was giving up the throne because his strength was exhausted and he was very tired. After Mayerling Franz Joseph had the courage and stamina to carry the mission with which he believed God had entrusted him on to the end. But he too was very tired.

Notes

The following abbreviations have been used for manuscript sources:

K.A.   Kriegsarchiv, Vienna.
P.R.O.   Public Records Office, London.
Sal.P.   Salisbury Papers, Christ Church, Oxford.
St. A.   Haus- Hof- und Stattsarchiv, Vienna.

PROLOGUE

1. Walburga Lady Paget, *Scenes and Memories*. Smith, Elder, London, 1912, p. 218.
2. Mrs. Hugh Fraser, *A Diplomatic Wife in Many Lands*. Hutchinson, London, 1911, Vol. II, pp. 539–40.
3. Quoted, Joseph Redlich, *Emperor Francis Joseph of Austria*. Macmillan, London, 1929, p. 408.
4. Quoted, Philipp Fürst zu Eulenberg-Hertefeld, *Das Ende König Ludwigs II und andere Erlebnisse*. Fr Wilh. Grund Verlag, Leipzig, 1934, Vol. II, p. 163.

1   THE EMPEROR—RULER AND STATESMAN

1. Schwarzenberg to Metternich, 29.7.1850. Metternich archives. Quoted Redlich, *op. cit.*, p. 50.
2. Quoted Egon Caesar Count Corti, *Mensch und Herrscher*. Styria Verlag, Graz, Vienna, Altötting, 1952, p. 78.
3. Quoted Redlich, *op. cit.*, p. 91.
4. Fischof, *Österreich und die Bürgerschaften seiner Bestände*, p. 177. Quoted Viktor Bibl. *Der Zerfall Österreichs*. Rikola Verlag, Vienna, Munich, Leipzig, Berlin, 1924, Vol. II, p. 221.
5. Quoted Redlich, *op. cit.*, p. 126.
6. Nicholas I to Frederick William IV.
7. Bavarian Minister to King of Bavaria, 16.11.1857. Bavarian Geheimes Staatsarchiv. Quoted Egon Cesare Count Corti, *Elisabeth*. Verlag Anton Pustet, Salzburg-Leipzig, 1935, p. 65.
8. Quoted Comte de Hübner, *Neuf Ans de Souvenirs d'un Ambassadeur d'Autriche à Paris sous le Second Empire 1851–1859*. Plon, Paris, 1905, Vol. II, p. 73.
9. Manzoni, quoted H. Montgomery Hyde, *Mexican Empire*, Macmillan, London, 1946, p. 73.
10. The Hon. Evelyn Ashley—*The Life and Correspondence of Henry John Temple Viscount Palmerston*. Richard Bentley and Sons, London, 1879, Vol. II, p. 386.
11. Franz Joseph to Elisabeth, 8.7.1859. Quoted Corti, *Mensch und Herrscher, op. cit.*, p. 238.
12. Friedjung, *Österreich von 1848 bis 1860*, Vol. I, pp. 181–2. Quoted Adolf Schwarzenberg, *Prince Felix zu Schwarzenberg*. Columbia University Press, New York, 1946, p. 119.

13. Budapest.
14. *Bismarck's Table Talk*. Introduced by Charles Low. H. Grevel and Co., London, 1895, p. 81.
15. Helmuth von Moltke, *Gesammelte Schriften und Aufsätze*. Berlin, 1891, Vol. III, pp. 426–7.
16. Quoted Gordon A. Craig, *The Battle of Königgrätz*. Weidenfeld and Nicolson, London, 1965, p. 38.
17. *Österreichs Kampfe im Jahr, 1866, k.k. Generalstabsbureau für Kreiggeschichte*, 2nd ed. Vol. III, p. 222. Quoted Emil Franzel, *1866 Il Mondo Casca*. Herold Verlag, Vienna–Munich, 1968, Vol. II, p. 599.
18. Kriegsarchiv. Quoted Franzel, *Il Mondo Casca, op. cit.*, Vol. II, p. 629.
19. Quoted Adam Wandruszka, *Schicksalsjahr 1866*. Styria Verlag, Graz, 1966, p. 13.
20. Moering Diary, 17.7.1866. Quoted Wandruschka, *op. cit.*, p. 272.
21. Quoted Eduard von Wertheimer, *Graf Julius Andrassy*. Deutsche Verlags Anstalt, Stuttgart, 1910–13, Vol. I, p. 200.
22. Queen Victoria to the Princess Royal, 15.2.1878. Quoted Elizabeth Longford, *Victoria R.I.*, p. 411. Weidenfeld and Nicolson, London, 1962.
23. Otto Frass, *Quellenbuch zur Österreichische Geschichte*. Birkenverlag, Vienna, 1962, Vol. III, p. 261.
24. von Biegeleben, 24.2.1871. Quoted Oskar Regele, *Österreichs Krieg, 1866*. Article in *Der Österreichisch-Ungarische Ausgleich von 1867*, edited by Dr. Peter Berger. Herold Verlag, Vienna–Munich, 1967, p. 300.
25. General von Schnürer, *Denkwürdigkeiten*. Verlag v. Reimer Hobhay, Berlin, 1927, Vol. I, p. 278.
26. Franz Schnürer—*Briefe Kaiser Franz Josefs an seine Mutter*—p. 377. Quoted Corti, *Mensch und Herrscher, op. cit.*, p. 449.
27. Lord Frederick Hamilton, *The Vanished Pomps of Yesterday*. Hodder and Stoughton, London, 1919, p. 120.
28. Michael Petrovich, *The Emergence of Russian Panslavism 1850–60*. Columbia University Press, 1956, p. 24. Quoted Virginia Cowles, *The Russian Dagger*. Collins, London, 1969, p. 37.
29. Horace Vernet. Quoted Cowles, *op. cit.*, p. 21.
30. George Earle Buckle, *The Letters of Queen Victoria*. John Murray, London, 1928, Second Series, Vol. III, p. 54.
31. The building in which the Ministry of Foreign Affairs was housed.
32. Franz Joseph to Elisabeth, Ragusa, 1.5.1875. Georg Nostitz-Rieneck, *Briefe Kaiser Franz Josephs an Kaiserin Elisabeth, 1859–1898*. Herold Verlag, Vienna–Munich, 1966, Vol. I, p. 177.
33. Hübner Diary, 10.4.1876. Quoted Corti, *Mensch und Herrscher, op. cit.*, pp. 490–1.
34. Quoted Theodor von Sosnosky, *Die Balkanpolitik Österreich-Ungarns seit 1866*. Deutsche Verlags Anstalt, Stuttgart–Berlin, 1913, Vol. I, pp. 154–5.
35. He had recently been created Lord Beaconsfield but will be referred to by the name by which he is more generally remembered.
36. George Earle Buckle (in succession to W. F. Monnypenny), *The Life of Benjamin Disraeli, Earl of Beaconsfield,* John Murray, London, 1920, Vol. VI, p. 217.

37. Andrassy to Plener, quoted Sosnowsky, *op. cit.,* Vol. II, p. 19.
38. Buckle, *Letters of Queen Victoria, op. cit.,* Second Series, Vol. II, p. 316.
39. Buckle, *Disraeli, op. cit.,* Vol. VI, p. 321.
40. Buckle, *Disraeli, op. cit.,* p. 329.
41. Quoted Oscar Jaszi, *The Dissolution of the Habsburg Monarchy.* University of Chicago Press, 1929, p. 115.
42. W. N. Medlicott, *The Congress of Berlin and After.* Methuen, London, 1938, p. 148.
43. St. A. Quoted Corti, *Mensch und Herrscher, op. cit.,* p. 520.
44. Lord Odo Russell to Lord Salisbury, 15.2.1879. Sal. P.
45. Quoted *Erinnerungen an Franz Joseph I.* Edited Eduard von Steinitz. Verlag fur Kulturpolitik, Berlin, 1931, p. 87.
46. Oskar Freiherr von Mitis, *Das Leben des Kronprinzen Rudolf.* Insel Verlag, Leipzig, 1928, p. 414.
47. Quoted Corti, *Mensch und Herrscher, op. cit.,* p. 273.

2 THE EMPEROR AND THE EMPRESS

1. Quoted Louis Eisenmann, *Le Compromis Austro-Hongrois de 1867.* Société Nouvelle de Librarie et d'Edition (Librarie Georges Bellais), Paris 1904, p. 123.
2. Count Egon Caesar Corti. *Elisabeth.* Anton Pustet Verlag, Salzburg, Leipzig, 1935, p. 28.
3. *Ibid.,* p. 30.
4. Quoted Hans Flesch-Brunningen, *Die Letzten Habsburger in Augenzeugenberichten.* Karl Rauch Verlag, Düsseldorf, 1967, p. 124.
5. Quoted Redlich, *op. cit.,* p. 217.
6. Franz Joseph to Elisabeth, Verona, 26.6.1859. Nostitz-Rieneck, *Briefe, op. cit.,* Vol. I, pp. 26–8.
7. *Ibid.* to *ibid.,* Verona, 8.7.1858, Nostitz-Rieneck, *Briefe, op. cit.,* Vol. I, p. 35.
8. Franz Schnürer, *Briefe Kaiser Franz Josephs an seine Mutter 1838–72.* Munich, 1930. Quoted Corti, *Mensch und Herrscher, op. cit.,* pp. 262–3.
9. Sir A. Morier to Lord Bloomfield, Budapest, February 4th, 1866. Quoted Corti, *Elisabeth, op. cit.,* p. 142.
10. Franz Joseph to Archduchess Sophie, Ofen, February 17th, 1866. Quoted Corti, *Elisabeth, op. cit.,* p. 143.
11. Sophie to Rudolf, July 5th, 1866. Quoted Corti, *Elisabeth, op. cit.,* p. 151.
12. Konyi, *Die Reden des Franz Deak,* Vol. III, p. 578. Quoted Corti, *Elisabeth, op. cit.,* p. 152.
13. Elisabeth to Franz Joseph, Budapest, 5.7.1866. Quoted Corti, *Elisabeth, op. cit.,* p. 156.
14. Franz Joseph to Elisabeth, 7.8.1866, Vienna. Nostitz-Rieneck, *Briefe, op. cit.,* Vol. I, pp. 57–8.
15. Franz Joseph to Elisabeth, 20.8.1866. Nostitz-Rieneck, *Briefe, op. cit.,* Vol. I, p. 61.
16. Quoted Corti, *Elisabeth, op. cit.,* p. 176.
17. Quoted Corti, *Elisabeth, op. cit.,* p. 181.
18. Edmund von Glaise-Horstenau, *Franz Joseph's Weggefährte, Das Leben des*

Generalstabschef Grafen Beck. Amalthea Verlag, Zürich, Leipzig, Vienna, 1930, p. 229.

19. Fraser, *op. cit.*, Vol. II, pp. 541–5.
20. Landgräfin Fürstenberg to her sister, 5.2.1868, Rechberg archives. Quoted Corti, *Elisabeth, op. cit.*, p. 191.
21. Elisabeth to Franz Joseph, Gödöllö, April 30th, 1869. Quoted Corti, *Elisabeth, op. cit.*, p. 201.
22. Fraser, *op. cit.*, Vol. II, pp. 541–5.
23. Quoted Kark Tschuppik, *The Reign of the Emperor Francis Joseph 1848–1916.* G. Bell, London, 1930, p. 148.
24. Ferenczy Archiv. Quoted Corti, *Elisabeth, op. cit.*, p. 202.
25. Quoted Corti, *Elisabeth, op. cit.*, p. 232.
26. Archduchess Valerie's Diary. Quoted *ibid.*, p. 443.

3 THE EMPEROR AND THE IMPERIAL FAMILY

1. Quoted Theo Aronson, *The Coburgs of Belgium.* Cassell, London, 1969, p. 52.
2. Memorandum by Max, 30.9.1861, on the question of accepting the crown of Mexico. Quoted Egon Caesar Corti, *Maximilian und Charlotte von Mexiko.* Amalthea Verlag, Zürich, Leipzig, Vienna, 1924, p. 214.
3. Franz Joseph to Napoleon III, 3.7.1867. Quoted Corti, *Mensch und Herrscher, op. cit.*, p. 399.
4. Lord Bloomfield to Lord Clarendon, 27.1.1869. Quoted Sir Sidney Lee, *King Edward VII.* Macmillan, London, 1925, Vol. I, p. 292.
5. Hamilton, *op. cit.*, p. 66.
6. *Ibid.*, p. 50.
7. Sir Philip Magnus, *King Edward VII.* John Murray, London, 1964, p. 76.
8. Karl Erdmann Edler. Quoted Fred Hennings, *Ringstrassen Symphonie.* Herold Verlag, Vienna, Munich, 1963, Vol. II, p. 35.
9. *The Times,* February 23rd, 1887.
10. Quoted Hennings, *op. cit.*, Vol. II, p. 69.
11. Quoted Princess Fugger, *The Glory of the Habsburgs.* Harrap, London, 1931, p. 11.
12. Victor Tissot, *Vienne et la Vie Viennoise.* E. Dentre, Paris, 1881, 23rd edn., p. 136.

4 ARCHDUKE ALBRECHT AND THE ARMY

1. Quoted Heinrich Ritter von Srbik, *Aus Österreichs Vergangenheit.* Otto Müller Verlag, Salzburg, 1949, p. 120.
2. Quoted Carl von Duncker, *Feldmarschall Erzherzog Albrecht.* F. Tempsky Verlag, Vienna, Prague, 1897, p. 199.
3. Quoted Srbik, *op. cit.*, p. 125.
4. Quoted Srbik, *op. cit.*, p. 134.
5. Sir Henry Newbolt.
6. Glaise-Horstenau, *op. cit.*, p. 48.
7. Archduke Albrecht, '*Wie soll Österreichs Heer organisiert sein?*' Verlag von Tendler and Company, Vienna, 1868, p. iv.
8. Jaszi, *op. cit.*, p. 467.

9. Rudolf Kizling, *Feldmarschall Erzherzog Albrecht. Neue Österreichische Biographie.* Amalthea Verlag, Zürich, Leipzig, Vienna, 1960.
10. Since they never appeared again, Albrecht presumably destroyed them. See Kisling, *op. cit.*

5 ARCHDUKE JOHANN SALVATOR

1. Albrecht to Crenneville, 10.2.1861. Quoted Srbik, *op. cit.*, pp. 137–8.
2. Mauro Musci, *Storia civile e militare del regno della due Sicili sotto il governo di Ferdinando II del 1830 al 1849.* Naples, 1855. Quoted Harold Acton. *The Last Bourbons of Naples.* Methuen, London, 1961, p. 60.
3. The Archduke ceased to use his second name after 1870, but will be referred to as 'Johann Salvator' in order to distinguish him from the better known Archduke Johann (1782–1859), a brother of the Emperor Franz I.
4. Johann Salvator to Grand Duchess Maria Antonia, Salzburg, 30.4.1864, St. A.
5. *Ibid.* to *ibid.*, 27.11.1864, St. A.
6. *Ibid.* to *ibid.*, 17.12.1864, St.A.
7. Johann Salvator to Grand Duchess Maria Antonia, 7.12.1866, Schönbrunn, St.A.
8. *Ibid.* to *ibid.*, 9.2.1868, St.A.
9. Johann Salvator to Grand Duchess Maria Antonia, 4.2.1870, St.A.
10. *Ibid.* to *ibid.*, 29.2.1868, St. A.
11. Johann Salvator to Grand Duchess Maria Antonia, Vienna, 10.4.1868, 21.4.1868, St. A.
12. *Ibid.* to *ibid.*, Vienna, 16.3.1869, St. A.
13. *Ibid.* to *ibid.*, 31.1.1869.
14. Quoted Paul Vasili, *La Société de Vienne.* Nouvelle Revue, Paris, 1885, p. 50.
15. Johann Salvator to the Grand Duchess Maria Antonia, 15.7.1872, St. A.
16. *Ibid.* to *ibid.*, 12.12.1872, St. A.
17. *Ibid.* to *ibid.*, 22.12.1872, St. A.
18. *Ibid.* to *ibid.*, 12.12.1872, St. A.
19. Oskar Regele, *Feldzeugmeister Benedek.* Herold Verlag, Vienna, Munich, 1960, p. 436.
20. Johann Salvator to Grand Duchess Maria Antonia, Temesvar, 5.2.1874, St. A.
21. Johann Salvator to Grand Duchess Maria Antonia, 12.8.1874, St. A.
22. *Betrachtungen über die Organisation der Österreichischen Artillerie.* L. W. Seidel u. Söhne, Vienna, 1875.
23. *Betrachtungen, op. cit.*, p. 52.
24. Johann Salvator to Grand Duchess Maria Antonia, Cracow, 7.3.1875, St. A.
25. St. A. Quoted Mitis, *op. cit.*, p. 88.
26. Johann Salvator to Grand Duchess Maria Antonia, Cracow, 7.3.1875, St. A.
27. *Ibid.* to *ibid.*, Cracow, 10.11.1875, St. A.
28. Archduke Johann Salvator to Grand Duchess Maria Antonia, Brod, 1.9.1878, St. A.
29. Johann Salvator to Grand Duchess Maria Antonia, Livno, 21.9.1878, St. A.
30. Johann Salvator to Grand Duchess Maria Antonia, Livno, 21.9.1878, St. A.
31. *Ibid.* to *ibid.*, 25.12.1878, St. A.

32. *Ibid.* to *ibid.*, Gmunden, 24.3.1879, St. A.
33. *Ibid.* to *ibid.*, 16.6.1879, St. A.

6   CROWN PRINCE RUDOLF

1. Quoted Corti, *Elisabeth, op. cit.*, p. 132.
2. Alfred von Arneth, *Aus meinem Leben.* Stuttgart, 1893, Vol. II, pp. 301–2.
3. Quoted Magnus, *op. cit.*, p. 101.
4. Quoted Mitis, *op. cit.*, pp. 43–4.
5. St. A. Quoted Mitis, *op. cit.*, pp. 23–4.
6. St. A. Quoted Mitis, *op. cit.*, pp. 23–4.
7. Quoted *ibid.*, St. A.
8. Quoted Mitis, *op. cit.*, p. 28.
9. Quoted Mitis, *op. cit.*, p. 33.
10. Louise of Belgium, *My Own Affairs.* Cassell, London, 1921, p. 106.
11. Quoted Mitis, *op. cit.*, pp. 254–5.
12. Quoted Richard Barkeley, *The Road to Mayerling.* Macmillan, London, 1959, pp. 40–1.
13. Crown Prince Rudolf, *Notes on Sport and Ornithology.* Gurney and Jackson, London, 1889, pp. 22–3.
14. *Ibid.*, p. 24.
15. Rudolf, *Sport and Ornithology*, p. 22.
16. *Ibid.*, p. 2.
17. *Ibid.*, p. 106.
18. *Der Österreichischer Adel und sein Constitutioneller Beruf. Mahnruf an die aristokratische Jugend.* Munich, 1878.
19. St. A. Quoted Mitis, *op. cit.*, p. 156.
20. *Die Lage Wiens und Unsere Zukunft.*
21. Quoted Mitis, *op. cit.*, pp. 250–2.
22. Franz Joseph to Elisabeth, 7.11.1869. Nostitz-Rieneck, *op. cit.*, Vol. I, p. 100.
23. Crown Prince Rudolf, *Travels in the East.* Richard Bentley and Son, London, 1884, p. 51.
24. Rudolf to Bombelles, 29.11.1878. Quoted Mitis, *op. cit.*, p. 62.
25. Rudolf to Latour, quoted Mitis, *op. cit.*, pp. 61–2.
26. Quoted Mitis, *op. cit.*, pp. 63–6.
27. Rudolf to Bombelles, 18.8.1879. Quoted Mitis, *op. cit.*, pp. 66 and 416.
28. Festetics Diary, 5.11.1879. Gödöllö. Quoted Corti, *Mensch und Herrscher, op. cit.*, p. 533.
29. Quoted Corti, *Elisabeth, op. cit.*, p. 311.

7   THE YOUNG MEN AND LOVE

1. Quoted Francis Gribble, *The Life of the Emperor Francis Joseph.* Eveleigh Nash, London, 1914, pp. 237–8.
2. Johann Salvator to Grand Duchess Maria Antonia, Cracow, 18.8.1875, St. A.
3. Quoted P. Heinrich, *Erzherzog Johann.* Adolph W. Künast, Vienna, 1901, p. 57.
4. Quoted Heinrich, *op. cit.*, p. 57.
5. Quoted Heinrich, *op. cit.*, p. 58.

6. Johann Salvator to Grand Duchess Maria Antonia, Vienna, 8.7.1883, St. A.
7. St. A. Quoted Mitis, *op. cit.,* p. 257.
8. St. A. Quoted *ibid., op. cit.,* p. 72.
9. Quoted Hector Bolitho, *Further Letters of Queen Victoria.* Thornton Butterworth, London, 1938, p. 177.
10. Quoted James Pope-Hennessy, *Queen Mary.* George Allen and Unwin, London, 1959, p. 38.
11. Quoted Joanna Richardson, *My Dearest Uncle.* Cape, London, 1961, p. 188.
12. Rudolf to Latour, 2.2.1880, and 13.2.1880, St. A. Quoted Mitis, *op. cit.,* p. 72.
13. Rudolf to Latour, Brussels, 7.3.1880, St. A. Quoted Mitis, *op. cit.,* p. 72.
14. Prince of Wales to Queen Victoria, Laeken, 9.9.1862. Quoted Magnus, *op. cit.,* p. 68
15. Rudolf to Latour, Brussels, 11.3.1880, St. A. Quoted Mitis, *op. cit.,* p. 73.
16. Quoted Egon Caesar Corti and Hans Sokol, *Der Alte Kaiser.* Styria Verlag, Graz, Vienna, Cologne, p. 14.
17. Rudolf to Latour, 16.1.1881, St. A.
18. Rudolf to Latour, Brussels, 25.1.1881, St. A.
19. Rudolf, *Travels in the East, op. cit.,* pp. 51, 66.
20. Rudolf, *Travels in the East, op. cit.,* p. 311.
21. Festetics Diary. Quoted Corti/Sokol, *Der Alte Kaiser, op. cit.,* p. 15.
22. Quoted, *op. cit.,* p. 15.
23. Quoted, *op. cit.,* p. 16.

8 CONFLICT OF IDEAS

1. Rudolf to Latour, 16.4.1880, St. A. Quoted Mitis, *op. cit.,* p. 78.
2. Rudolf to Latour, Prague, 2.12.1881, St. A. Quoted Mitis, *op. cit.,* pp. 263–5.
3. Quoted Corti, *Der Alte Kaiser, op. cit.,* p. 21.
4. Rudolf to Latour, 13.10.1879, St. A. Quoted Mitis, *op. cit.,* pp. 416–17.
5. Rudolf to Szeps, Prague, 9.11.1882. *Kronprinz Rudolf Politische Briefe an einen Freund, 1882–1889.* Edited Julius Szeps. Rikola Verlag, Vienna, Munich, Leipzig, 1922, pp. 17–20.
6. Rudolf to Szeps, Prague, 24.11.1882. *Kronprinz Rudolf Politische Briefe, op. cit.,* pp. 20–1.
7. Rudolf to Szeps, Reichstads, 28.6.1882. *Kronprinz Rudolf Politische Briefe, op. cit.,* pp. 7–9.
8. Rudolf to Szeps, Prague, 1883. *Kronprinz Rudolf Politische Briefe, op. cit.,* pp. 27–32.
9. Quoted in Mitis, *op. cit.,* pp. 267–70.
10. Rudolf to Szeps, Laxenburg, 29.8.1883. *Kronprinz Rudolf Politische Briefe, op. cit.,* p. 58.
11. Heinrich, *op. cit.,* p. 29.
12. Corti, *Der Alte Kaiser, op. cit.,* p. 95.
13. Johann Salvator to Grand Duchess Maria Antonia, Vienna 20.1.1883, St. A.
14. *Bemerkungen zu den Betrachtigungen über die Organisation der Österreichischen Artillerie.* Luckhardt Verlag, Kassel, 1875.
15. *Psychologisches und Physiologisches aus der Österreichischen Armee.* Luckhardt, 1874.
16. Beck to Franz Joseph, Vienna, 12.9.1875, K.A.

17. Johann Salvator to Weilen, 26.6.1884. *Neues Wiener Journal*, 15.2.1925.
18. Minister of War to Franz Joseph, 13.4.1880, K.A.
19. Memorandum from Archduke Albrecht, 19.4.1880, K.A.
20. Archduke Johann Salvator. *Drill oder Erziehung.* Vienna: *Organ der Militär-Wissenschaftliche Vereine,* Vol. XXVII, 1883.
21. Helmulth von Moltke, *Militärische Werke,* Vol. II, p. 195. Quoted Craig, *op. cit.,* p. 210.
22. Johann Salvator to Grand Duchess Maria Antonia, Vienna, 17.11.1883, St. A.

9 AN UNEASY RELATIONSHIP

1. Johann Salvator to Grand Duchess Maria Antonia, 10.6.1881, St. A.
2. *Ibid.* to *ibid.,* Gmunden, 15.7.1881, St. A.
3. Johann Salvator to Grand Duchess Maria Antonia, Komorn, 11.1.1881, St. A.
4. Johann Salvator to Grand Duchess Maria Antonia, Komorn, 15.1.1881, St. A.
5. Heinrich, *op. cit.,* pp. 76–7.
6. Werner Richter, *Kronprinz Rudolf von Österreich.* Eugen Rentsch Verlag, Erlenbach, Zürich, Leipzig, 1941, p. 103.
7. Johann Salvator to Grand Duchess Maria Antonia, Vienna, 31.5.1883, St. A.
8. Johann Salvator to Grand Duchess Maria Antonia, Vienna, 17.11.1883, St. A.
9. Rudolf to Szeps, 4.4.1882. *Kronprinz Rudolf Politische Briefe, op. cit.,* p. 4.
10. The Austro-Hungarian Monarchy in Words and Pictures.
11. Johann Salvator to Grand Duchess Maria Antonia, Linz, 25.3.1884, St. A.
12. *Ibid.* to *ibid.,* Linz, 30.5.1884, St. A.
13. Johann Salvator to Weilen, 18.1.1885. *Neues Wiener Journal,* 15.2.1925.
14. Quoted, Field-Marshal Viscount Montgomery of Alamein, *A History of Warfare.* Collins, London, 1968, p. 19.
15. Rudolf to Franz Ferdinand. 26.11.1884. Quoted Roland Krug von Nidda, *Der Weg nach Sarajevo.* Amalthea Verlag, Vienna, Munich, Zürich, p. 16.
16. *Die Stunde,* Vienna, 22.9.1923.
17. Quoted Hans Schaffelhofer, *Johann Orth.* Verlag Josef Faber, Vienna–Krems, 1952, p. 64.
18. Johann Salvator to Grand Duchess Maria Antonia, Linz, 24.8.1884, St. A.
19. Rudolf to Franz Ferdinand, 22.8.1884. *Franz Ferdinand Nachlass.* Quoted Corti, *Der Alte Kaiser, op. cit.*
20. Johann Salvator to Grand Duchess Maria Antonia, Linz, 24.8.1884, St. A.
21. Quoted Glaise-Horstenau, *op. cit.,* pp. 276–7.
22. Quoted Glaise-Horstenau, *op. cit.,* p. 279.
23. Heinrich Friedjung, *Historische Aufsätze.* J. G. Cotta'sche Buchhandlung Nachfolger, Stuttgart, Berlin, 1919, p. 335.
24. Rudolf to Szeps, Laxenburg, 1.8.1885. *Kronprinz Rudolf Politische Briefe, op. cit.,* p. 121.
25. Johann Salvator to Weilen, Linz, 18.1.1885. *Neues Wiener Journal,* 15.2.1925.
26. Johann Salvator to Grand Duchess Maria Antonia, Linz, 17.12.1884, St. A.
27. Johann Salvator to Grand Duchess Maria Antonia, Linz, 1.3.1885, St. A.
28. The Slav minority in Hungary.
29. Johann Salvator to Grand Duchess Maria Antonia, 17.12.1885, St. A.

10 THE BULGARIAN THRONE

1. Quoted Robert K. Massie, *Nicholas and Alexandra*. Gollancz, London, 1968, p. 9.
2. David Dilks, *Curzon in India*. Rupert Hart Davis, London, 1969, Vol. I, p. 194.
3. See Mitis, *op. cit.*, pp. 309–11.
4. Quoted Mitis, *op. cit.*, pp. 312–16.
5. Rudolf to Szeps, Vienna, 1.1.1886. *Kronprinz Rudolf Politische Briefe, op. cit.*, pp. 128–9.
6. *The Times*, 18.10.1886.
7. *The Times*, 13.11.1886.
8. *The Times*, 12.11.1886.
9. Queen Victoria to Lord Salisbury, 17.11.1886. Buckle, *Letters of Queen Victoria, op. cit.*, Third Series, Vol. I, p. 223.
10. Phipps to Iddesleigh, Vienna, 11.11.1886, P.R.O.
11. Johann Salvator to Grand Duchess Maria Antonia, Linz, 12.12.1886, St. A.
12. *The Times*, 13.12.1886.
13. Heinrich, *op. cit.*, p. 72.
14. See Mitis, *op. cit.*, Facsimile reproduction of letter facing p. 96.
15. Rudolf to Kalnoky, Vienna, 10.1.1887, St. A.
16. Johann Salvator to Grand Duchess Maria Antonia, Linz, 8.2.1887, St. A.
17. See Mitis, *op. cit.*, pp. 91–2.
18. Buckle, *Letters of Queen Victoria, op. cit.*, Third Series, Vol. I, pp. 229–30.
19. Buckle, *Letters of Queen Victoria, op. cit.*, Third Series, Vol. I, p. 230.
20. Johann Salvator to Grand Duchess Maria Antonia, Linz, 28.2.1887, St. A.
21. Johann Salvator to Grand Duchess Maria Antonia, Linz, 13.4.1887, St. A.
22. *Ibid.* to *ibid.*, Linz, 28.2.1887, St. A.
23. To congratulate Johann Salvator on his lecture 'Drill or Education'.
24. Johann Salvator to Grand Duchess Maria Antonia, Linz, 13.4.1887, St. A.

11 THE BEGINNING OF THE END

1. Johann Salvator to Grand Duchess Maria Antonia, Ostend, 29.7.1887, St. A.
2. Ferdinand of Tuscany to Grand Duchess Maria Antonia, Salzburg, 19.10.1889, St. A.
3. Franz Joseph to Taaffe, Radmer, 7.10.1887, St. A.
4. Franz Joseph to Johann Salvator, Eisenerz, 11.10.1887, St. A.
5. Johann Salvator to Grand Duchess Maria Antonia, London, 23.9.1887, St. A.
6. Johann Salvator to Grand Duchess Maria Antonia, Southampton, 2.10.1887, St. A.
7. Johann Salvator to Grand Duchess Maria Antonia, Cherbourg, 11.10.1887, St. A.
8. Johann Salvator to Grand Duchess Maria Antonia, Lisbon, 4.12.1887, St. A.
9. Johann Salvator to Grand Duchess Maria Antonia, Nice, 7.1.1887, St. A.
10. British Military Attaché, Vienna, 21.12.1887, P.R.O., F.O. 7/119.
11. Johann Salvator to Weilen, Arco, 30.1.1888, *Neues Wiener Journal*, 31.5.1925.
12. *Ibid.* to *ibid.*, Arco, 6.2.1888, *Neues Wiener Journal*, 31.5.1925.
13. Johann Salvator to Laaba, Arco, 13.2.1888, *Österreichische National Bibliothek, Handschriften Sammlung*.

14. von Warsberg to Kalnoky, Venice, 23.5.1888, St. A.
15. Johann Salvator to Weilen, Orth, 22.11.1888, *Neues Wiener Journal*, 15.2.1925.
16. Rudolf to Szeps, Laxenburg, 21.8.1888, *Kronprinz Rudolf Politische Briefe, op. cit.*, pp. 163–4.
17. Buckle, *Letters of Queen Victoria, op. cit.*, Third Series, Vol. I, p. 504.
18. Buckle, *Letters of Queen Victoria, op. cit.*, Third Series, Vol. I, p. 327.
19. Kinsky to Kalnoky, Newmarket, 25.6.1887. Quoted Mitis, *op. cit.*, pp. 371–4.
20. Rudolf to Frischauer, Vienna, 13.7.1887. St. A.
21. Rudolf to Stephanie, Bruck, 31.7.1887. Quoted Stephanie Lonyay (Princess of Belgium), *I Was to be Empress*. Ivor Nicolson and Watson, London, 1937, pp. 213–14.
22. Rudolf to Stephanie, Belovar, 12.9.1888. Quoted Juliana von Stockhausen, *Im Schatten der Hofburg*. F. H. Kerle Verlag, Heidelberg, 1952, pp. 116–17.
23. Paget to Salisbury, Vienna, 5.10.1888, P.R.O., F.O. 7/1135.
24. Quoted Magnus Edward VII, *op. cit.*, p. 210.
25. Magnus *ibid.*
26. See Fritz Judtmann, *Mayerling ohne Mythos*. Verlag Kremayr und Scheriau, Vienna, 1968, pp. 16–20.
27. Rudolf to Stephanie, Berlin, 21.3.1887. Quoted Stephanie, *op. cit.*, p. 205.
28. Ernst Edler von Planitz, *Die volle Wahrheit über den Tod des Kronprinzen Rudolf von Österreich 1889*. H. Piehler Verlag, Berlin, 55th edn., 1900, Vol. I, pp. 456–7.
29. Kinsky to Kalnoky, Newmarket, 25.6.1887. Quoted Mitis, *op. cit.*, p. 374.
30. Paget to Salisbury, Vienna, 21.2.1888, P.R.O., F.O. 7/1131.
31. Archduke Otto.
32. Rudolf to Stephanie, Vienna, 5.3.1888. Quoted Stephanie, *op. cit.*, pp. 221–2.
33. Paget to Salisbury, Vienna, 17.10.1888, P.R.O., F.O. 7/1135.
34. Franz Joseph to Frau Schratt, 14.2.1888. Quoted Corti, *Der Alte Kaiser, op. cit.*, p. 107.
35. Franz Joseph to Elisabeth, Vienna, 31.12.1888, Nostitz-Rieneck, *Briefe, op. cit.*, Vol. I, p. 203.
36. Paget to Salisbury, Vienna, 27.4.1887, P.R.O., F.O. 7/1115.
37. Johann Salvator to Weilen, Orth, 22.11.1888, *Neues Wiener Journal*, 15.2. 1925.
38. Rudolf to Szeps, Vienna, 8.11.1888, *Kronprinz Politische Briefe, op. cit.*, p. 166.

12 MAYERLING I

1. Rudolf to Szeps, Vienna, 27.12.1888, *Kronprinz Rudolf Politische Briefe, op. cit.*, p. 168.
2. Walburga Lady Paget, *Embassies of Other Days*. Hutchinson, London, 1923, Vol. II, p. 465.
3. Countess Marie Larisch, *My Past*. Eveliegh Nash, London, 1913, p. 166.
4. Paget, *Embassies, op. cit.*, Vol. II, p. 467.
5. Quoted Corti, *Elisabeth, op. cit.*, p. 269.
6. Paget to Salisbury, Vienna, 1.2.1889, P.R.O., F.O. 7/1146.
7. Paget to Salisbury, Vienna, 5.2.1889 Sal. P.
8. *The Times*, 31.1.1889.
9. *The Times*, 1.2.1889.
10. Sir Augustus Paget to Queen Victoria, Vienna, 5.2.1889 and 7.2.1889, Sal. P.

11. Reuss to Bismarck, Vienna, 5.2.1889. Quoted Albert E. J. Hollaender. *Streiflichter auf den Kronprinzen Tragödie von Mayerling*. In: *Festschrift für Heinrich Benedikt*. Verlag Notring der wissenschaftlichen Verbände Österreich, Vienna, 1957, p. 140.

12. Sir Augustus Paget to Lord Salisbury, Vienna, 5.2.1889, Sal. P.

13. *Ibid*. to *ibid.*, Vienna, 15.2.1889, Sal. P.

14. Paget to Queen Victoria, Vienna, 15.2.1889, Sal. P.

15. *Denkschrift der Baronin Hélène Vetsera über die Katastrophe in Mayerling*. Edited Ernst von Planitz. H. Piehler Verlag, Berlin, 5th edn., 1899.

16. Quoted Judtmann, *op. cit.*, p. 315.

13   MAYERLING II

1. St. A. *See* Mitis, *op. cit.*, pp. 385–99.

2. *See* Judtmann, *op. cit.*, p. 93.

3. *Neues Wiener Tagblatt*, Sonntags-Beilage, 24.4.1932.

4. Quoted Corti, *Der Alte Kaiser, op. cit.*, pp. 121–3. *See also* Judtmann, *op. cit.* Facsimile reproduction of Corti's notes from the Archduchess's diary between pp. 151–2.

5. *Neues Wiener Tagblatt*, Sonntags-Beilage, 15.7.1931–13.9.1931.

6. Judtmann, *op. cit.*

7. Quoted Judtmann, *op. cit.*, p. 145.

8. Quoted Judtmann, *op. cit.*, p. 146.

9. Quoted *ibid.*, p. 307.

10. Quoted Judtmann, *op. cit.*, p. 307.

11. Arthur Polzer-Hoditz, *Kaiser Karl*. Amalthea Verlag, Zürich, Leipzig, Vienna, 1929, pp. 586–7.

12. *Erinnerungen und Gedanken des Botschafters Anton Graf Monts*. Edited by Karl Friedrich Nowak and Friedrich Thimme. Verlag für Kulturpolitik G.M.B.H., Berlin, 1932, pp. 105–9.

13. Philip of Coburg to Queen Victoria. Quoted Hollaender, *op. cit.*, p. 148.

14. Quoted Judtmann, *op. cit.*, p. 146.

15. *Das Mayerling Original. Offiziellen Akt der K. K. Polizeipräsidium*. Wilhelm Frick Verlag, Munich, Stuttgart, Vienna, Zürich, 1955, p. 106.

16. Quoted Stephanie Lonyay, *op. cit.*, p. 204.

17. Quoted Rudolf Neck, *Über die Abschiedsbriefe des Kronprinzen Rudolfs*. Mitteilungen der Österreichischen Staatsarchives, Vienna, 1958, Vol. II, pp. 494–501.

18. Neck, *op. cit.*, pp. 500–1.

19. Mitis, *op. cit.*, p. 306.

20. Corti, *Elisabeth, op. cit.*, p. 422.

21. Quoted Jean de Bourgoing, *Briefe Kaiser Franz Josephs an Frau Katherina Schratt*. Ullstein Verlag, Vienna, 1949, p. 135.

22. Quoted Wilhelm Polzer, *Licht über Mayerling*. Verlag Oskar Karinger, Graz, 1954, p. 212.

14   CAPE HORN

1. *See* Judtmann, *op. cit.*, p. 302.

2. Larisch, *op. cit.*, pp. 278–9 and 284–9.

3. Marie Stubel, *Die Wahrheit über Johann Orth. Die Stunde,* 28.9.1923.
4. Heinrich, *op. cit.,* p. 121.
5. Johann Salvator to Grand Duchess Maria Antonia, Fiume, 15.4.1889, St. A.
6. *Ibid.* to *ibid.,* Fiume, 19.6.1889, St. A.
7. Johann Salvator to Professor Budevich, Orth, 22.7.1889. *Handschriften Sammlung Nationalbibliothek,* Vienna.
8. *Neue Freie Presse,* Vienna, 14.6.1925. *Wie Johann Orth aus dem Österreichischen Kaiserhaus auschied.* Reproduction of original letter in the State Archives, Vienna.
9. Ferdinand of Tuscany to Grand Duchess Maria Antonia, Salzburg, 19.10.1889, St. A.
10. *Neue Freie Presse,* 14.6.1925.
11. Johann Salvator to Grand Duchess Maria Antonia, 8.10.1889, St. A.
12. Johann Salvator to Grand Duchess Maria Antonia, Paris, 21.10.1889, St. A.
13. Johann Salvator to Kalnoky, London, 2.11.1889, St. A.
14. Johann Salvator to Grand Duchess Maria Antonia, Hamburg, 10.11.1889, St. A.
15. Johann Salvator to Kalnoky, Hamburg, 25.11.1889, St. A.
16. Austro-Hungarian Embassy, London, to Kalnoky, 9.11.1889, St. A.
17. *The Daily News,* London, 18.11.1889.
18. *The Times,* 23.10.1889.
19. Heinrich, *op. cit.,* p. 155.
20. Kalnoky to Johann Salvator, Vienna, 16.12.1889, St. A.
21. Austro-Hungarian Consul-General to His Imperial Majesty's Ambassador in London, 25.1.1890, St. A.
22. Deym to Kalnoky, London, 4.2.1890, St. A.
23. Taaffe to Kalnoky, Vienna, 9.2.1890, St. A.
24. Taaffe to Kalnoky, Vienna, 25.2.1890, St. A.
25. von Burian, Sofia, to Kalnoky, telegrams, 3.3.1890; letter, 9.3.1890, St. A.
26. Kalnoky to Calice, Vienna, 4.3.1890, St.A.
27. Kalnoky to von Burian, Vienna, 14.3.1890, St. A.
28. Johann Salvator to Franz Joseph, Birstein, 10.3.1889, St. A.
29. Karl Freiherr von Hasenhauer, 'Johann Orth's Abschiedsbriefe', *Neues Wiener Journal,* 2.2.1930.
30. Johann Salvator to Grand Duchess Maria Antonia, Chatham, 25.3.1890, St. A.
31. Heinrich, *op. cit.,* p. 183.
32. Milli Stubel to Marie Schenk, La Plata, 10.7.1890, St. A.
33. Dr. Bachrach to Obersthofmarschallamt, Vienna, 18.3.1911, St. A.

EPILOGUE

1. *Franz Ferdinand Nachlass.* Quoted Corti. *Der Alte Kaiser, op. cit.,* p. 143.

Selected Bibliography

This book is a study of personalities and their interaction on each other within the framework of the Hapsburg mystique. Discussion of politics has therefore been confined to the minimum necessary in order to enable the general reader to understand why the differences between the older and younger generations of the family arose.

The account of Franz Joseph and his attitude towards his relations owes much to the unique documents quoted by Count Corti in his biographies of the Emperor and the Empress.

Freiherr von Mitis's book on Rudolf remains the classic work on the Crown Prince. Von Mitis was Director of the State Archives when he wrote it and therefore had full access to such of Rudolf's papers as have been preserved—a great many were destroyed.

The literature on Mayerling is immense, and some of it does not greatly contribute to the elucidation of what occurred. The works on this subject listed in the bibliography are confined to those which pertain to the theme of this book. Amongst them Professor Judtmann's *Mayerling ohne Mythos* (published in an English translation by Messrs Harrap in 1971) is of exceptional interest, and I am indebted to it, as any serious student of the tragedy must be, for a great deal of valuable factual information. The theory in the first part of Chapter 13 as to what may have occurred at Mayerling on the morning when the Crown Prince's death was discovered is, however, my own.

In an attempt to analyse the character of Archduke Johann Salvator and his relationship with Crown Prince Rudolf, I have examined and quote from a number of manuscripts in the Haus-Hof- und Staatsarchiv and in the Kriegsarchiv in Vienna. These also throw some light on the attitude of Archduke Albrecht.

The following bibliography lists printed works which may be of interest to the reader who wishes to make a further study of the personalities and their problems which I describe, together

Selected Bibliography

with some sources, manuscript and otherwise which, so far as I know, have not previously been intensively evaluated.

PRINTED SOURCES

ALBRECHT, Archduke. *Wie soll Österreichs Heer organisiert sein?* Verlag von Tendler, Vienna, 1868.

ANDERSON, M. S. *The Eastern Questions 1774–1923.* Macmillan, London, 1966.

ARNETH, Alfred von. *Aus meinem Leben.* Stuttgart, 1893, Vol. II.

ARONSON, Theo. *The Coburgs of Belgium.* Cassell, London, 1969.

BAREA, Ilse. *Vienna.* London, 1966.

BARDOLF, Carl Freiherr von. *Soldat im alten Österreich.* Eugen Diederischer Verlag, Jena, 1938.

BARKELEY, Richard. *The Road to Mayerling.* Macmillan, London, 1959.

BEAMAN, A. Hulme. *M. Stambuloff.* Bliss Sands and Foster, London, 1895.

BENEDIKT, Heinrich. *Kaiseradler über dem Apennin.* Herold Verlag, Vienna, Munich, 1964.

—— *Monarchie der Gegensätze.* Ullstein Verlag, Vienna, 1947.

BIBL, Viktor. *Der Zerfall Österreichs.* Rikola Verlag, Vienna, Munich, Leipzig, Berlin, 1924, Vol. II.

—— *Kronprinz Rudolf.* Gladius Verlag, Leipzig, Budapest, 1938.

BLAKE, Robert. *Disraeli.* Eyre and Spottiswood, London, 1966.

BOURGOING, Jean de. *Briefe Kaiser Franz Josephs an Frau Katherina Schratt.* Ullstein Verlag, Vienna, 1949.

BUCKLE, George Earle (in succession to W. F. Monnypenny). *The Life of Benjamin Disraeli Earl of Beaconsfield.* John Murray, London, 1920, Vol. VI.

—— *The Letters of Queen Victoria.* John Murray, London, Second Series, Vol. III, 1928; Third Series, Vol. I, 1930.

CHRISTOPH, Paul. *Grossherzogtum Toskana.* Bergland Verlag, Vienna, 1957.

CORTI, Egon Caesar Count. *Alexander of Battenberg.* Cassell, London, 1954.

—— *Maximilian und Charlotte von Mexiko.* Amalthea Verlag, Zürich, Leipzig, Vienna, 1924.

—— *Elisabeth.* Anton Pustet Verlag, Salzburg, Leipzig, 1935.

—— *Mensch und Herrscher.* Styria Verlag, Graz, Vienna, Altötting, 1952.

—— and SOKOL, Hans. *Der Alte Kaiser.* Styria Verlag, Graz, Vienna, Cologne, 1955.

COWLES, Virginia. *The Russian Dagger.* Collins, London, 1969.

CRAIG, Gordon A. *The Battle of Königgrätz.* Weidenfeld and Nicolson, London, 1965.

CRANKSHAW, Edward. *The Fall of the House of Habsburg.* Longmans, London, 1963.

Selected Bibliography

Das Mayerling Original. Offiziellen Akt der K. K. Polizeipräsidium. Wilhelm Frick Verlag, Munich, Stuttgart, Vienna, Zürich, 1955.

Denkschrift der Baronin Helene von Vetsera über die Katastrophe in Mayerling. Edited Ernst von Planitz. H. Piehler Verlag, Berlin, 5th edition, 1899.

Die Stunde, Vienna 11.8.1923. Leopold Wölfling. *Die letzten Habsburger.*

—— —— 7.9.1923–7.10.1923. Memories of Marie Stubel: *Die Wahrheit über Johann Orth.*

DUNCKER, Carl von. *Feldmarschall Erzherzog Albrecht.* F. Tempsky Verlag, Vienna, Prague, 1897.

EISENMANN, Louis, *Le Compromis Austro-Hongrois de 1867.* Sociète Nouvelle de Librarie et d'Edition (Librarie Georges Bellais), Paris, 1904.

ENGEL JANOSI, Friedrich. *Geschichte auf dem Ballhausplatz.* Styria Verlag, Graz, 1953.

—— *Einige neue Dokumente zum Tod des Kronprinzen Rudolf.* Mitteilungen des Osterreichischen Staatsarchivs, 1964/65.

Erinnerungen und Gedanken des Botschafters Anton Graf Monts. Edited Karl Friedrich Nowak and Friedrich Thimme. Verlag für Kulturpolitik, Berlin, 1932.

Erinnerungen an Franz Joseph I. Edited Eduard von Steinitz. Verlag für Kulturpolitik, Berlin, 1931.

ERNST, Otto. *Franz Joseph I in seinen Briefe.* Rikola Verlag, Vienna, Leipzig, Munich, 1924.

EULENBERG-HERTEFELD, Philipp Fürst zu. *Das Ende König Ludwigs II und andere Erlebnisse.* Fr. Wilhelm Gronow Verlag, Leipzig, 1934, Vols. I, II.

FLESCH-BRUNNINGEN, Hans. *Die letzten Habsburger in Augenzeugenberichten.* Karl Rauch Verlag, Düsseldorf, 1967.

FRANZEL, Emil. *Erzhaus des Abendlandes.* In: *Virtute Fideque.* Herold Verlag, Vienna, Munich, 1963.

—— *Kronprinzen Mythos und Mayerling Legenden.* Herold Verlag, Vienna, Munich, 1963.

—— *1866 Il Mondo Casca.* Herold Verlag, Vienna, Munich, 1968, Vols. I. II.

Franz Joseph und seine Zeit. Edited J. Schnitzer. R. Lechner (Wilhelm Müller), Vienna, 1898, 2 vols.

FRASER, Mrs. Hugh. *A Diplomatist's Wife in Many Lands.* Hutchinson, London, 1911, Vol. II.

FRIEDJUNG, Heinrich. *The Struggle for Supremacy in Germany 1859–1866.* Macmillan, London, 1935.

—— *Historische Aufsätze.* J. G. Cotta'sche Buchhandlung Nachfolger, Stuttgart, Berlin, 1919.

Gestalten der Geschichte Österreichs. Edited Dr. Hugo Hantsch. Tyrolia Verlag, Innsbruck, Vienna, Munich, 1962.

Selected Bibliography

GLAISE-HORSTENAU, Edmund von. *Franz Josephs Weggefährte. Das Leben des Generalstabschef Grafen Beck.* Amalthea Verlag, Zürich, Leipzig, Vienna, 1930.

HANTSCH, Hugo. *Die Geschichte Österreichs.* Styria Verlag, Graz, Vienna, Cologne, 2nd edn., 1955, Vol. II.

HAMILTON, Lord Frederick. *The Vanished Pomps of Yesterday.* Hodder and Stoughton, London, 1919.

HASLIP, Joan. *The Lonely Empress.* Weidenfeld and Nicolson, London, 1965.

HEINRICH, P. *Erzherzog Johann.* Adolph W. Künast, Vienna, 1901.

HENNINGS, Fred. *Ringstrassen Symphonie.* Herold Verlag, Vienna, Munich, 1963–64, 3 vols.

HOLLAENDER, Albert E. J. *Streiflichter auf die Kronprinzen Tragödie von Mayerling.* In: *Festschrift für Heinrich Benedikt.* Verlag Notring der wissenshaftlichen Verbände Österreich, Vienna, 1957.

HUMMELBERGER, Walter. *Marie Caspar und Josef Bratfisch.* In: *Jahrbuch der Vereines für Geschichte der Stadt Wien.* Verlag Ferdinand Berger, Horn, 1964, Vol. 20.

HUHN, A. von. *The Struggle of the Bulgarians for National Independence.* John Murray, London, 1886.

JASZI, Oscar. *The Dissolution of the Habsburg Monarchy.* University of Chicago Press, Chicago, 1929.

JOHANN SALVATOR, Archduke. *Betrachtungen über die Organisation der Österreichischen Artillerie.* Seidel, Vienna, 1874.

—— *Geschichte des K. K. Linien Regiments Erzherzog Wilhelm No. 12.* L. W. Seidel und Sohn, Vienna, Vol. I, 1877, Vol. II, 1880.

—— *Drill oder Erziehung. Organ der Militär-Wissenschaftliche Vereine.* Vienna, Vol. XXVII, 1883.

JUDTMANN, Fritz. *Mayerling ohne Mythos.* Kremayr und Scheriau, Vienna, 1968.

KANN, Robert A. *The Multinational Empire.* Columbia University Press, New York, 1950, Vol. II.

KIZLING, Rudolf. *Feldmarschall Erzherzog Albrecht. Neue Österreichische Biographie.* Amalthea Verlag, Zürich, Leipzig, Vienna, 1960.

k.k. Kriegsarchivs. Die Okkupation Bosniens und die Hercegovina durch k.k. Truppen im Jahre 1878. Verlag des k.k. Generalstabs, Vienna, 1879.

Kronprinz Rudolf Politische Briefe an einen Freund 1882–1889. Edited Julius Szeps. Rikola Verlag, Vienna, Munich, Leipzig, 1922.

LAABA, M. *Psychologisches und Physiologisches aus der Österreichischen Armee.* Firma Luckhardt, Leipzig, Cassel, Berlin, 1874.

—— *Bemerkungen zu den Betrachtigungen über die Organisation der Österreichischen Artillerie.* Firma Luckhardt, Kassel, 1875.

LARISCH, Countess Marie. *My Past.* Eveliegh Nash, London, 1913.

Selected Bibliography

Linzer Tagespost. Linz, 25.9.1887; 4–7.10.1887.

Linzer Zeitung. Linz, 4.10.1887; 6.10.1887.

LOEHR, Clemens. *Mayerling.* Amalthea Verlag, Vienna, Munich, Zürich, 1968.

LONGFORD, Elizabeth. *Victoria R.I.* Weidenfeld and Nicolson, London, 1964.

LONYAY, Count Carl. *Rudolf. The Tragedy of Mayerling.* Hamish Hamilton, London, 1950.

LONYAY, Stephanie (Princess of Belgium). *I was to be Empress.* Ivor Nicholson and Watson, London, 1937.

LOUISA OF TUSCANY. *My Own Story.* Eveliegh Nash, London, 1911.

LOUISE OF BELGIUM. *My Own Affairs.* Cassell, London, 1921.

MACARTNEY, C. A. *The Hapsburg Empire. 1790–1918.* Weidenfeld and Nicolson, London, 1969.

MAGNUS, Sir Philip. *King Edward VII.* John Murray, London, 1964.

MARGUTTI, Lt.-General Baron von. *The Emperor Francis Joseph and His Times.* Hutchinson, London, 1921.

MAY, Arthur J. *The Habsburg Monarchy, 1867–1914.* Harvard University Press, 1951.

MEDLICOTT, W. N. *The Congress of Berlin and After.* Methuen, London, 1938.

MITIS, Oskar Freiherr von. *Das Leben des Kronprinzen Rudolf.* Insel Verlag, Leipzig, 1928.

MOLDEN, B. *Kalnoky. Allgemeine Deutsche Biographie.* Dundes und Humboldt Verlag, Leipzig, 1906, Vol. LI.

NECK, Rudolf. *Über die Abschiedsbriefe des Kronprinzen Rudolfs. Mitteilungen des Österreichischen Staatsarchivs.* Vienna, 1958, Vol. XI.

Neue Freie Presse, Vienna, 14.6.1925. *Wie Johann Orth aus dem Österreichischen Kaiserhaus auschied.*

Neues Wiener Journal, Vienna, 15.2.1925 and 31.5.1925. *Unbekannte Briefe von Johann Orth.*

—— Vienna 2.2.1930. Karl Freiherr von Hasenauer: *Johann Orths Abschiedsbriefe.*

Neues Wiener Tagblatt, Sonntags-Beilage, Vienna, 24.4.1932. Johann Loschek: *Was ich von Mayerling weiss.* Copyright Carl Duncker Verlag, Berlin, 1932.

—— Vienna, 1.1.1933. *Johann Orth an seine Mutter. Der letzte Brief.* Translation and commentary Sandra Bauer.

NIDDA, Roland Krug von. *1866—Königgrätz.* Amalthea Verlag, Vienna, Munich, Zürich, 1966.

NOSTIZ-RIENECK, Georg. (Editor) *Briefe Kaiser Franz Josephs an Kaiserin Elisabeth 1859–1898.* Herold Verlag, Vienna, Munich, 1966, 2 vols.

PAGET, Walburga Lady. *Scenes and Memories.* Smith Elder, London, 1912.

—— *Embassies of Other Days.* Hutchinson, London, 1923, Vol. II.

Selected Bibliography

PLANITZ, Ernst Edler von. *Die volle Wahrheit über den Tod des Kronprinzen Rudolf von Österreich 1889.* H. Piehler Verlag, Berlin, 55th edition, 1900, 2 vols.

POLZER-HODITZ, Arthur Graf, *Kaiser Karl.* Amalthea Verlag, Zürich, Leipzig, Vienna, 1929.

POLZER, Wilhelm. *Licht über Mayerling.* Verlag Oskar Karinger, Graz, 1954.

PRZIBRAM, Ludwig Ritter von. *Erinnerungen eines alten Österreichers.* Deutsche Verlags Anstalt, Stuttgart, 1910–12, 2 vols.

REDLICH, Josef. *Emperor Francis Joseph of Austria.* Macmillan, London, 1929.

REGELE, Oskar. *Feldzeugmeister Benedek.* Herold Verlag, Vienna, Munich, 1960.

RICHTER, Werner. *Kronprinz Rudolf von Österreich.* Eugen Rentsch Verlag, Erlenbach, Zürich, Leipzig, 1941.

RUDOLF, Crown Prince. *Travels in the East.* Richard Bentley and Son, London, 1884.

—— *Der Österreichische Adel und sein Constitutionelle Beruf.* Adolf Ackermann, Munich, 1878.

—— *Notes on Sport and Ornithology.* Gurney and Jackson, London, 1889.

RUMBOLD, Sir Horace. *The Austrian Court in the Nineteenth Century.* Methuen, London, 1909.

—— *Recollections of a Diplomatist.* Edward Arnold, London, Second impression, 1901, Vol. I.

RUTKOWSKI, Ernst R. *Gustav Graf Kalnoky. Mitteilungen des Österreichischen Staatsarchivs,* Vol. XIV, 1951.

SCHAFFELHOFER, Hans. *Johann Orth.* Josef Faber Verlag, Vienna, Krems/Donau, 1952.

SCHWARZENBERG, Adolf. *Prince Felix zu Schwarzenberg.* Columbia University Press, New York, 1946.

SCHWEINITZ, General von. *Denkwürdigkeiten.* Verlag von Reimar Hobbing, Berlin, 1927.

SETON-WATSON, R. W. *The Rise of Nationality in the Balkans.* Constable, London, 1917.

SKEDL. Dr. Arthur and WEISS, Dr. Egon. *Der Politische Nachlass des Grafen. Eduard Taaffe.* Rikola Verlag, Vienna, Berlin, Leipzig, Munich, 1922

SOSNOSKY, Theodor von. *Die Balkanpolitik Österreich—Ungarns seit 1866.* Deutsche Verlags Anstalt, Stuttgart, Berlin, 1913, 2 vols.

SRBIK, Heinrich Ritter von. *Aus Österreichs Vergangenheit.* Otto Müller Verlag, Salzburg, 1949.

STEED, Henry Wickham *The Hapsburg Monarchy.* Constable, London, 1914, 3rd edn.

STOCKHAUSEN, Juliana von. *Im Schatten der Hofburg.* F. H. Kerle Verlag, Heidelberg, 1952.

Selected Bibliography

SZEPS, Berta. *My Life and History.* Cassell, London, 1938.

TAYLOR, A. J. P. *Bismarck. The Man and Statesman.* Hamish Hamilton, London, 1959.

—— *The Habsburg Monarchy, 1809–1918.* Hamish Hamilton, London, new edn., 1955.

The Times. July 1886–December 1890.

TISSOT, Victor. *Vienne et la Vie Viennoise.* E. Dentre, Paris. 23rd edn. 1881.

TSCHUPPIK, Karl. *The Reign of the Emperor Francis Joseph, 1848–1916.* G. Bell, London, 1930.

URBAS, Emmanuel. *Kronprinz Rudolf. Preussische Jahrbücher,* Vol. 215. Verlag von Georg Stilke, Berlin, 1929.

VASILI, Paul. *La Société de Vienne.* Nouvelle Revue, Paris, 1885.

WANDRUSZKA, Adam. *Schicksalsjahr 1866.* Styria Verlag, Graz, 1966.

—— *The House of Habsburg.* Sidgwick and Jackson, London, 1964.

WERTHEIMER, Eduard von. *Graf Julius Andrassy.* Deutsche Verlags Anstalt, Stuttgart, 1910–1913, 3 vols.

WILCZEK, Count. *Happy Retrospect. Reminiscences, 1837–1922.* G. Bell, London, 1934.

WÖLFLING, Leopold (Ex-Archduke Leopold of Tuscany). *My Life Story.* Hutchinson, London, 1930.

MANUSCRIPT SOURCES

GERMAN FOREIGN OFFICE ARCHIVES: Österreich No. 46 1A. (Microfilmed in Foreign Office Library, London.)
Kronprinz Rudolf von Österreich.

HAUS-HOF-UND STAATSARCHIV VIENNA:
OMaA III/B 125b, Karton 446.
OMaA III/B 125a, Kartons 427, 429, 430.
14 Minist. d. k.u.k. Hauses Einzel. Abhandlungen XIX 62, Karton 14.
Nachlass Kronprinz Rudolf, Kartons 13, 16, 19.

KRIEGSARCHIV, VIENNA: *Qualifikationsliste* Archduke Johann Salvator.
Akt 80—3/3
Akt $\frac{70—1}{39}$.
Präsidial Fall Laaba.
Dienstbeschreibung FA 82 414. Ferdinand Prinz von Sachsen Coburg-Gotha.

PUBLIC RECORDS OFFICE LONDON: Dispatches from the British Ambassador in Vienna. F.O. 7/1093–1149.

SALISBURY PAPERS, CHRIST CHURCH, OXFORD: Bound Volumes A/9, A/39. A/45, A/48.

Index

Index

Index

Index

Sodich, Captain, 242
Solferino, battle of, 11–12, 16, 66–7
Stambulov, Stefan, 158–9, 160, 169
Stephanie, Crown Princess, 111–18, 146, 150, 160, 186–8, 190–1, 200, 205, 225–6, 228
Stockau, Count, 206
Stoilov, 169
Strauss, Johann, 2, 61, 151, 191
Stubel, Marie, 230
Stubel, Milli, 106–10, 189, 230–1, 242–3
Sucich, 242–3
Sweden, Prince Oskar of, 160
Szeps, Moritz, 125–30, 132, 149, 153, 181, 193–4, 197
Szögyeny-Marich, Count Ladislaus von, 144, 208–9, 213, 225–6

Taaffe, Count, 119–27, 129, 132, 149, 201–2, 205–6, 223, 233, 235, 237, 239
Tegethof, Admiral, 15
Tisza, Count, 130, 201
Tuscany, Grand Ducal Family of, 75–7

Valerie, Archduchess, 43, 46, 95, 104, 119, 226
Vetsera, Baron Albin, 195–6
Vetsera, Baroness Hélène, 195–8, 209
Vetsera, Mary, 194–8, 200, 202–6, 208–9, 211–12, 214–16, 218–22, 224, 226–9

Victor Emmanuel II, King of Italy, 13, 15, 37, 81–2
Victoria, Queen, 19, 22, 24, 26, 53, 56, 93, 98, 101, 110–12, 114, 124–5, 153, 158–9, 166, 182–3, 208
Vienna, the city and its inhabitants, 16, 57, 59–61
Vienna, Congress of, 11
Vienna, Court of, 2, 30, 55–8, 201, 203
Villafrance, Peace of, 11

Wales, Prince of (later King Edward VII), 53, 59, 93–4, 98, 101, 110, 114, 124–5, 183–7, 196
Widerhofer, Hofrat Dr. Hermann, 201, 203–4, 215–16, 219–20, 227
Weilen, Ritter von, 143, 179, 193
Wiener Zeitung, 125, 202–4
Wilczek, Count Hans, 105
Wilhelm I, Emperor of Germany, 12, 20–1, 23, 182, 184
Wilhelm II, Emperor of Germany, 2, 182, 184–6, 198
Wilhelm, Archduke, 62–3, 85–6, 88, 118
Winterhalter, 4, 95
Wodiczka, 220
Wurtemberg, Prince Philip of, 62

Zwerger, 214